NEW FRONTIERS
IN THEOLOGY

*Discussions among German
and American Theologians*

VOLUME I
THE LATER HEIDEGGER AND THEOLOGY

NEW FRONTIERS
IN THEOLOGY

*Discussions among German
and American Theologians*

Volume I

The Later Heidegger and Theology

Edited by

James M. Robinson · John B. Cobb, Jr.

Southern California School of Theology at Claremont

HARPER & ROW, PUBLISHERS

New York, Evanston, and London

LIBRARY OF CONGRESS CATALOG CARD NUMBER: 63-10506

CONTENTS

NEW FRONTIERS IN THEOLOGY
Volumes in preparation

II. THE NEW HERMENEUTIC

Contributors:

Ernst Fuchs
Gerhard Ebeling
Amos Wilder
John Dillenberger
Robert Funk

III. THEOLOGY AS HISTORY

Contributors:

Wolfhart Pannenberg
William Hamilton
Kendrick Grobel
Martin J. Buss

Foreword to the Series

German theology has played a leading role in the creative theological thinking of modern times. American theology has shown a characteristic openness in hearing, adapting, and assimilating the significant movements of German theology.

As long as this relationship was characterized by a considerable time lag in the translation and introduction of German theological trends in America, the American role was of necessity often that of receiving the results of a largely terminated German discussion, so that the ensuing American discussion could hardly affect the ongoing German discussion. In recent years the greatly increased number of personal contacts among German and American theologians, and the steady flow of translations, indicate the possibility of a more direct interaction between German and American theology.

This series of "discussions among German and American theologians" is intended to provide a means for such a theological interaction. Rather than translating the finished systems of mature scholars, it proposes to identify future trends at the germinal stage of programmatic essays, and by means of critical discussion to share constructively in their development. Accordingly, each volume will present in translation such a programmatic essay, introduced by Professor Robinson with an analysis of the German situation in which it emerged and in terms of which it has its significance. This will be followed by constructive and critical contributions to the issue by American theologians of promise. Finally, reappraisals of the issue in the light of these American contributions will be presented both by Professor Cobb and by the German author of the essay under analysis.

Editors' Preface

One may learn from Heidegger to what an extent thought is dependent upon language. Heidegger has found assistance for his thought in archaic or unusual terms and usages, which have created difficulties both for the German reading public and for translators of Heidegger. The present volume seeks to state Heidegger's thought in language that, on the one hand, respects Heideggerian language as inherently related to his thought and, on the other hand, moves within the English idiom with sufficient naturalness to make possible English-language thinking about the subject matter of Heidegger's thought. Although the translations of Heidegger available in English have proved helpful, they do not present the consistency or the finality that would free the present volume from the responsibility of seeking afresh for adequate English articulation. In quoting Heidegger, the reference is to the German edition, followed in brackets by allusion to the English translation when such is available, although for the sake of consistency and clarity the translation is usually new. The translation of Ott's "What is Systematic Theology?" and of his "Response to the American Discussion" is by James M. Robinson.

A few translational problems have to do with terms that are sufficiently central, that pose problems sufficiently complicated, that invite misunderstandings sufficiently serious, and that have been previously solved in sufficiently diverging ways that they call for an explicit statement of the policy followed in the present volume.

Existenziell and *existenzial* have been translated as "existentiell" and "existentialist." The opportunity to translate *existenzial* as "existential," a translation made all the more inviting by Bultmann's practice of spelling the German word *existenial,* has not been used. For the English word "existential" has, since the translation of Barth and Kierkegaard, become so deeply embedded in English usage as the equivalent to existentialism's *existenziell* that a reversal in usage can hardly be expected. And for Heidegger's position it is essential that *existenzial* not be understood in the way English usage leads us to understand "existential." Nor is it fitting that the foreign loan-word *existenziell* replace the now common term "existential." *Existenziell,* as the less technical German term, is most fittingly translated with the familiar and less technical English term "existential," while the more technical and specifically Heideggerian term *existenzial* can more justifiably be translated with an adjective that sounds technical to the English ear, such as "existentialist." If "existential" describes an ontic concern for one's existence, "existentialist" refers primarily to an ontological analysis of the structures of existence.

Das Sein and *das Seiende* have been translated as "being" and "beings" (*das Seiende* occasionally "a being"). The use of the same root with diverging endings keeps before the reader the relatedness and yet distinctiveness of the two terms, a dialectic that is the focus in Heidegger's use of the terms. This terminological tension has the precedent both of the German and of the Greek (*to einai* and *ta onta*). The plural "beings" is an exact translation of the Greek that Heideggar cites when he sets up his term *das Seiende.* Indeed in one passage he actually affirms the superiority of the Greek plural over the German singular, and hence by implication endorses the plural English translation: "It is no coincidence that the Greek language speaks most sharply and clearly, in referring in the neuter plural to what we call *das Seiende.* For beings (*das Seiende*) are in each instance specific and hence form a plurality, whereas being (*das Sein*) is unique, absolutely singular in unconditional singularity."[1] Hence this way of distinguishing the terms is consistent with the terminological tradition and preserves the tension of the two terms

[1] *Der Satz vom Grund* (1957; 2nd ed., Pfullingen: Günther Neske, 1958), p. 143.

more adequately than do such translations of *das Seiende* as "entity," "essent," or "what-is," where roots are employed that do not relate beings to being so clearly. Of course it is indispensable that the terms be also clearly distinguishable. The precedent of capitalizing "being" has not been adopted, although such a policy could appeal to Heidegger's occasional practice of capitalizing a pronoun referring to being. For the danger that "being" will, in the reader's mind, gradually become hypostasized or even deified must at all costs be avoided, if one is to understand Heidegger correctly. Since capitalization is thus not available to keep the distinction between the terms automatically visible, special care has been taken to avoid formulations in which the intended meaning could be in doubt.

Geschichtlich and *historisch* have been translated as "historic" and "historical." The two English adjectives are well established in English usage, and convey overtones corresponding to some extent to the German terms with which they are here equated. "Historical" calls to mind the factual, what the historian has proved to have happened by the "historical-critical method" (*historisch-kritische Methode*). "Historic" suggests past events of such significance as to continue to play a role in subsequent times, much as Martin Kähler in his famous book of 1892, *Der sogenannte historische Jesus und der biblische, geschichtliche Christus,* defined the historic Christ as the kerygmatic picture of Jesus that has affected the world through the centuries.

These policies with regard to translation have been applied in editing the American contributions insofar as this proved suitable. But the author's own usage has been retained where it seemed materially relevant, specifically in Michalson's use of "historical."

The volume has grown out of considerable discussion among its contributors. Preliminary papers were circulated and criticized. Copies of the papers were sent to Heinrich Ott at an early point, and one of the editors was able to discuss them with him personally. Then the San Francisco Theological Seminary at San Anselmo was host to a meeting of the American contributors.

The discussion was enriched by the participation of several members of the faculty at San Anselmo, including Professors Surjit Singh and Martin Anton Schmidt. The editors wish to express their special appreciation to Professor Arnold B. Come and to President Theodore A. Gill for making this meeting possible. Ott's written response to the first drafts was also read at the San Anselmo meeting. Each writer then had the opportunity to revise his essay in the light of the discussion. On the basis of this revision Ott prepared his Response, which is published as the conclusion of this volume.

Needless to say, discussion has by no means removed differences of opinion either as to the value or as to the meaning of the later Heidegger for theology. Inconsistencies of interpretation as well as disagreements of judgment will be found by the careful reader, and each author alone bears the responsibility and deserves the credit for his contribution. At the same time, the editors have tried to minimize the difficulties afforded the reader by standardizing terminology and by omitting some controversial interpretations not essential to the argument.

This project could not have been undertaken apart from the encouragement and assistance of President Ernest C. Colwell of the Southern California School of Theology at Claremont. For his counsel and for the generous aid provided by the school in a variety of ways we are sincerely grateful. Dean Thomas Trotter has read and commented helpfully on the manuscript. Our student assistants, Ernst Eberhard Fincke, Frederic Fost, and Duane Priebe, have given of their time and thought far beyond the demands of their jobs, and to them too we owe a debt of gratitude.

I. The Issue

1. The German Discussion of the Later Heidegger

JAMES M. ROBINSON

Southern California School of Theology

Immediately after the Second World War, Jean-Paul Sartre published a manifesto entitled "Existentialism Is a Humanism."[1] Thereupon Jean Beaufret of Paris wrote Martin Heidegger inquiring as to his position, to which Heidegger replied in the autumn of 1946 with an open "Letter on Humanism."[2] Here Heidegger explicitly repudiates the existentialism of Sartre, who only three years before, with the appearance of *Being and Nothingness,* had been hailed as Heidegger's French equivalent. "Sartre on the contrary expresses the basic statement of existentialism thus: existence precedes essence. Here he takes *existentia* ('existence') and *essentia* ('essence') in the meaning current in metaphysics, which since the time of Plato has said that *essentia* precedes *existentia.* Sartre turns this sentence around. But the reversal of a metaphysical sentence remains a metaphysical sentence. As such it remains with metaphysics in the forgetfulness of being."[3]

Heidegger explains Sartre's failure to attain to the kind of thinking he himself intended as follows: "The adequate reproduction of and participation in this other thinking that leaves

[1] *L'Existentialisme est un Humanisme* (Paris: Les Editions Nagel, 1946). English translation by Bernard Frechtman, *Existentialism* (New York: Philosophical Library, 1947).

[2] "Brief über den Humanismus," in *Platons Lehre von der Wahrheit* (Bern: Franke, A. G., 1947), pp. 53–119; republished separately as *Über den Humanismus* (Frankfurt a. M.: Vittorio Klostermann, 1949).

[3] *Über den Humanismus,* p. 17.

subjectivity behind is indeed rendered difficult by the fact that when *Being and Time* was published, the third Division of the first Part, entitled 'Time and Being,' was held back.[4] In 'Time and Being' everything is turned around. The Division in question was held back because thinking failed in adequately articulating this turn, and did not achieve its goal by means of the language of metaphysics."[5] Although this comment seems to turn away from *Being and Time* as well as from Sartre, Heidegger also emphasizes the continuity in the turn from *Being and Time* to "Time and Being." "This turn is not an alteration of the standpoint of *Being and Time*. Rather it is only in the turn that the thought which was attempted arrives into the proximity of the dimension out of which *Being and Time* was experienced, though experienced out of the basic experience of the forgetfulness of being."[6]

Various kinds of ambiguous allusions to this turn have occurred in the writings of Heidegger ever since. In reply to a recent question as to whether he had changed his position, Heidegger answered: "I have forsaken an earlier position, not to exchange it for another, but because even the former position was only a pause on the way. What lasts in thinking is the way. And ways of thought conceal within them the mysterious factor that we can walk on them forwards and backwards; even the way back first leads us forward."[7]

The relevance for theology of this turn or change of position is made explicit by Heidegger himself. "As long as anthropological-sociological conceptualizing and the conceptualizing of ex-

---

[4] *Sein und Zeit,* First Half, appeared in Vol. VIII of the *Jahrbuch für Philosophie und phänomenologische Forschung.* It has been republished separately by the Neomarius Verlag in Tübingen. The English translation by John Macquarrie and Edward Robinson, *Being and Time* (New York and Evanston: Harper & Row, Publishers, 1962), is based on the 8th German ed. of 1957, which contains minor alterations introduced in the 7th ed. of 1953. Cf. the outline of the total work as originally proposed, in *Sein und Zeit,* p. 39. [*Being and Time*, p. 64.] Heidegger's address on "Time and Being" at the meeting of "old Marburgers" in October, 1962, held at Marburg, was apparently derived from the unpublished third Division of the first Part.

[5] *Über den Humanismus,* p. 17.
[6] *Ibid.,* p. 17.
[7] *Unterwegs zur Sprache* (Pfullingen: Günther Neske, 1959), pp. 98 f.

istentialism are not overcome and pushed to the side, theology will never enter into the freedom of saying what is entrusted to it."[8]

Although the turn in Heidegger's thought began to be debated in philosophical publications as early as 1953,[9] the relevance of this turn for theology was not immediately seen. Rather, Heidegger's thought continued to be treated by theologians generally as a single position that had already been classified.[10] Only in 1959 did the explosive potentialities of "the later Heidegger" for theology become evident, when a young Privat-Dozent at Basel, Heinrich Ott, presented a monograph[11] arguing that the later Heidegger shows us that the philosophy of Heidegger as a whole is more compatible with Barthian theology than with Bultmannian theology. The significance of this monograph was enhanced by Heidegger's positive appraisal of it.

The annual meeting of Bultmann's former pupils, the "old Marburgers,"[12] chose as its topic the same year the relation of Heidegger to theology. This meeting was climaxed by a day-long seminar conducted by Heidegger on "Christian Faith and Thinking." He concluded by remarking that the door remains open for a nonmetaphysical God, and he proposed that the next year's

[8] From a letter to Heinrich Ott on the appearance of the latter's *Denken und Sein. Der Weg Martin Heideggers und der Weg der Theologie* (Zürich: EVZ-Verlag, 1959). Ott quotes the sentence in his essay, "What is Systematic Theology?" translated on p. 110 of this volume.

[9] Karl Löwith, *Heidegger. Denker in dürftiger Zeit* (1953. 2nd ed.; Göttingen: Vandenhoeck und Ruprecht, 1960). Citation is from the 2nd ed. See also Walter Schulz, "Über den philosophiegeschichtlichen Ort Martin Heideggers," *Philosophische Rundschau*, I (1953–54), 65–93, 211–232.

[10] Hermann Diem, *Gott und die Metaphysik, Theologische Studien, Heft 47* (Zürich: EVZ-Verlag, 1956) continued the traditional Barthian rejection of Heidegger, whereas the use of the later Heidegger by Friedrich Gogarten and Ernst Fuchs seemed to be merely a continuation of the traditional Bultmannian use of Heidegger. Cf. Gogarten, *Demythologizing and History* (London: S C M Press, 1955; German ed., 1953); *The Reality of Faith: the Problem of Subjectivism in Theology* (Philadelphia: The Westminster Press, 1959; German ed., 1957). Fuchs, *Hermeneutik* (Bad Cannstatt: R. Müllerschön Verlag, 1954; 2nd ed., 1958), pp. 62–72.

[11] *Denken und Sein. Der Weg Martin Heideggers und der Weg der Theologie* (Zürich: EVZ-Verlag, 1959).

[12] This meeting of "old Marburgers" was held at Höchst in Germany's Odenwald in October, 1959.

meeting should continue the discussion under the theme, "New Testament Exegesis and Systematic Theology." This topic arose from the sentiment that if there is to be any theology at all it must be a nonspeculative clarification of faith from within faith, so that the need for systematic theology in addition to exegetical theology was put in question. The meeting of 1960[13] followed this proposal with a paper on the New Testament by Herbert Braun[14] and one on systematic theology by Heinrich Ott.[15] The latter is included in this volume. Wilhelm Anz replied to this paper by Ott from a Bultmannian perspective.[16]

The debate begun at the 1960 meeting of old Marburgers has been continued by Ernst Fuchs and Gerhard Ebeling. Fuchs published a highly critical review of Ott's book,[17] and this has been supplemented by contributions of his pupils.[18] In the semester following the meeting, Ebeling conducted a seminar on "The Philosophy of M. Heidegger and Theology" in which Heidegger himself participated. The theses presented by Ebeling have been published,[19] together with most of the papers just mentioned, in a special issue of the leading Bultmannian periodical, edited by Ebeling, the *Zeitschrift für Theologie und Kirche*.

[13] This meeting was held in the *Kirchliche Hochschule* in Bethel bei Bielefeld, Germany, in October, 1960.

[14] "Die Problematik einer Theologie des Neuen Testaments," *Zeitschrift für Theologie und Kirche, Beiheft* 2 (1961), pp. 3–18.

[15] "Was ist systematische Theologie?" *ZThK, Beiheft* 2 (1961), pp. 19–46. English translation "What is Systematic Theology?" is on pp. 77–111 of this volume.

[16] "Verkündigung und theologische Reflexion," *ZThK, Beiheft* 2 (1961), pp. 47–80.

[17] *PhR,* VIII (January, 1961), 106–108.

[18] Eberhard Jüngel, "Der Schritt zürück. Eine Auseinandersetzung mit der Heidegger-Deutung Heinrich Otts," *ZThK,* LVIII (1961), 104–122. Jüngel was an assistant at the *Kirchliche Hochschule* in Berlin-Zehlendorf and is now instructor in New Testament in the theological house in the Russian Sector of Berlin. Helmut Franz, "Das Denken Heideggers und die Theologie," *ZThK, Beiheft* 2 (1961), pp. 81–118. Franz had already published in 1959 a small volume *kerygma und kunst* (Saarbrücken: Minerva-Verlag), which was a highly original attempt to theologize in the style of the later Heidegger.

[19] "Verantworten des Glaubens in Begegnung mit dem Denken M. Heideggers," *ZThK, Beiheft* 2 (1961), pp. 119–124.

It is this debate about the later Heidegger in the German discussion of the last decade that the present essay proposes to
analyze.

I. THE LATER HEIDEGGER

The very fact that one speaks of the "later" Heidegger presupposes some turn in his career in terms of which the distinction
of "early" and "late" is to be understood. This turn is both a
movement within Heidegger's own thought and a movement
within the understanding of Heidegger by his contemporaries.
Walter Schulz opens his interpretation of the later Heidegger
with a summary of the course of Heidegger's career in both these
respects. The role of *Being and Time* is described as follows:
"The appearance of Heidegger's first larger work, *Being and
Time* (1927), drew the attention of the philosophical world to
this thinker. In contrast to the 'existential misunderstanding,' to
the effect that Heidegger wished to describe or even proclaim the
nihilistic, heroic man of the time just after the First World War,
those who penetrated more deeply into this work recognized that
here a new beginning in philosophy was being attempted. Heidegger sought to overcome traditional ontology which defined man
in terms of the way *things* are. He sought to do this by showing
that man is a being of quite his own kind, namely *Dasein,* which
in its being is concerned with its being and is this being. The so-
called 'existentialist analysis' of the first and only part of this
work to appear sought to reveal the characteristics of this *Dasein,*
the 'existentials' in their inner connection. Yet it was at first less
noticed that Heidegger had not carried through the existentialist
analysis for its own sake, but rather in order to awaken anew
the question as to the meaning of being. The phenomenological
descriptions which in fact comprised the concrete content of the
work were convincing even without this 'background.' "[20]

When, two years later, two smaller works, *What is Meta-*

[20] *PhR,* I (1953–54), pp. 65 f.

physics?[21] and *Vom Wesen des Grundes*[22] appeared, they hardly seemed to alter the current view of *Being and Time*. They merely seemed to be intended to clarify the metaphysics implicit in the existentialist analysis. *What is Metaphysics?*, which was built upon the analysis of anxiety in *Being and Time*, seemed merely to lay hold of the finitude of *Dasein*, which as "thrown projection" rests only upon itself. *Vom Wesen des Grundes* traced *Dasein* back to freedom as the inner source of its possibility. Hence both pamphlets seemed merely to be supporting the existentialist analysis of *Being and Time* by showing *Dasein* grounding itself transcendentally in itself. Though Heidegger[23] has suggested that his lecture of 1930 "On the Essence of Truth" gave some insight into the turn in his thought, this lecture was published only in 1943,[24] and, as Schulz has shown,[25] the published form makes the turn more explicit than did the original lecture.

Heidegger's notorious address as Rector of the University of Freiburg in 1933 on "The Self-Assertion of the German University"[26] was still prior to the turn. But the lecture on "The

21 *Was ist Metaphysik?* (1929. 8th ed.; Frankfurt a. M.: Vittorio Klostermann, 1960). A Postscript was added in 1943, an Introduction in 1949. The English translation by R. F. C. Hull and Alan Crick in *Existence and Being* (London: Vision Press, 1949) contains the lecture (pp. 353–380) and the Postscript (pp. 380–392). *Existence and Being* is also published as a Gateway Paperback Edition (Chicago: Henry Regnery Company, 1960). The lecture appears on pp. 325–349 and the Postscript on pp. 349–361 in this edition. The Introduction is translated by Walter Kaufmann, "The Way Back into the Ground of Metaphysics," in *Existentialism from Dostoevsky to Sartre* New York: Meridian Books, Inc., 1956), pp. 206–221.

22 *Vom Wesen des Grundes* appeared in 1929 in the *Festschrift* for E. Husserl and also as a separate pamphlet. The 2nd ed. of 1931 appeared in Halle: Max Niemeyer. The 4th ed. appeared in Frankfurt a. M.: Vittorio Klostermann, 1955. There also appeared in 1929 *Kant und das Problem der Metaphysik* (2nd ed.; Frankfurt a. M.: Vittorio Klostermann, 1951). This book has been subjected to wide criticism by Kant scholars—criticisms which Heidegger accepts in the preface to the 2nd ed.

23 *Über den Humanismus*, p. 17.

24 3rd ed., Frankfurt a. M.: Vittorio Klostermann, 1954. English translation by R. F. C. Hull and Alan Crick, *Existence and Being*, pp. 319–351, paperback edition, pp. 292–324.

25 *PhR*, I (1953–54), 88–90.

26 *Die Selbstbehauptung der deutschen Universität* (Breslau: Gottl. Korn, 1933). This lecture has not been reprinted. One importance of this lecture

Origin of the Work of Art" in 1935[27] and the lecture at Rome in 1936 on "Hölderlin and the Essence of Poetry"[28] reflected the turn taking place. The way in which this turn was experienced is reported by Schulz:[29] "In connection with the commentaries on Hölderlin and the corresponding discussions of art, Heidegger took his departure from the tradition with a radicality that left far behind it the overcoming of the traditional approaches that the existentialist analysis of *Being and Time* had in certain respects carried through. Now the epoch of metaphysics, lasting from Plato to Nietzsche, is held to be an 'error.' To be sure, it is not an error to be condemned, or that could in principle have been avoided. Rather it is an error in which thinking was 'led astray' by being. *Being*—this was now the center of Heidegger's thought. It was clear that Heidegger placed this concept of being—and the concept of the 'holy,' which was apparently somehow equivalent to it—at the center of his works, and that it was from this center that he dismantled[30] the tradition so radically. But it was less clear exactly what he really meant with this term 'being.' The following publications and lectures,[31] which

for the analysis of the turn in Heidegger's thought is that it reveals the extent to which the turn, which at some points seems so abstract, is related to the down-to-earth course of political reality. The renunciation of self-assertion in the later Heidegger is materially a repudiation of this lecture.

[27] "Der Ursprung des Kunstwerkes," in *Holzwege* (1950. 3rd ed.; Frankfurt a. M.: Vittorio Klostermann, 1957), pp. 7–68.

[28] *Hölderlin und das Wesen der Dichtung* (Munich: Langen und Müller, 1937), reprinted in *Erläuterungen zu Hölderlin* (Frankfurt a. M.: Vittorio Klostermann, 1944); 2nd enlarged ed., entitled *Erläuterungen zu Hölderlins Dichtung*, 1951, pp. 31–43. English translation by Douglas Scott, *Existence and Being*, pp. 291–315, paperback ed. pp. 270–291.

[29] *PhR*, I (1953–54), 66.

[30] The German verb *destruieren* and noun *Destruktion* used by Heidegger in this connection are not fully equivalent to the English "destroy" and "destruction," for which one has as German equivalents *zerstören* and *Zerstörung*. Rather they suggest dismantling the history of metaphysics so as to learn from its inevitable defects and to lay bare its foundation. Karl Löwith in *Heidegger. Denker in dürftiger Zeit*, 2nd ed., p. 17, circumscribes the term *Destruktion* with the following: "dismantling to the point of exposing the foundations, and, beyond that, undermining metaphysics as such."

[31] The postwar publications of Heidegger are as follows: *Platons Lehre von der Wahrheit. Mit einem Brief über den "Humanismus"* (1947. 2nd ed.; Bern: Francke Verlag, 1954). The letter on humanism appeared separately as *Über den Humanismus* (Frankfurt a. M.: Vittorio Klostermann,

came one behind the other, each more extraordinary than the preceding, did not give any directly illuminating information, but increased the odd helplessness in which the scholarly world found itself with regard to Heidegger."[32]

1949). *Aus der Erfahrung des Denkens,* written in 1947 (Pfullingen: Günther Neske, 1954). *Der Feldweg* (1949. 2nd ed.; Frankfurt a. M.: Vittorio Klostermann, 1956). *Vorträge und Aufsätze* (1954. 2nd ed.; Pfullingen: Günther Neske, 1959). The pamphlet *Die Frage nach der Technik* in the series *Opuscula. Aus Wissenschaft und Dichtung* (Pfullingen: Neske Verlag, 1962) is a reprint of the first essay in this volume. *Was heisst Denken?* (Tübingen: Max Niemeyer Verlag, 1954). "Ein Briefwechsel mit Martin Heidegger," in Emil Staiger, *Die Kunst der Interpretation. Studien zur deutschen Literaturgeschichte* (Zürich: Atlantis Verlag, 1955, 2nd ed. 1957), pp. 34–49. *Zur Seinsfrage* (1956. 2nd ed.; Frankfurt a. M.: Vittorio Klostermann, 1959). English translation by William Kluback and Jean T. Wilde, *The Question of Being* (New York: Twayne Publishers, 1958). *Was ist das—die Philosophie?* (Pfullingen: Günther Neske, 1956). English translation by William Kluback and Jean T. Wilde, *What is Philosophy?* (New York: Twayne Publishers, 1958). *Gespräch mit Hebel,* No. 4, in the *Schriftenreihe des Hebelbundes Sitz Lörrach e.V.,* 1956. *Hebel—Der Hausfreund* (Pfullingen: Günther Neske, 1957). *Identität und Differenz* (Pfullingen: Günther Neske, 1957). English translation by Kurt F. Leidecker, *Essays in Metaphysics: Identity and Difference* (New York: Philosophical Library, 1960). *Der Satz vom Grund* (1957. 2nd ed.; Pfullingen: Günther Neske, 1958). *Einführung in die Metaphysik* (1957. 2nd ed.; Tübingen: Max Niemeyer Verlag, 1958). English translation by Ralph Manheim, *An Introduction to Metaphysics* (New Haven: Yale University Press, 1959). *Gelassenheit* (1959. 2nd ed.; Pfullingen: Günther Neske, 1960). *Unterwegs zur Sprache* (1959. 2nd ed.; Pfullingen: Günther Neske, 1960). "Der Weg zur Sprache" in *Die Sprache* published by the Bavarian Academy of Fine Arts (Darmstadt: Wissenschaftliche Buchgesellschaft, 1959), pp. 93–114, is an essay found in *Unterwegs zur Sprache,* pp. 239–268. "Aufzeichnungen aus der Werkstatt," *Neue Zürcher Zeitung,* Sept. 27, 1959, Blatt 5, Nr. 2898(69). *Nietzsche* (2 vols., Pfullingen: Günther Neske, 1961). "Aus einer Erörterung der Wahrheitsfrage," in the "almanach" *Zehn Jahre Neske Verlag* (Pfullingen: Neske Verlag, 1962), pp. 19–23.

[32] Heidegger's bibliography does not facilitate clarity in tracing the course of his thought. There are two sources of difficulty. First, several volumes contain collected essays, many of which antedate by several years their publication in the collection (*Holzwege, Vorträge und Aufsätze, Identität und Differenz, Unterwegs zur Sprache*). Secondly, other volumes contain lectures and university courses given in the past but only recently published. These have been partially reworked before publication in such a way that the original version and the later revisions can hardly be distinguished (*Vom Wesen der Wahrheit, Einführung in die Metaphysik, Nietzsche*). Bibliographical remarks at the end of most volumes clarify these matters to some extent. The English reader suffers the additional handicap that most of the later writings remain untranslated, and he may be confused by the fact that the translation of the earlier Heidegger's major work, *Being and*

Schultz brought order into this confusion by interpreting the turn in Heidegger's thought as the consistent, even necessary result of his having brought Western metaphysics to its ultimate outcome. German idealism had eliminated substance as an unalterable substratum in which selfhood can be grounded and had instead viewed the mind as mediating itself in a dialectic movement. However, the later Schelling failed in his attempt to establish a ground in which this dialectic movement of the mind is itself grounded. As a result, there emerged the irreducible facticity of man's selfhood. Whereas Schelling and Kierkegaard attempted to ground this facticity of man in God, Heidegger accepted the irreducibility of that facticity as such, that is to say, he sought to interpret *Dasein* only in terms of its own structure. This problem of analyzing the whole of *Dasein* in terms of its own structure is resolved by the successive analyses of the existentials. "Being-in-the-world" is meaningful in terms of "care," and this in turn can be grounded in "temporality." But rather than providing a ground outside *Dasein,* temporality has been recognized as itself an existential. Put otherwise: To understand *Dasein* as "thrown" does not relate it to a "thrower" outside *Dasein,* but rather relates it to *Dasein's* own projection of itself. *Dasein* is grounded in *nothing* outside itself.

It is this "nothing" upon which *What is Metaphysics?* focuses attention, in answering the question of metaphysics as to what is beyond *Dasein. Dasein,* held out into nothing, is beyond all beings, and has in this sense attained ultimate transcendence, the goal of metaphysics. Transcendence beyond all beings leads neither to God, nor to the cosmos as the sum total of all beings, nor to an established Cartesian subject upon which a world of

---

Time, has just now been published. Furthermore, Heidegger's recent concern for overcoming metaphysics has been obscured by the positive use of metaphysics in the titles of two recent English translations. One title, *Introduction to Metaphysics,* is the literal translation of the German title, but this title dates from 1935, when the first draft of this book was written. The second title, *Essays in Metaphysics: Identity and Difference,* is an expansion of the German title *Identität und Differenz.* The expansion is peculiarly misleading since the essays included are intended as the overcoming of metaphysics.

objects can be built, but rather to nothing. Thus the metaphysical question is answered in "nothing," and this answer to the metaphysical question is at the same time the end of metaphysics. For the outcome of the metaphysical question demonstrates the futility of the question, which consisted in seeking the "something" in which *Dasein* is grounded, whereas *Dasein* is in fact grounded in nothing. Heidegger's completion of metaphysics is the end of metaphysics.

The end of metaphysics is the experience of the ultimate impotence of *Dasein*. For the recognition that *Dasein* cannot transcend to a ground outside itself, but only to nothing, does not ground man in a Cartesian sense in himself, in self-reliance or Nietzsche's "will to power." Rather it involves the ultimate renunciation of one's role as the grounded subject that has both grasped its own ground and provided the ground for all other beings as its objects. For the nothing to which *Dasein* transcends is not at *Dasein's* disposal, but comes upon *Dasein* in anxiety, which is not fear of something specific, but rather a vague dread, simply being afraid—of *nothing*.

This ultimate impotence or facticity of *Dasein* leads Heidegger to give up the whole metaphysical attempt to ground *Dasein* outside itself, a renunciation that Heidegger calls "overcoming" metaphysics. This renunciation replaces a heroic self-assertion over against nothing. This is the turn in Heidegger's thought, necessitated by the course of that thought itself. Once this turn is made, the nothing that emerged when metaphysics sought to ground *Dasein* in something outside itself ceases to emerge as nothing, and instead being dawns. If it was metaphysics' engrossment with analyzing beings that prevented it from catching sight of being, then the arrival at nothing, by ending the engrossment with beings, corresponds to the unveiling of being.

This turn in direction brings with it a reversal of the basic mood of Heidegger's philosophy. Rather than calling man "the one who stands in nothing's place," Heidegger now speaks of him as the "shepherd of being." Instead of anxiety, there emerges gratitude for being's "favor." Once the Promethean direction of metaphysics is renounced, the positive emerges. "Renunciation does not take away, it gives."[33]

If Schulz interprets the turn in Heidegger's thought as the logically necessary outcome of Western metaphysics, with the implication that the follower of Heidegger, and indeed Western philosophy as a whole, must go along with Heidegger in this turn, Karl Löwith interprets the turn in Heidegger's thought as less the "consequence of his point of departure" than "the result of an about-face" equivalent to a conversion,[34] a move in which the consistent Heideggerian would hardly participate. For what is at stake is whether *Dasein* is to be grounded "in its own, 'authentic' being, or in the wholly other 'being,' which on its own initiative brings mankind's *Dasein* into its own."[35] There has been a decisive "shift of emphasis from *Dasein* which is resolved for itself and asserts itself in confrontation with 'nothing,' to being, which gives itself, and for whose understanding one's own *Dasein* was originally the 'foundation,' whereas, later, *Dasein* has merely to correspond to the claim of being and hence is no longer fundamental."[36] Löwith's interpretation amounts to saying the "existential misunderstanding" of *Being and Time* was the correct understanding of it, and that Heidegger has in old age given up that "heroic nihilism" and turned to religion as a "return to his theological beginning."[37]

---

[33] *Der Feldweg*, p. 7.

[34] *Heidegger. Denker in dürftiger Zeit* (2nd ed.), p. 7. Whereas Schulz speaks of a *Kehre* ("turn"), Löwith speaks here of *Umkehr*, a term that uses the same root but implies more a reversal of direction with religious overtones, since it is the term also used to mean "repentance" (cf. "return" as the Biblical term for repentance). On p. 21, Löwith describes the turn *in malam partem* as a religious "conversion" and "regeneration." Schulz, *Der Gott der neuzeitlicher Metaphysik* (2nd ed.; Pfullingen: Günther Neske, 1959), p. 54, also suggests that we have to do with "the secularized form of Christian conversion." Similarly, Hermann Diem, *Gott und die Metaphysik*, p. 18.

[35] Löwith, *Heidegger*, p. 7.

[36] *Ibid.*, pp. 17 f., n. 2.

[37] *Ibid.*, p. 21. On p. 20, when Löwith remarks that no one can honestly claim to understand what Heidegger means by "being," he adds: "Those who will come nearest to understanding it are believers, who think they find in Heidegger's ontological talk of 'revelation' and 'unveiling' an access to the Christian revelation of a God who too is not a being—believers who

The subtitle of Löwith's book, "thinker in a needy time," derived from Heidegger's characterization of Hölderlin as the poet who stands "in the no-more of the departed gods and the not-yet of the coming (God),"[38] is intended to suggest the later Heidegger's understanding of himself as the prophet of a new age marked by the imminent advent of being.[39] Such an eschatological hope is for Löwith no more than "wishful thinking";[40] and Heidegger's philosophizing in terms of an understanding of his time is for Löwith little better than keeping in step with the fads, far beneath the timeless "primal wisdom of the Greeks."[41]

If authentic existence had meant anticipating one's own death, the urgent need for our times is now seen to consist in recovering the dimension of the whole and the holy. The original claim to be initiating a "universal phenomenological ontology" as a scientific philosophy has given way; that is to say, Heidegger has given up the attempt to provide a phenomenological basis for his view, and positions are merely asserted, when not simply veiled in silence. Heidegger's thinking has become a meditation, and even a thanking of being for its favor in unveiling itself. Language is no longer understood as the articulation of the intelligibility of our "being-in-the-world," but is rather the "house of being." Resolve is no longer the determination to be oneself rather than being an impersonal "one," but, by an etymological play on words, means one's openness to being.[42] Freedom is no longer understood as one's ability to be, but rather as one's letting being be. The mean-

as such do not pretend to comprehend with the reason the God of revelation." In a footnote he indicates how Heidegger's *Habilitationsschrift* of 1916, *Die Kategorien- und Bedeutungslehre des Duns Scotus*, says in theological language what the later Heidegger is saying in terms of "being."

[38] *Erläuterungen zu Hölderlins Dichtung* (2nd ed.), p. 44.
[39] *Heidegger. Denker in dürftiger Zeit* (2nd ed.), p. 12.
[40] *Ibid.*, p. 17.
[41] *Ibid.*, p. 12. One may recall Löwith's volume *Meaning in History* (Chicago: University of Chicago Press, 1949), in which the philosophical concern for history is traced back to primitive Christian eschatology.
[42] By emphasizing the prefix in *Ent-schlossenheit*, Heidegger suggests the negation of *Verschlossenheit*, which means being closed or shut up in oneself.

ing of being has been replaced by the "truth" or unveiling of being.[43]

Löwith's basic protest is that Heidegger has not adequately conceded this reversal of position, but has in later years reinterpreted his earlier position to make it conform to his later position.[44] Löwith quotes *Being and Time* to the effect that it attempts a hermeneutic of *Dasein* because existence is the point from which philosophical inquiry arises and to which it returns. Having thus quoted *Being and Time* as intending existentialism, Löwith proceeds to contrast this original meaning of the basic categories of *Being and Time* with the meaning the later Heidegger has found in them, especially in his "Letter on Humanism" of 1946. In *Being and Time* man is defined as *Dasein* because his essence is "there-ness," the fact that he is and has to be himself; in the "Letter on Humanism" man is *Da-sein* because he is where being becomes clear, where *its* "there-ness" emerges. "Care" is no longer primarily *Dasein*'s concern for its own being, but rather has become care for being in and of itself. *Dasein*'s burden, in that it rests upon itself, has been replaced by gratitude for being's favor. "Existence" is no longer transcending oneself in projecting one's world, but, as "ek-sistence," means "ec-statically" standing-out into the truth of being. Man's thrown-ness is no longer the brute facticity of his being there, in terms of which he must in resolve project his existence, but is a throw of being, suggesting man's nearness to being. Hence the correlative term "projection" no longer refers to man's resolute laying hold of the existence that lies before him, but refers rather to being's act of sending man into ek-sistence, into openness to being, as his true nature. Anxiety in confrontation with nothing turns into shyness in the presence of being. The self-assertion of a *Dasein* responsible for itself gives way to "sacrifice" for the sake of preserving the truth of being.

[43] *Heidegger. Denker in dürftiger Zeit*, pp. 8–18. In this last instance Löwith concedes that already in *Being and Time* the concept "meaning" had been divorced from existential meaning when it was defined as the "horizon of projection."

[44] *Heidegger. Denker in dürftiger Zeit* (2nd ed.), p. 18, n. 2.

If *Being and Time* could say that "only so long as there is *Dasein,* is there being," the "Letter on Humanism" interprets this sentence to mean that only so long as being gives itself is there *Dasein.*[45]

Löwith, one of Heidegger's outstanding pupils of the twenties, returned to Germany in 1952 after teaching *Being and Time* as existentialism for eighteen years in Rome, Japan, and the United States, and indeed in Heidegger's own Marburg from 1928 to 1934.[46] It is understandable that he should take offense at Heidegger for having changed the official interpretation of the work that is at the basis of Löwith's own position. This relation of Löwith to the turn in Heidegger's thought is in interesting contrast to that of Heinrich Ott. If the "Letter on Humanism" was for the mature Löwith Heidegger's postwar repudiation of Heideggerianism, it was for the youthful Ott, then in his last year of studies at the *Gymnasium* in Basel, a first introduction to Heidegger. What was for Löwith an unfortunate reinterpretation was for Ott simply Heidegger's authoritative statement, a solid basis on which to enter into a valid understanding of his thought. And this basis seemed to suggest a more obvious correlation with Barthian theology, which Ott was already reading, than with Bultmannian theology, which had laid claim on Heidegger. It is thus as a spokesman for the later Heidegger and Barthian theology that Heinrich Ott subsequently emerged. For him "the later Heidegger" includes both the concept of a turn in Heidegger's career and the validity of the reinterpretation of *Being and Time*

---

[45] The original German sentence was: "Nur solange Dasein ist, gibt es Sein." The German idiom "es gibt," literally "it gives," means "there is." This indefinite "there" or "it" is identified with being, in the sense that being gives or unveils itself. Thus Heidegger's interpretation of what the sentence means is technically a meaning which could be associated with the sentence, but is hardly what Heidegger meant when he wrote the sentence in *Being and Time*. Cf. Löwith, *Heidegger. Denker in dürftiger Zeit* (2nd ed.), pp. 22–28.

[46] On p. 21, Löwith comments bluntly: "After all it was no mere misunderstanding, when so many hearers of Heidegger's lectures and readers of *Being and Time* understood the author then differently from the way he understands himself today."

that brings it into a more direct relation to the position after the turn.

Ott summarizes the main lines or the movements in Heidegger's thought as follows: "The point of departure for the question of being is in the existentialist analysis of *Being and Time;* then comes the turn, that shift which becomes perceptible in Heidegger's postwar publications and which is characterized by a far-reaching change in point of view as well as in the methods of thought and in terminology, yet with an unaltered theme."[47] Ott's first objective in his presentation of Heidegger is to interpret *Being and Time* as an analysis of *Dasein* whose only purpose is to provide a point of departure for the question of being, the unaltered theme of Heidegger's whole career. Put negatively, Ott's objective is to show that the direction even of *Being and Time* is misunderstood when its analysis of *Dasein* is seen as an end in itself, as might be the case in existentialism. Put polemically, his objective is to show that the Bultmannian use even of *Being and Time* is only to a certain degree legitimate, in that Bultmann used *Being and Time* in terms of a concern and a purpose different from that of Heidegger. Thus, although Ott emphasizes the turn in Heidegger's thought and builds primarily upon the later Heidegger, he would, at least by implication, maintain that a position built upon the later Heidegger could lay claim to the early Heidegger with more appropriateness than can Bultmannian theology. In substance this amounts to a preference for the interpretations of *Being and Time* by Walter Schulz and the later Heidegger himself rather than for those by Karl Löwith and the handbooks on existentialism.

Ott traces the turn through three interrelated dimensions of Heidegger's thought: the turn from nothing to being, the overcoming of metaphysics, and the "step backwards."

The stages in the turn with regard to the first of these dimensions may be summarized as follows. Still within the earlier period, in his inaugural address at the University of Freiburg in

[47] *Denken und Sein,* pp. 26 f.

1929 on *What is Metaphysics?*, Heidegger introduced the concept of "nothing." This theme was foreign to *Being and Time;* yet *What is Metaphysics?* carried it through in the method characteristic of *Being and Time,* namely, in an analysis of the situation of *Dasein.* Then in the Postscript to that address, written in 1943, and in the Introduction to it, written in 1949, nothing is brought increasingly into relation to being. Thus the history of being—the forgetfulness of being in metaphysics, the end of metaphysics in nothing, the replacement of nothing with being once metaphysics is renounced—gradually emerges as the central theme of the later Heidegger.

The address of 1929 analyzes the situation of the *Dasein* of the university audience, i.e., of science itself. Science is concerned with establishing what is, and nothing else. Thus science inevitably has to do with the concept of "nothing." However this inevitable emergence of the concept within science does not mean that nothing is merely negation by reason. Nothing is not first constituted by a logical inference of nonexistence. Rather, nothing is rooted in a region prior to logical inference, in *Dasein* itself. *Dasein* is inevitably characterized by anxiety, which is not fear of a specific danger but rather a vague dread in which the very givenness of beings ceases to be a matter of course, and their contingency, the oddity that they are at all, is sensed. *Dasein's* anxiety brings home the question, "Why are there beings at all, and not, rather, nothing?" Anxiety is not fear of something, but of nothing. Thus anxiety reveals nothing, and in so doing reveals beings as beings, that is, draws attention to the really rather surprising fact that there are things at all—which is thus seen to be anything but a matter of course. Thus anxiety, by revealing beings as beings (via the concept "nothing"), makes science possible. Nothing, given in *Dasein* prior to all logical operations, is the condition of the possibility of the form of *Dasein* called science.

In the Postscript of 1943 Heidegger raises the question whether this nothing, which is by its very nature not a being, is not actually being itself. For the being of beings is by *its* very nature not a being. "This which is wholly other than all beings is that-which-is-not. But this nothing functions as being." Somewhat more carefully formulated, "nothing, as that which is other than the beings, is the veil of being."[48] Nothing, by pointing to the contingency of the beings, draws our attention to their being, so that the possibility of their not being functions as a veil through which we catch sight of the surprising fact that they are. Being dawns upon us first as a question to ponder, that is, in the form of nothing. Yet this unveiling of being is increasingly described positively as the occurrence of being itself, as the voice of being calls upon us, revealing the beings as being, that is, unveiling being as "the marvel of all marvels, that beings are."[49] Here one observes the turn taking place, as the emergence of being in the move from nothing to being.

The condition of the possibility of *Dasein* confronting the being of beings had been located simply in the fact that *Dasein* is suspended in nothing. But when thus confronted by nothing, the prior condition of the possibility of *Dasein* actually confronting the being of beings is now seen to be that being gives itself to *Dasein* even more basically than *Dasein* is held out into nothing.[50] Thus the flow of Heidegger's thinking has turned: rather than thought moving via *Dasein* to being, being moves to *Dasein* and thus into thought. Prior to the turn, thinking is conceived as basically derived from *Dasein's* initiative; after the turn, thinking is envisaged as given to *Dasein* by the initiative of being.

The turn in Heidegger's thought in terms of overcoming metaphysics is externally documented by the observation that up through the address of 1929 on *What is Metaphysics?* and the lecture course, *An Introduction to Metaphysics,* given in 1935, the term metaphysics was used in a positive sense. This suggests that Heidegger initially proposed to purify and thus revitalize metaphysics. But in his subsequent writings the term tends increasingly to be used in a pejorative sense. Heidegger now con-

---

[48] *Was ist Metaphysik?* (8th ed.), pp. 45, 51. [*Existence and Being,* pp. 384, 392; paperback ed., pp. 353, 360.]
[49] *Ibid.,* pp. 45 f. [*Existence and Being,* p. 386; paperback ed., p. 355.]
[50] *Denken und Sein,* pp. 82 f.

ceives of his task as that of "overcoming metaphysics," which is
the title he chose when publishing his notes on the topic dating
from 1936–1946.[51] Heidegger in retrospect even defines his essay
What is Metaphysics? as moving beyond metaphysics, and actually as involved in overcoming metaphysics. He explains the ambiguity: "It belongs to the nature of such transitions that they
to a certain extent must still speak the language of what they are
helping to overcome."[52]

Heidegger's criticism of metaphysics can be summarized as
follows: Metaphysics is *Dasein's* effort to ground itself, so that
all beings are ultimately grounded in some supreme being, itself
an uncaused cause (*causa sui*). The investigation of this problem
has been the traditional task of ontology. Since this supreme being
was often conceived of by metaphysics as God, Heidegger speaks
of "the onto-theo-logical nature of metaphysics."[53] Furthermore,
metaphysics, especially since Descartes, is an objectifying kind of
thought in which the subject establishes itself as the basis of
reality and builds the world of reality upon itself. The subject
forms propositions (*Vorstellungen*) by placing the object before
it (*vor-stellen*), the result of which is that reality becomes only
the subject's picture, his world view. It is in this context that Heidegger understands modern science and technology as the outcome of metaphysics. Here man's relation to nature is no longer
that of finding a *modus vivendi* in conformity to nature, but
rather that of obliging nature to assume a shape assigned to it
by man. Western metaphysics has on the one hand produced a
concept of God that the modern world has rejected, so that "God
is dead," and on the other hand has produced a technological
scientific progress that has become the world's fate.

The positive achievement of *Being and Time* consists in having
posed once and for all the question of the meaning of being, and

---

[51] "Überwindung der Metaphysik," in *Vorträge und Aufsätze,* 1954, pp.
71–99.
[52] *Was ist Metaphysik?* (8th ed.), Nachwort, p. 43. [*Existence and Being,*
Postscript, pp. 380 f.; paperback ed., p. 350.]
[53] Cf. "Die onto-theo-logische Verfassung der Metaphysik," in *Identität
und Differenz,* 1957, pp. 35–73. [*Essays in Metaphysics,* pp. 33–67.]

in having taken the first step in limiting the pervasive subjectivity of objectifying conceptualization by rooting objective thought in something more primal than a metaphysically understood subject. Instead, thought is rooted in the structure of *Dasein*, as when science is rooted in the existentialist category "being-in-the-world." Thus, when the turn in Heidegger's thought is defined as the overcoming of metaphysics, *Being and Time* can itself be defined as already beginning this turn, although it is clearly not yet around the turn. Rather the defect of *Being and Time* lies in its "failure to recognize that there is thought that is more rigorous than conceptual thought."[54] To force being into a concept is precisely not to understand the truth of being. It was in fact such conceptualizing thinking that had led the West into forgetting being.

Heidegger concedes to metaphysics that it is an effort at thinking "beyond" (*meta-*) beings in order to conceptualize them as such, i.e., as beings. To the extent that metaphysics is aware of beings as beings, it senses them as being. It investigates beings in the light of their being. But it does not directly face the light itself, it does not direct itself to the problem of being as such. Or, to change the figure, if philosophy is a tree whose roots are metaphysics (Leibniz), Heidegger would direct attention to the soil in which the roots grow. This light or this soil is the condition of the possibility of metaphysics. At the same time it constitutes the limitation of metaphysics, in that metaphysics does not concern itself with this presupposition of its own occurrence.

This light or soil is, of course, being itself. Metaphysics, in its concern with beings, does recognize them as being, and to this extent senses the being of beings. But here "being" is a static concept, expressed by the German abstract noun, *Seiendheit*, which one might better translate "being-ness." Metaphysics does not really understand the true nature of being, and hence can be spoken of as "forgetting being." For being in its true sense Heidegger uses the verbal noun, *Sein*.

Now the "essence" of being is its happening. The German

54 *Über den Humanismus*, p. 41.

word here translated "essence" is *Wesen,* a Middle High German infinitive meaning "to be" (compare the Old High German and Anglo-Saxon, *wesan*). This term survives today only as the German past participle, *gewesen* ("been") and as the English past tense "was." The original Indo-Germanic meaning is reflected in the Indian root, *vas,* meaning "remain," "abide," "reside," "camp." Heidegger uses the term in this verbal sense of coming to reside, arriving, taking place. Thus being essentially takes place —and this is what metaphysics had ignored. In Heidegger's most recent writings the verbal noun *Anwesen,* where the prefix accentuates the temporal meaning of arriving, tends to replace the verbal noun *Sein.* The "being of beings" is formulated "the arriving of what arrives" (*das Anwesen des Anwesenden*).[55]

The same point is made by another etymological reflection, which is involved in the statement that metaphysics does not reach the truth of being. For metaphysics conceives of truth as the correspondence of the subject's concept and the object's reality (*adaequatio rei ad intellectum*).[56] But originally truth is un-hiddenness, un-veiling. The Greek term for truth is *a-letheia,* composed of the negating alpha privative and the root of the verb *letho* or *lanthano,* which means to escape notice, to be hidden, or, in the middle and passive, to forget. Thus being's truth is its no longer escaping notice, its unveiling, the act of its making itself known.

The essence of being and the truth of being tend to converge in Heidegger's focal understanding of being as an event of unveiling or revealing. This event of being has to do both with beings and with thought. It is this understanding of being that is involved in overcoming metaphysics and arriving at non-conceptual thought.

Non-conceptual thinking may seem at first sight to be a con-

---

[55] Cf., for example, *Unterwegs zur Sprache,* p. 122.

[56] In *Vom Wesen der Wahrheit* (3rd ed., 1954), p. 8, Heidegger points out that this concept of truth originally meant the correspondence of created beings to the divine intellect, which provided the basis for assuming the correspondence of the human intellect to created beings. Only in the period of Cartesian subjectivism has the metaphysical concept to truth meant simply the correspondence of the objective world to man's intellect.

tradiction in terms, in that words are after all inseparable from concepts. Yet Heidegger's later thinking is non-conceptual in that it does not think of language as composed of or seeking after clearly defined and rationally fixed concepts, whose static and compartmentalized nature would insure their clarity. Rather Heidegger asks how it is that certain subject matters have come to be articulated with certain concepts. Rather than thinking of this as a somewhat arbitrary choice on the part of the thinker, who largely for convention's sake uses certain terms, Heidegger holds that the initiative resides in language—more exactly, in being as it calls forth language. By means of this primal call of being something happens to us, the subject matter of thought clarifies or obscures itself for us. Thought is not primarily our action, but something that comes upon us when being clears itself to our thought. A concept is the occurrence of the clearing or veiling of the subject matter. Thus each concept has its history—not just in retrospect as the history of ideas, but in itself, as the very nature of what a concept is. "Being" is not a fixed concept, but an occurrence that happens to us, something that dawns on us, and the various views about being that have been held over the centuries are the necessary result of the way in which being has on various occasions shown itself. This is a more primal grasp of the nature of thinking than that characteristic of the subject-object approach.

The overcoming of metaphysics is sometimes referred to by Heidegger as a "step backwards," the renunciation of the desire to produce a system of concepts and thus have a viewpoint. This step backwards refers neither to a return to an earlier position in the history of philosophy nor to some logical inference still to be drawn within conceptual thinking. Rather it has to do with the kind of movement involved in thinking. It involves thinking back behind opinions and viewpoints into the dimension out of which the subject matter of thought comes to encounter us. It is the return to the soil out of which metaphysics grew.

To be sure, such a step backwards is extremely difficult. Heidegger's effort to take this step makes use of the combination of two paths. The one consists in including the background of the concepts, their history, even their sound, within concepts, so that they themselves are understood as historic. His frequent etymological play on words is not play, but is a serious effort at understanding. The other approach consists in a rapprochement of his thought to poetry. Heidegger holds that many poets, especially Hölderlin, Trakl, and Hebel, thought the subject matter of thought much more primally than did the metaphysical philosophers. Composing poetry and thinking being are two forms of language rooted in the same truth of being. Thus the poetic, hauntingly suggestive rather than conceptually explicit style of the later Heidegger is not to be seen as a weakening of his intellectual rigor, but rather as a serious experiment in a new mode of thought.

If the position of the early Heidegger could be focused by the Bultmannians upon the historicness of *Dasein,* Ott proposes to approach the position of the later Heidegger by focusing upon the history of being. Already in *Being and Time* Heidegger had argued that the question of being was to be pursued in terms of the history of ontology. Heidegger is "the thinker about thinking," as Ott puts it. In his seminar of 1959 on "Christian Faith and Thinking" Heidegger said that in his seminars and lectures he never thinks of matters in and of themselves, but only in their relatedness to specific historic events.[56a] Insisting that one must think historically, he investigated the question as to what thinking is by inquiring what a specific thinker thought it to be.

Since in some respects Heidegger's emphasis upon thought as historic and upon his own role as a thinker about thought calls Hegel to mind, Heidegger's position gains sharper profile through his comparison of his own procedure with that of Hegel.[57] The subject matter of both Hegel's and Heidegger's thought is thought itself; but for Hegel this means the absolute concept,

---

[56a] Cf. Heidegger's call for "perseverance in authentically historic thinking" and his criticism of "the increasing flight from the historic tradition," *Der Satz vom Grund,* p. 138.

[57] "Die Onto-theo-logische Verfassung der Metaphysik," in *Identität und Differenz,* pp. 35–73. [*Essays in Metaphysics,* pp. 33–67.]

whereas for Heidegger the subject matter is the ontological difference between being and the beings. The nature of Hegel's treatment of the history of thought is "to take it up and resolve it" (*aufheben*) into the absolute truth, whereas Heidegger's stance toward the history of thought is characterized by the step backwards into the sphere overlooked by metaphysics. Thus, if Hegel focused his attention upon the thoughts of earlier thinkers, Heidegger proposes to penetrate through their thoughts to their subject matter, which Heidegger distinguishes from the thoughts themselves by referring to it as "what is not thought" (*das Ungedachte*). What is not thought is not simply nothing, but is rather the hidden power of thought, the subject matter that is never fully grasped in any thought. This subject matter of thought is both back of and ahead of thought. It is the origin and the goal of thought, the condition of the possibility of thought and the theme of thought. Thus thought is encompassed, closed in on both sides, by its subject matter—a pattern which for Heidegger replaces the subject-object schema.

The basic experience out of which Heidegger philosophizes is amazement that thinking happens. Hence his concern with what is not thought is that it is "what is to be thought" (*das Zu-Denkende*), that which brings thought into motion. Hence what is not thought cannot simply be the various beings, since the existence of various entities does not in itself necessitate thought. Rather what is to be thought is being itself, in its distinctness from the beings, that is, in its ontological difference. This difference is not a separation, as if being were some entity alongside the beings. It is rather their being, seen in itself. Being speaks to us through the beings, by unveiling to us that they are. It is because of their being that beings become the theme of thought. It is this unveiling of the being of beings that sets thought in motion. Modern science, in that it has focused exclusively upon beings and has forgotten being, has, in the pregnant sense intended by Heidegger, ceased to think. For being and what is to be thought tend to converge.

Since the basic subject matter of thought is being, the history of thought is rooted in the history of being. Thinking takes place in the way being gives itself to be thought. Being, as the condition of the possibility of the history of thought, must itself have a history, must itself be historic. The epochs in the history of thought are basically epochs in the history of being. For being is not a static entity but an event. Hence Heidegger speaks of being in terms of *Lichtungsgeschichte,* "clearing history." Being, again and again, in different times and ways, clears out the underbrush of thinking so as to make itself clear to thought. If the truth of being is its unveiling of itself to thought, the history of being is the history of these clearings.

Since whether this happens or how it happens is not at the disposal of the thinker, thinking about being has a fate-like character. Heidegger speaks of the *Geschick* of being. This term, not to be confused with *Geschichte* (history), derives from the verb *schicken,* which means to send, ordain. (Compare the obsolete usage of the cognate English verb, "shift," meaning to distribute or apportion.) Thinking's lot is cast by being. Being speaks to thought, and what it speaks is thought's lot. Thus the noun *Geschick* is quite comparable to the English noun "fate," derived from the Latin *fatum,* meaning "what is spoken." Thus the historicness of thinking is often referred to with the adjective *geschicklich,* "fateful" (not to be confused with *geschichtlich,* "historic"). This adjective, though difficult to translate, refers to this fateful nature of thought, the dependence of thought upon what is sent into it. This may sound as if being were here hypostasized, but, since being is not itself a being, such an inference would be incorrect. Instead, the emphasis upon the activity of being rather than of thought is to be understood in terms of Heidegger's consistent effort to overcome the subjectivity of thought.

There is then a fate-laden movement in the course of Western thought. Being gave itself at different times differently to thought. It is the fate of thinking that being has been described in different periods with different terms, such as nature, truth, logos; just as the movement from the Greek meaning of *physis* to the Latin meaning of *natura* and to the modern scientific concept of "nature" is not simply a matter of philology but also and more basically a matter of clearing history.

The general course of this history is sketched by Heidegger in terms of the concepts used successively for being: "There is being only from occasion to occasion in this and that fate-laden contour: *physis, logos, hen, idea, energeia,* substantiality, objectivity, subjectivity, will, will to power, will to will."[58] This series of interpretations of being reflects the occurrence of being from early Greek thought via Plato and Aristotle to the Middle Ages, Descartes, German idealism, Nietzsche, and, finally, modern technology.

Why this clearing history is at the same time referred to by Heidegger as "forgetting being" can be made clear from his presentation of the beginning of this path with Plato and its end with technology. Whereas the Greek word for truth, *a-letheia,* implies that truth is self-disclosure, Plato's parable of the cave treats truth as a function of the subject's point of view, that is, the question of truth becomes that of the correctness of one's view. This shifts the location of truth. It ceases to be a trait of the beings as they unveil themselves, and becomes a matter of the subject's approach to the beings.[58a] Truth is subjugated to idea, which is ety-

[58] *Identität und Differenz,* p. 64. [*Essays in Metaphysics,* p. 59.]

[58a] Here we have a striking instance of the antithesis between what the term "Heidegger" symbolizes down to the present and what the later Heidegger himself maintains. Ernst Heitsch, the most theologically interested classical philologian of German today, has presented in the journal for classical philology *Hermes* (Vol. 90, 1962, 24–33) a detailed refutation of the "subjectivistic" interpretation of *aletheia,* for whose popularity he holds "Heidegger" as popularly understood responsible, although he concedes this "subjectivistic" view had the support of classical philologians through Friedländer, whose *Platon* I, 2nd. ed. 1954, 242 is cited: "There is no such thing as hiddenness and unhiddenness in and of themselves. (Un)hiddenness does not exist unless it is (un)hidden for someone." On the basis of a study of "non-philosophical *aletheia,*" as Heitsch's essay is entitled, he confirms the philological presupposition of Heidegger's discussion of *a-letheia,* to the effect that the alpha privative was "heard" by the Greek ear, but uses the evidence to repudiate the "subjectivism" of "Heidegger" and to favor "the opposite of Heidegger, Nikolai Hartmann" (p. 25, n. 2). The counter-thesis of Heitsch to Friedländer is as follows: "It is an easy suggestion that (un)hiddenness presupposes an observer and consequently that the understanding of *aletheia* oriented etymologically to the fact that it is

mologically related to the Greek infinitive *idein,* to see or view. Thus Heidegger identifies in Plato the origin of the secondary concept of truth as *adaequatio rei ad intellectum.* This is the same as the beginning of metaphysics, of subjectivism, or, as Heidegger also puts it, of humanism: the primacy of man over all beings. Thus something happened in Plato's thinking, something of which Plato himself was not aware. Through Plato's thoughts one reaches what was not thought, the fate-laden ordinance of being in which it veiled itself for the West, an occurence which only made itself known via the long history of thought.

The other end of this metaphysical tunnel is modern technology. Subjectivity reached its last philosophical stage in Nietzsche's will to power, where being is only the value posited by the will. Ultimately the will wills nothing external to itself; the will wills itself. This first became fully clear after Nietzsche in technology, which Heidegger characterizes as the will to will. Here man actualizes his will by constructing the world to conform to it. In this sense the will to will is the last stage in the process whereby metaphysics has altered the world by placing man as the subject in the center of it. Thus the completion of metaphysics eventuates in technology, which according to Heidegger does not itself think.

Under technology[59] Heidegger understands not simply the machines of production, but also objectified nature, an engineered culture, professional politics, superimposed ideals—the whole artificial stance of modern man toward beings as a whole. He characterizes technology as follows: Man's relation to beings is reduced

a composite subjectivizes the concept of truth. But this view does not get beyond externals and obscures the decisive distinction between *aletheia* and the German word 'truth.' What is decisive is that *aletheia* as unhiddenness pertains to the object, but 'truth' pertains to the statement (made by the subject). *Aletheia* is primarily a quality of the world, i.e. of the sum total of objects, whereas the German word is a quality of the judgment about the objects" (p. 31). Thus Heitsch arrives at the same material position as that of the later Heidegger. However, lest one assume that this leaves Bultmann with the "subjectivism" attributed to Heidegger, it should be noted that Heitsch defends his own "objective" interpretation of *aletheia* by reference (p. 31, n. 1) to Bultmann (*ZNW,* 27, 1928, 134).

[59] Cf. "Die Frage nach der Technik," *Vorträge und Aufsätze,* pp. 13–44.

to mathematical calculation; what cannot become a statistic is no longer said to be, and the mathematical solution is held to be an explanation of being. The will to will thus achieves security by putting all beings at its disposal. Man's reduction of reality to his object reaches in technology the acute stage of a revolt against or attack upon reality. Man "challenges" reality. (*Stellen,* the verb normally meaning "to place," can mean "to challenge," "to stand someone down.") The subject places its object before it, first as its propositions (*Vor-stellungen*), then in technology as the product (*her-stellen,* i.e.,—"to produce") it has ordered (*be-stellen*). Reality thus becomes what man has posited or placed, which leads Heidegger to name reality from this point of view *Ge-stell,* a thing that is placed somewhere or that is stood up or erected, a "stand." Reality as the sum of such stands is for technology stock or inventory. Even the picturesque and scenic is merely tourism's stock, and man himself becomes only manpower, part of the cold war's arsenal.

This characterization of technology means that the will to will has eliminated the fate-ladenness of existence, the initiative of being pressing in upon thought. Thus technology is unhistoric. Yet technology itself has come upon thought as an action of being, and is itself an epoch in the history of being. When one recognizes that the essence of technology is rooted in the history of being, one is freed from a romantic, nostalgic flight from technology, and on the other hand one has historically relativized technology so as to transcend it and be free from it. Man cannot overcome technology with a technological understanding of technology, but only by hearing in it a claim of being upon us. Thus, even as forgetfulness of being, the history of being bears in upon us determining world history.

Man does not create history by initiating a causal chain that produces the connection of history; rather it is the sharing of a common fate in the history of being that produces a common history under which a whole culture or epoch stands. One does not have freedom of choice merely to take or leave the situation in which one is placed and finds oneself. Yet the very fact that

Heidegger has uncovered the forgetfulness of being is a return to a more primal thinking. This fact sometimes leads Heidegger to prophetic utterances about a return by the West to more contemplative thinking, which cherishes being.

II. THE LATER HEIDEGGER AND THE THEOLOGY OF HEINRICH OTT

The question of the relation between the thought of the later Heidegger and theological thought is obviously much broader than the question of the theological implications that Heinrich Ott finds in the later Heidegger. Ott is not the only theologian to have concerned himself thus far with the thought of the later Heidegger, nor even the first. The Bultmannians have remained in close contact with Heidegger down through the years, and especially Friedrich Gogarten and Ernst Fuchs have made use of his more recent writings. Yet Ott is the first theologian to have attempted in a programmatic and concentrated way a statement of the theological implications specifically of the later Heidegger. Hence his position has presented the concrete point of departure for the theological discussion of the later Heidegger.

Heinrich Ott was born at Basel in 1929 and began to read Barth as well as Heidegger while still a pupil in the *Gymnasium*. He remained in Basel for the study of theology and made so favorable an impression on Barth that Barth accepted him as a doctoral candidate and assigned him a choice topic: a critique of the theology of Rudolf Bultmann. For two semesters Ott studied in Marburg under Bultmann and during that time lived in the Bultmann home. The result of his intensive study was a dissertation on "History and *Heilsgeschichte* in the Theology of Rudolf Bultmann."[60] This book closes with a call for a positive, constructive criticism of Bultmann, which would make use of what he then termed the "newer Heidegger." Four years later, when Ott

---

[60] *Geschichte und Heilsgeschichte in der Theologie Rudolf Bultmanns,* Vol. 19 of *Beiträge zur historischen Theologie* (Tubingen: J. C. B. Mohr, 1955).

published his Heidegger volume on "Thinking and Being,"[61] he began by quoting this passage from the earlier book to indicate his own approach to the later Heidegger:

"Our investigation sought to clear the ground for a productive criticism of Bultmann. Perhaps the course of the immanent criticism carried through thus far has already indicated the lines along which one should think further. One must seek in connection with Bultmann (1) a concept of reality of a historic type that overcomes the Bultmannian cleavage with a synthesis embracing both 'significance' and 'corporeality,' 'history' and 'nature'; (2) a comprehensive interpretation of understanding as the actualizing of historic being that goes beyond the limits of Bultmann's hermeneutic; (3) a synthetic concept of time that takes into account both the eminent significance of the historic Now and the reality of past and future as such; (4) the primal essence of language. The fourth point also indicates that such ontological reflection does not stand apart from but rather very close to practical church life. For what is involved is language as it occurs in scripture and confession, in exegesis and dogmatics, in preaching and prayer, i.e., language as the medium of all the church's and theology's activity. Further thinking along these four lines could perhaps use as its concrete point of departure the work especially of the newer Heidegger, a thinker who has inspired Bultmann in his theological thought but who speaks up from time to time just where Bultmann's limits are met, as we could observe again and again. His work may contain a flood of perspectives important for theology that have probably never been correctly exploited."[62]

This program had undergone some modification by the time of *Denken und Sein* in 1959. The intervening four years and the general rejection by the Bultmannians of his criticism of Bultmann had convinced Ott that "Bultmann's most personal position is not reached by such a formal ontological criticism, since

[61] *Denken und Sein. Der Weg Martin Heideggers und der Weg der Theologie* (Zürich: EVZ-Verlag, 1959).

[62] *Geschichte und Heilsgeschichte in der Theologie Rudolf Bultmanns*, pp. 210 f.; *Denken und Sein*, p. 7.

that position rests upon an ultimate basic religious decision, which transcends all purely formal considerations. This decision can be defined as 'eschatological paradoxical dualism' and doubtless has its ultimate basis in the dualism of law and gospel."[63] Rather than assuming his proposals will be accepted by Bultmann into an improved Bultmannian theology, Ott now proposes to present a theology that can claim to be more truly Heideggerian. To be sure this would not "disprove Bultmann," but it would break down one of Bultmannianism's major elements of strength in the present situation.[64] Hence Ott proposes to "prove that Bultmann may legitimately appeal to Heidegger only to a very limited extent."[65] Of course the outcome of such an argument may very well be that the Bultmannians, like the Barthians, will turn away from Heidegger altogether, rather than join Ott in a theology corresponding to the later Heidegger.

The theological position in terms of which Ott approaches a correlation between the later Heidegger and theology is more nearly that of Barth. To be sure Barth had disassociated himself from any correlation with existentialism and Kierkegaard just at the time when Heidegger was introducing Kierkegaardian motifs into philosophy, as if Barth wished intentionally to avoid a correlation with Heidegger. Barth's rare references to Heidegger have been consistently critical,[66] so that Ott's project could hardly

---

[63] *Denken und Sein*, p. 8. From note 8 of "What is Systematic Theology?," p. 95 below, one observes that we have to do with a basic distinction between the Reformed tradition in which Ott stands and the Lutheran tradition in which Bultmann stands. The potentiality for a positive use of the law-and-gospel pattern for approaching the later Heidegger has been developed by the Lutheran theologian Gerhard Ebeling, in his "Verantworten des Glaubens in Begegnung mit dem Denken M. Heideggers," *ZThK, Beiheft* 2 (1961), p. 122. In his pamphlet devoted to overcoming Bultmann's supposedly "dualistic" view of history, *Die Frage nach dem historischen Jesus und die Ontologie der Geschichte (Theologische Studien*, Heft 62, Zurich: EVZ-Verlag, 1960), Ott advocates the "single reality of history" and yet concedes (p. 33): "One can speak of a genuine duality at most when one confronts the *old and new aeon.*"

[64] Cf. James M. Robinson, "Basic Shifts in German Theology," *Interpretation*, XVI (1962), 76–97, esp. pp. 96 f.

[65] *Denken und Sein*, p. 8.

[66] Eberhard Jüngel, "Der Schritt zurück," *ZThK*, LVIII (1961), 122, speaks of the "irony" of Barth's misunderstanding of the statements of the

count on support from Barth. In fact, the Barthian rejection of the interpretation of the later Heidegger as presented by Walter Schulz[67] had already been supplied by Hermann Diem.[68] Hence Ott's attempt to achieve a positive relation between the later Heidegger and Barthian theology indicates a new alternative within the Barthian movement.

Since the publication of Ott's book there has appeared an essay by Karl Barth on the relation of philosophy and theology that well illustrates the ambiguous relation of Ott's undertaking to Barthianism.[69] Here Barth concedes that philosophy and theology may be concerned with the same problem. The theologian describes this problem as the relation of Creator and creature, while philosophers have treated it under a variety of terms. In this connection Barth speaks specifically of Heidegger's treatment of the relation of being and *Dasein*. Now Barth's basic criticism of philosophy has to do with the question of sequence or priority. He holds that philosophy tends consistently to give priority to man, whereas theology must give priority to God. Presumably Barth conceives of Heidegger as giving priority to *Dasein* over

---

later Heidegger that involve "a hidden kinship" between Barth and Heidegger.

[67] Walter Schulz's address, "Der 'Gott der Philosophen' in der neuzeitlichen Metaphysik," 1956, was published in his volume *Der Gott der neuzeitlichen Metaphysik* (Pfullingen: Günther Neske, 1957, 2nd ed.; 1959).

[68] Diem's address in reply to Schulz, *Gott und die Metaphysik,* appeared as number 47 in the series *Theologische Studien* edited by Karl Barth (Zürich: EVZ-Verlag, 1956). See also the dissertations of Diem's pupils Lother Steiger, *Die Hermeneutik als dogmatisches Problem; Eine Auseinandersetzung mit dem transzendentalen Ansatz des theologischen Verstehens* (Gerd Mohn: Gütersloher Verlagshaus, 1961), and Gerhard Noller, *Sein und Existenz; Die Überwindung des Subjekt-Objektschemas in der Philosophie Heideggers und in der Theologie der Entmythologisierung* (Munich: Chr. Kaiser Verlag, 1962), and Eduard Thurneysen's association of Ott with "Heidegger's existentialistic philosophy" in his article "Warum nicht Gollwitzer? Ein Wort zum Kampf um die Nachfolge Karl Barths in Basel," published in the *Kirchenblatt für die reformierte Schweiz,* numbers 118–119 of 1962, and reprinted in *Evangelische Theologie,* XXII (1962), 271–277.

[69] "Philosophie und Theologie," in *Philosophie und Christliche Existenz, Festschrift* for Heinrich Barth, ed. by Gerhard Huber (Basel and Stuttgart: Hebling und Lichtenhan, 1960), pp. 93–106.

being. Yet this "existential misunderstanding" of *Being and Time* does not fit at least the later Heidegger, whose turn consisted in giving being strict priority in his thinking. Thus, in terms of the condition Barth sets up for a positive relation between philosophy and theology, the later Heidegger would seem to provide the kind of philosophy Barth would advocate. Though Barth himself gives no indication of modifying his traditional rejection of Heidegger, one may find here some material justification of Ott's present position as Barth's successor.

If Ott's dissertation had been in intent a conversation with Bultmann, designed to lead Bultmann toward a revision of his position, one may say that *Denken und Sein* is addressed to Barth or at least to the Barthian position, to lead it, without violating its basic principles, into a confrontation with the later Heidegger. However it should not be overlooked that Ott is also addressing himself to Heidegger, who might be led by Ott's empathetic and noncritical interpretation of his thought to see in its theological development a path for his own reflection. As a matter of fact Heidegger concluded his seminar on "Christian Faith and Thinking" at the conference of old Marburgers in October, 1959, with the suggestion that although he could not, in view of his repudiation of metaphysics as such, accept a metaphysical concept of God, the door remained open with regard to other possible approaches to theology. And there have been some indications that Heidegger was at least initially more impressed by Ott's theological correlation than were the theologians.

A. *Being and God*

Any discussion of God in terms of the philosophy of Heidegger encounters the common association of Heidegger with the atheism of Sartre in distinction to the dimension of transcendence in Jaspers' thought. Ott argues that the association of atheism with Heidegger is part of the basic misunderstanding of Heidegger as if he were an existentialist. This error leads to treating the ontological structures set up as existentials as if they were ontic statements about man's existential dilemma. For example, "being-in-the-world" as a focal existential is at times taken to mean that man's existence is only worldly or immanent, so as to exclude the possibility of contact with a transcendent God.

Heidegger himself had already corrected this misunderstanding as early as 1929. "The ontological interpretation of *Dasein* as 'being-in-the-world' makes neither a positive nor a negative decision about the possibility of being in relation to God. Rather it is only the clarification of transcendence that achieves an *adequate concept of Dasein,* in terms of which being *(Seiendes)* one can now *inquire* as to how the matter stands ontologically with regard to *Dasein*'s relation to God."[70] This is further explained in the "Letter on Humanism." "In the designation 'being-in-the-world,' 'world' does not at all mean earthly beings in distinction from a heavenly being, nor does it refer to the 'worldly' in distinction from the 'spiritual.' 'World' in that designation does not refer to any being or realm of beings, but to openness for being. Man is and is man to the extent that he is ek-sistent."[71]

Not only does Heidegger explicitly reject the attribution to him of atheism;[72] he even goes on to say that his leaving open the question as to God is not a matter of indifference, but is rather intended to point out that a more adequate category than metaphysics is needed for theology. "Only from the truth of being can the essence of the holy be thought. Only from the essence of the holy is the essence of deity to be thought. Only in the light of the essence of deity can that be thought and said which the word 'God' should name. Do we not have to be able first to understand and hear carefully all these words, if we as men, i.e., as ek-sistent beings, are to experience a relation of God to man? For how could man in contemporary world history even ask seriously and

---

[70] *Vom Wesen des Grundes* (4th ed.), p. 39, n. 1.

[71] *Über den Humanismus,* p. 35.

[72] *Über den Humanismus,* p. 36. Heinz-Horst Schrey, "Die Bedeutung der Philosophie Martin Heideggers für die Theologie," *Martin Heideggers Einfluss auf die Wissenschaften* (Heidegger *Festschrift,* Bern: A. Francke AG. Verlag, 1949), p. 15, speaks in the context of these remarks by Heidegger of an "ironic atheism" which, as a form of negative theology, is "nothing other than an indirect indication of a feeling of the inadequacy of our human conceptions of God."

rigorously whether God is drawing near or withdrawing himself, if man neglects first of all to think his way into the only dimension in which such a question can be asked? But that is the dimension of the holy, which even as a dimension remains closed if the openness of being does not become clear and in its clearing is not near to man. Perhaps the outstanding characteristic of this age consists in the closedness of the dimension of the whole. Perhaps that is the sole bane."[73]

Ott's basic assumption with regard to Heidegger's attitude toward the relation of philosophy to Christian faith is that Heidegger maintains that only a metaphysical philosophy should be regarded by faith as "foolishness."[74] This would leave open the possibility of a positive relation of Heidegger's own philosophy to faith. Ott builds on such quotations as the following: "Thus the theological character of ontology is not merely due to the fact that Greek metaphysics was later taken up and transformed by the ecclesiastical theology of Christianity. Rather it is due to the manner in which beings as beings have from the very beginning disconcealed themselves. It was this unconcealedness of beings that provided the possibility for Christian theology to take possession of Greek philosophy—whether for better or for worse may be decided by the theologians, on the basis of their experience of what is Christian; only they should keep in mind what is written in the First Epistle of Paul the Apostle to the Corinthians: 'Has not God made foolish the wisdom of the world?' (1 Cor. 1, 20). The 'wisdom of the world,' however, is that which, according to 1, 22, the 'Greeks seek.' Aristotle even calls 'philosophy proper' 'what is sought.' Will Christian theology make up its mind one

---

[73] *Über den Humanismus,* pp. 36 f. The religious overtones in *heil* ("whole") and *Unheil* ("bane") are more evident in German (cf. *Heilsgeschichte*) than in English.

[74] *Denken und Sein,* p. 147 and *passim.* The alternate position, to the effect that Heidegger regards all philosophy, including his own, as "foolishness" for Christian faith, is advocated by Helmut Franz (cf. pp. 70–75 below), who explicitly rejects Ott's position in "Das Denken Heideggers und die Theologie," *ZThK, Beiheft* 2, 1961, p. 114. (cf. *kerygma und kunst,* Saarbrücken: Minerva-Verlag, 1959), p. 65. Cf. Ott's reply in "What is Systematic Theology?", p. 106 below, n. 13.

day to take seriously the word of the apostle, and thus also the conception of philosophy as foolishness?"[75] In Ott's view, this opens the door to a theology that would join Heidegger in his "step backwards" to overcome metaphysics.

Such an understanding of Heidegger's relation to theology becomes clearer in the essay on "The Onto-theo-logical Nature of Metaphysics," where Heidegger says of the uncaused cause or *causa sui:* "This is the fitting name for the god in philosophy. To this god man can neither pray nor sacrifice. Before the *causa sui* man can neither fall to his knees in awe nor sing and dance. Accordingly, godless thinking that must give up the god of philosophy, god as *causa sui,* is perhaps nearer to the divine God. This means only that such thinking is freer for him than onto-theo-logics would like to admit. This comment may let some small light fall on the path toward which a thinking that carries through the step backwards, back out of metaphysics into the essence of metaphysics, is moving."[76]

As long as this step backwards has not been made, the most appropriate thing to do with regard to God would be to remain silent: "He whose experience of theology, both that of Christian faith and that of philosophy, is rooted in an unbroken heritage, prefers nowadays to remain silent about God in the realm of thought. For the onto-theo-logical character of metaphysics has become questionable to thought, not on the basis of any atheism, but because of the experience of a thinking that has seen in onto-theo-logics the still unthought unity of the essence of metaphysics."[77] Yet now that Heidegger has advanced beyond (or stepped behind) metaphysics into more primal thought, Ott sees the possibility of moving beyond a silence with regard to a metaphysical concept of God into explicit nonmetaphysical language about God.

Ott takes his point of departure in the following statement by

[75] *Was ist Metaphysik?* (8th ed.), pp. 19 f. [*Existentialism from Dostoevsky to Sartre*, p. 218.]

[76] *Identität und Differenz*, pp. 35–73, esp. p. 70. [*Essays in Metaphysics*, pp. 33–67, esp. p. 65.]

[77] *Identität und Differenz*, p. 51. [*Essays in Metaphysics*, p. 47 f.]

Heidegger: "Readiness for anxiety is a Yes to the urgent call to fulfill the highest claim, which only man's nature encounters. Only man of all the beings experiences, when called upon by the voice of being, *the wonder of all wonders: that* beings *are.*"[78] Heidegger maintains that when man is held out into nothing he becomes aware of the contingency of beings and thus is struck with the fact that they are at all. Their being calls to him. Now Ott infers[79] that if their being is experienced as a wonder, this amounts to experiencing them as God's creation. To be sure such a concept of God the Creator would have to be clearly distinguished from a metaphysical first cause, if such a theology is to correspond to Heidegger's thought. For it was the metaphysical concept of a first cause that provided an answer so fully "settling" the question as to stultify it and even to lead to the question being forgotten. Ott denies that this would be the outcome in terms of the Biblical concept of God as Creator. The Bible "answers" the question as to why there are beings by giving the question permanence, in that the awe in the question is carried over in the answer, as awe before the Creator. For God the Creator is not at man's disposal, but in his independence and sovereignty holds the believer in awe. Faith in this Creator is the continuing experience of the strangeness that beings are, it is "the uncompromising persistence of the basic question as to 'why there are beings rather than nothing.' "[80] Thus Ott finds a correspondence between the Biblical faith in God the Creator and the philosopher's basic question. He even describes this as the philosopher's encounter with God, the "secularized Christianity" of Heidegger's thought.[81]

The first attempt to work out a correlation between the Christian concept of God and Heidegger's philosophy consisted in a correlation between the believer's numinous awareness of the world as creation and the philosopher's amazement at the being of beings. The being of beings is understood as creation. The

---

[78] *Was ist Metaphysik?* (8th ed.), pp. 46 f. [*Existence and Being*, 1949, p. 386; paperback ed., p. 355.]
[79] *Denken und Sein*, p. 86.
[80] *Ibid.*, p. 88.
[81] *Ibid.*, p. 87.

theological term "creation" indeed tends to correspond to the philosophical term "being," precisely in the parallel ambiguity of both terms. Being has often been understood metaphysically as the sum total of all beings, thus obscuring the Heideggerian meaning of being, the awareness that the beings *are* at all. Just so the theological term "creation" is often taken to mean the sum total of all creatures, thus obscuring the more basic meaning of the term, the awareness that all creatures are God's creation. The Christian language corresponding to the being of beings would then be the creation of creatures. Again and again in the Bible the people of God experience their being as the wonder of deliverance, and commemorate this awareness in the language of blessing or thanksgiving. When one recalls that for Heidegger primal thinking is gratitude for the favor of being and thus becomes thanking,[82] one may suspect that the Biblical analogy, rather than being a derivative of philosophical thought, is indeed the ultimate origin of Heidegger's insight. For here the thanksgiving emerges as the linguistic formulation of the reverent awareness that one's being is God's creation.[83]

It was in this direction that Ott's thinking was directed in the first, historical part of *Denken und Sein*, consisting of lectures given in the Winter Semester, 1957–58. In the latter, systematic half of *Denken und Sein*, consisting of lectures given in the Summer Semester of 1958, Ott enters into another avenue of correlation.[84] Rather than correlating the doctrine of creation with amazement at the being of beings, Ott now seeks to fit the concept of God into the philosophical position provided by Heidegger. If being is not God—and it is clear that such an identification is contrary to Heidegger's intention, since being is not a being and

[82] *Was ist Metaphysik* (8th ed.), p. 49. [*Existence and Being*, pp. 389 f; paperback ed., pp. 358 f.]

[83] This latter point is the thesis of my essay "Heilsgeschichte und Lichtungsgeschichte," *Evangelische Theologie*, XXII (1962), 113–141. This essay is to appear in English under the title "The Historicality of Biblical Language" in a volume edited by Bernhard W. Anderson on *The Relevance of the Old Testament for Christian Faith*.

[84] Cf. esp. "The Question as to the Being of God," *Denken und Sein*, pp. 138–152.

is not to be hypostasized—then God must be a being. And indeed Heidegger, when emphasizing that man is the only being that "exists," lists other beings that "are" but do not "exist"—and here God is listed alongside a rock, a horse, and an angel as things that are, that is to say, as a being.[85] Ott infers that if one is to talk about God in Heideggerian terms one would speak of God as a being[86]—which immediately confronts Ott with Barth's rejection of the *analogia entis*.

Ott argues that the Heideggerian understanding of being makes it possible to share the two basic objections that led Barth to reject the *analogia entis* and still affirm the being of God.[87] Barth's objection to subsuming God under the highest generalization, being, is that man in his thinking thereby gains control over God; God becomes a concept at man's disposal. Now this objection envisages the subjectivistic approach to thought, in which beings are reduced to objects of the subject's thoughts, against which Heidegger himself is reacting in his rejection of metaphysics. Hence the nonmetaphysical concept of being advocated by Heidegger is a concept intentionally freed of that to which Barth takes exception. Being, for Heidegger, is precisely not a most general concept that thought has at its disposal. Quite the reverse. Being is an occurrence of unveiling, a fate-laden happening upon thought. As thought's fate or lot, being is precisely not at thought's disposal. To speak of God's being and to speak of his freedom in self-revelation are for Ott congruous formulations.

Barth's other objection to the *analogia entis* had to do with the concept of analogy as a static similarity between God and man. Barth rejected the term analogy until he came to conceive of analogy (*analogia fidei* or *relationis* or *operationis*) as a correspondence effected by God in the act of faith. Now Ott holds that this emphasis is more radically carried through by Heidegger, who moves from the concept of analogy to that of correspond-

85 *Über den Humanismus,* pp. 14 f.
86 *Denken und Sein,* p. 142.
87 *Ibid.,* pp. 143–146.

ence, and affirms that thinking is simply the "response" to the call of being as it unveils itself and gives itself to thought.

Here again one has to do with a Heideggerian play on words. The German word for correspondence is *Entsprechung,* which, like the English "cor-re-spondence," had lost for the average ear its etymological affinity to "re-sponse" *(ent-sprechen).* "Correspondence" had lost the dynamic implications of "an-swering" and had taken on static implications, until heard in its primal etymological meaning by Heidegger. Thus, in the case of "analogy" just as in the case of "being," Ott holds that Heidegger has provided a way for implementing Barth's criticism of the *analogia entis* that is more adequate than Barth's own solution. Ott argues that Barth's valid criticisms of the *analogia entis,* which led him to remove the term "being" while retaining the term "analogy," can be better implemented in terms of Heidegger by removing the term "analogy" (in favor of "re-sponse") and retaining the term "being."[88]

Having in this way protected his Barthian and Heideggerian flanks, Ott moves constructively toward a clarification of God's being. The Bible says without inhibition[89] that God "is." Yet, as the cryptic name of God in Exodus 3:14 "I am who I am" indicates, to say God "is" does not for the Bible imply subsuming God under a higher generalization. Rather this predicate for God brings to expression his absolutely unique self-hood: "God is simply himself: He is he who he is, mysterious, glorious, unapproachable, not part of the world."[90] This is also for Ott the way Heideggerian philosophy would think of God's being: *"The being of God signifies,* in terms of the way we have understood 'being' thus far, *an occurrence of unveiling:* that God unveils himself to thought as he who he is! that he strikes upon thought

[88] Eberhard Jüngel, "Der Schritt zurück," *ZThK,* LVIII (1961), 116–122, argues that the position Ott presents on the basis of Heidegger as a criticism of Barth is in substance Barth's own position.

[89] Helmut Franz, "Das Denken Heideggers und die Theologie," *ZThK, Beiheft* 2 (1961), p. 109, brands this an "illusion." "It is precisely the Bible—both Old and New Testament—that speaks of God's being in anything but an uninhibited way."

[90] *Denken und Sein,* p. 146.

as a fate and gives himself to thought as the subject matter to be thought, that he encounters thought as a claim upon it and requires of the thinking person a correspondence in freedom."[91] God's being is not to be compared with that of beings in general, as if God shared in their being as the supreme being or the cause of all other beings. Rather God's being is to be conceived of as the fate-like occurrence that "God is thought about."[92] Thus Ott conceives of God as a being whose being is his revelation of himself, comparable to Heidegger's understanding of being as unveiling.

The two correlations Ott makes between Heidegger's ontology and the doctrine of God stand in some tension to each other. If amazement at the being of beings corresponds to numinous awareness that their being is God's creation, then awareness of God would seem to be latent in awareness of a being's being. When this correlation is applied to God as himself a being, the second correlation Ott proposes, confusion emerges. If awe-inspired awareness of a being's being corresponds to sensing a being as a creature, is then God a creature? If such awe at a being's being is ultimately reverence for a being's Creator, does God, as a being, have a Creator? It seems impossible thus to move from Ott's first correlation to his second correlation. Nor is the situation easier when one goes at the matter in the other direction. If God is a being, how then can amazement at the being of beings be correlated to God as their Creator, when Heidegger is fundamentally opposed to the grounding of being in a being? The objection to metaphysics is not just that it stultified the question of being, but that it grounded being in a supreme being. If God is a being, the second correlation Ott proposes, how is Ott to avoid the criticism that his first correlation is by implication metaphysical?

In the light of such problems and the discussion following his presentation at the 1960 meeting of old Marburgers, Ott has assumed a more cautious position. Whereas his address "What is

91 *Ibid.*, p. 148.
92 *Ibid.*, p. 149.

Systematic Theology?" spoke of his theology "fitting into" Heidegger's philosophy, the printed form of the address only speaks of a "correspondence" with Heidegger's philosophy. Heidegger introduced into the discussion at the 1960 meeting the idea of an *analogia proportionalitatis:* A is to B as C is to D. As philosophical thinking is related to being, when being speaks to thinking, so faith's thinking is related to God, when God is revealed in his word. Ott adopts this formulation, seeing in it primarily an emphasis upon the experiential nature of philosophical and believing thought. Thus theology in its speaking of God is not required to choose whether God is in Heideggerian terms a being, or nothing, or being itself, or that which is implicit in the awesome awareness of the being of beings. God would not "fit into" the Heideggerian system, but the whole of theology, operating within its own language, would have a structural correspondence to philosophy of the Heideggerian kind. It remains to be seen whether Ott can produce a theology under this definition that is still meaningfully related to Heidegger.

B. *Thinking and Theology*

For the later Heidegger, thinking is directly related to his understanding of the nature of man. Existence is a term used to define man not because of the traditional distinction between existence as actuality and essence as possibility; rather ek-sistence refers to man as the being who moves out of his subjectivity and stands out where being becomes clear. Man stands ec-statically within the truth of being. Man takes place as man when he is addressed by being. Man is the place where being clears so that one catches sight of it and exclaims "There!" This is the meaning the later Heidegger attributes to his designation of man as "being-there," *Da-sein.* Thus both Heideggerian terms for man, existence and *Dasein,* envisage man as the place where being opens up and reveals itself.

It is the place of man thus defined that is the origin of thinking. Thinking "carries out" man's nature. If man is the being where being itself dawns on the beings, then this basic "clearing" of being, which constitutes man's nature, is synonymous with thinking about being. Thus the act most fundamentally related to man's nature is the act of thinking. Thinking is indeed the form in which the action of being upon man manifests itself.

To be sure, Heidegger does not have in mind any and all thought, but rather thinking in the pregnant sense he sometimes refers to as basic or primal thinking. The objectifying conceptualization carried on by metaphysical philosophy and the mathematical calculation carried on by natural science are in this sense not "thought." Real thinking restricts itself to the unveiling of being. It has no practical goal. It does not, like science, provide information, or, like traditional philosophy, seek to solve the ultimate puzzles of the universe, nor does it produce wisdom for living or guidance for action. Real thinking has "renounced" such pragmatism and persists in understanding itself only as the unveiling of being. Such thought is called forth by being itself, so that thought has a fate-laden character. In distinction from scientific calculation, which derives from the initiative of the scientist, real thinking comes to the thinker from his subject matter. It is this receptive structure of thought, based in man's nature as ek-sistence, that is for Ott the basic insight of relevance for perceiving the nature of theology. "Here lies the key to understanding the whole of Heidegger's work and the key to the whole relevance of this thinker for theology!"[93]

This distinction between the self-appointed calculation of the scientist and the response of primal thinking to the call of being can also be expressed in terms of a path of thought. Thought is not a road upon which one can simply stand and observe its course. Rather it is like a woodland trail which can be seen only as one goes along it, so that the trail seems to open up only in one's movement along it—and yet the course of one's movement is determined by the trail. Thinking consists in following the trail of being by pushing aside the underbrush as one works one's way down the path, thereby revealing the clearing that is in fact the path upon which one is led.

[93] *Ibid.*, p. 164.

In his published works Heidegger has been more involved in relating thinking to poetry than to theology. "The poet's naming is of a like origin [to the thinker's speaking]. However what is alike is alike only in that it is something different from what it is like. Although composing poetry and thinking are most alike in the care in the use of words, they are at the same time furthest separated in their nature. The thinker speaks being. The poet names the holy. To be sure the question must be left open here as to how, when thought about in terms of the nature of being, composing poetry and thanking and thinking are dependent on each other and at the same time different."[94] This association of poetry with Rudolf Otto's concept of "the holy," as well as the introduction of the third category of thanking alongside poetic composition and thinking, suggest that we are in close proximity to the thinking involved in theology.

Ott's point of departure for defining theology in correspondence to Heidegger's understanding of thinking and of poetic composition is the conviction that theology of necessity is to be understood as primal thinking, rather than as an instance of the secondary thinking characteristic of metaphysics and science. Otherwise theology would be subordinate to and under the control of another dimension of thought that would be more primal. This subordination theology could hardly accept in view of its responsibility to devote itself fully and hence freely to the critical explication of Christian faith. Nor does Ott think that one should make a sharp cleavage between preaching and theology, with the one understood as primal thinking, the other as secondary, "scientific" thinking. For this would leave theology in the subject-object dilemma, in the subjectivism that distorts a true understanding of the subject matter.[95]

"What then follows from Heidegger's interpretation of think-

---

[94] *Was ist Metaphysik* (8th ed.), pp. 50 f. [*Existence and Being*, pp. 391 f; paperback ed. p. 360.]

[95] Cf. Ott's criticism of Ernst Fuchs in this regard in Ott's latest book *Dogmatik und Verkündigung* (Zürich: EVZ-Verlag, 1961), pp. 19 f. The alternate position to Ott's is suggested by Ebeling, *ZThK, Beiheft* 2 (1961), pp. 123 f. (Cf. pp. 75 f. below).

ing for theology? Theology should not understand itself, its thinking, as freely carried on by a subject who subjectivistically observes an object and talks about it. Rather theology should understand itself as an element of encounter, as encounter with what is to be thought, which shows itself, 'unveils' itself to thought and thus determines thought. What is to be thought by theology is faith. Faith, however, is not something in itself; instead, it is faith in God. He who does the thinking in theology is himself the believer. Hence theological thinking is the thinking of faith and from faith, a thinking from within the encounter. When theology speaks of God, it does not speak 'about' God *outside* the encounter of faith; rather it speaks *out of* the encounter. Its talk about God is the encounter of faith explaining itself. Theology is the movement of faith wishing to clarify itself: *fides quaerens intellectum.* A theology that was something other than thinking out of the encounter, something other than thinking *as encounter,* could from Heidegger's point of view be designated in no other way than as subjectivistic and metaphysical."[96]

The extent to which this Heideggerian approach to theology converges in Ott's mind with reflection from within theology itself becomes clear when one consults Ott's inaugural address as Private-Dozent at the University of Basel, entitled "Theology as Prayer and as Science."[97] Theology is classified among those sciences that are based in experience, in distinction from *a priori* sciences such as logic and mathematics based in reason itself. Now the "experience" that theology explicates is prayer. For in prayer the believer "gives his response to God's word that corresponds to this word. . . . In human language God's own language makes itself heard."[98] Prayer is the experience in which God can be experienced, not as a psychic phenomenon, but as a response in which God's word comes to expression. It is upon this experience of God that theology is based.

Here the structural parallel to Heidegger's understanding of

[96] *Denken und Sein,* p. 173 f. Cf. the whole of the section on "The Thinking of Theology," pp. 171–175.

[97] "Theologie als Gebet und als Wissenschaft," *Theologische Zeitschrift,* XIV (1958), 120–132.

[98] *Ibid.,* p. 123.

being pressing itself into thought and hence finding expression in language which "cor-re-sponds" to being can be clearly sensed. And just as Heidegger finds in the language of such poets as Hölderlin the "text" for his thinking, Ott explicates his position in the same essay by means of an interpretation of Anselm of Canterbury's *Proslogion,* which was Anselm's "address" to God in prayer.[99] This treatise, itself composed in the form of prayer, reflects the understanding of theology Ott had in mind. "Teach me to seek thee, and show thyself to me as I seek: for I am not able to seek thee unless thou teachest, nor to find thee unless thou showest thyself" (Chapter I). Here theology's relation to God corresponds to thinking's relation to being as seen by Heidegger. The fate-laden character of thinking, as response to the unveiling of being that is given to it to think, could hardly be more adequately stated in terms of theological thinking. Thus, as poetry most authentically reflects man's ek-sistence as standing in the clearing of being, so prayer is the mode that best represents the believer's being as response to the word of God.

The relation of theology to prayer need not rob theology of its critical rigor or scholarly character. To be sure the goal of theological scholarship is not a proof convincing to one standing outside of faith. Yet the structure of prayer as response to God's word includes a responsibility before God for one's theological formulations. Just as one can discuss previous decisions and with responsibility reaffirm or revise them, just so theological discussion is possible with those who share the encounter with God and for whom the theologian speaks (church dogmatics!). The rigor of theological responsibility also expresses itself in the rigor of its presentation, the systematic, methodical nature of its utterance. Thus theology is to be defined as a system of analytic statements, explicating the experience of encounter with God which Ott focuses in the term "prayer."

Bultmann has taken exception to this understanding of the

---

[99] Cf. also Ott's article "Anselms Versöhnungslehre," *ThZ,* XIII (1957), 183–199. Wilhelm Anz, *ZThK, Beiheft* 2, 1961, p. 57, in dependence on Ernst Haenchen, "Anselm, Glaube und Vernunft," *ZThK,* XLVIII (1951), 312–342, argues that Ott's use of Anselm is invalid, since according to Anselm it is temptation which necessitates theology.

relation of theology to Christian experience, by insisting in a letter to Ott on the occasion of the publication of *Denken und Sein* that theology in distinction from faith is an instance of objectifying thought. He illustrates his point by quoting Ott's statement that "theology alone permits the Thou, namely God, to remain a Thou."[100] Here God is not addressed as Thou, but is talked about as a Thou, so that the divine Thou becomes a neuter category rather than a personal address. Bultmann argues that this relative objectification is inevitable. To be sure faith itself implies thought, so that there is a continuity. But the continuity is paradoxical. Theology is on the one hand the self-explication of faith's encounter. Yet theology has turned from faith's stance of hearkening into the stance of reflective thinking. Lectures and publications are not a witness in which the theologian presents himself as a believer, but are more nearly an "unbelieving" thought-process of an objectifying kind. Bultmann senses some awareness of this on Ott's part when Ott describes theology as moving beyond the horizon of the existence of the individual, and when Ott distinguishes theology's methodological reflections from theology as prayer.[101] Indeed, one may inquire whether Ott conceives of his own publications as theology, and, if so, whether they are not at least as much on the objectifying or methodological side of the dialectic as they are on the encounter or prayer side of the dialectic.

C. *Language and Hermeneutic*

Any Heideggerian discussion of being and thinking already involves by implication a discussion of language. For Heidegger, the term language (*Sprache*) does not merely designate audible or verbal articulation. It is more basically related to the conveying of meaning. For example, a thing's identity with itself "speaks" this identity to us, calls upon our thinking to correspond and our speaking to respond to this speech that comes to us from

---

[100] "Theologie als Gebet und als Wissenschaft," *ThZ*, XIV (1958), 124.
[101] *Ibid.*, pp. 130 f.

the subject matter.[102] Hence human language that says nothing is not true language. And on the other hand, man may speak without vocal articulation.[103]

Being, as that which calls forth thinking, takes place as authentic language; and thinking, as the "answer to the word of the silent voice of being," "seeks the word" in which being can "become language" and thus be communicated.[104] Language, like thinking, is rooted in *Dasein* as the place where being clears and becomes perceived. Already in *Being and Time* language is understood as having its roots "in the existentialist constitution of *Dasein's* disclosedness."[105] But for the later Heidegger this means that language does not originate in man as his activity;[106] man's language is his response to being's call upon him.

Heidegger maintains that his approach to language is different from that current in philosophical and theological circles.[107] Language is not to be understood as functioning as a sign, to designate a given content by means of commonly accepted sounds. Nor is language to be understood as functioning to express ineffable inner experience, whereby it would be the speaker himself who comes to expression in his language, and language itself would always be inadequate because of its derivative, objectifying overtone. Such an understanding of language is regarded by Heidegger as secondary, resultant upon the forgetfulness of being characteristic of the West, which has produced a "degeneration of language," e.g., into scientific terminology. Heidegger himself defines language as "the house of being" in which man lives and

[102] *Identität und Differenz*, pp. 17 ff. [*Essays in Metaphysics*, pp. 16 f.]
[103] The fact that Heidegger's term "language" does not coincide fully with what the term usually designates can lead to confusion. However, Heidegger tends to some extent to replace "language" with a term designating its essence when he is not referring to man's speaking. Such terms are "calling" (*Ruf*), "tolling" (*Geläut*), "saying" (*Sage*), "showing" (*Zeige*). Man's role in these instances is that of listening.
[104] *Was ist Metaphysik?* (8th ed.), pp. 49 f. [*Existence and Being*, pp. 389–391; paperback ed., pp. 358–360.]
[105] *Sein und Zeit*, p. 160. [*Being and Time*, p. 203.]
[106] *Unterwegs zur Sprache*, pp. 249 ff., and *passim*.
[107] *Über den Humanismus*, p. 16; *Unterwegs zur Sprache*, pp. 14 ff.

over which the thinkers and poets stand watch, as their speech carries out the revelation of being.[108] "Language is the clearing-concealing arrival of being itself."[109] For being as it unveils itself calls attention to itself, calls forth thought, calls for a response. When thus identified with the unveiling of being, language rather than man can be said to do the speaking: "Language speaks."[110] Language itself speaking is the condition of the possibility of man having something to say, the condition of the possibility of authentic human language. Just as man is by his very nature caught up into the unveiling of being, just so language takes man up into its occurrence, so that he makes audible through his own speaking the silent voice of being. Language *needs* man as its loudspeaker and hence *uses* man.[111]

Language is conceived of as a movement, a path.[112] This path can be detected when one retraces its steps. A poem "calls up" things in such a way that they are present in their significance, in their little "world." Now this world is not the poet's subjective feeling, but rather the historic significance of beings. The world that the poet calls up is in fact called up to him by the things themselves in their being. The poet harkens to the silent tolling in things as their being unveils itself. His answer only carries into audible language (so that less perceptive persons may hear) what the things themselves have to say as they speak their world. Thus human language is basically "answer," and shares in the fate-laden character of thinking. Primal language is being itself, to which our language corresponds. This path of language from being to human words is the actual dimension in which thinking and being take place.

It is in terms of this particular understanding of language that Heidegger's study of linguistic articulation is to be understood.

---

[108] *Über den Humanismus,* p. 5; *Unterwegs zur Sprache,* p. 267.

[109] *Über den Humanismus,* p. 16.

[110] *Unterwegs zur Sprache,* p. 12 and *passim.*

[111] The German verb *brauchen* means both to "need" and to "use." Heidegger seems to intend both meanings. Cf. *Unterwegs zur Sprache,* pp. 30, 256.

[112] "Der Weg zur Sprache," *Unterwegs zur Sprache,* pp. 239–268.

His fascination with etymology is not primarily directed toward reviving archaic usages, nor is it primarily directed toward a philologically exact statement of the use of terms at a given period, such as the pre-Socratic usage of the term *a-letheia*. "The point is rather, on the basis of the early meaning of a word and its transformation, to catch sight of the material area into which the word speaks, and to reflect upon this area as the area within which the subject matter named by the word moves. Only in this way does the word speak, and this in connection with the meanings with which the subject matter has unfolded itself throughout the history of thinking and poetic composition."[113] It is in this way that poets serve an inspirative function for Heidegger, in that they lead him into a realm that had been closed off by the metaphysical-scientific tradition, a realm into which he seeks entry. Rather than presenting a historical-critical exegesis of a poem, he enters into dialogue with the poem about the subject matter to which the poem admits him. Thus the poet's word is not an *object* of our study, but is an event calling up to us a subject matter that calls forth a response from us. The crucial issue is not whether the interpreter confines himself to exegesis to the exclusion of eisegesis, but rather whether he succeeds in entering into the movement of the poet's words, which are derived from the subject matter. The decisive issue is whether he hears the call of being to which the poet's words answered— whether he hears that call with sufficient clarity to be himself called upon to answer. The understanding of a text consists in hearing through the human language what that language has to say, namely, the showing of being which once called forth that language and which still calls upon us in that language.

Heidegger traces the roots of his concern for language to the theological discipline traditionally called "hermeneutic." "The title 'hermeneutic' was familiar to me from my study of theology. At that time I was especially disturbed by the question as to the relation between the word of Holy Scripture and theo-

[113] *Vorträge und Aufsätze,* pp. 48 f. With regard to the philological validity of Heidegger's use of *a-letheia* see note 58a above.

logical speculative thought. It was, if you wish, the same relation, i.e., between language and being, only obscured and inaccessible to me, so that I sought in vain via many detours and false leads for a guiding thread. . . . Without this theological origin I would never have arrived on the path of thought. But origin remains always future."[114]

This is one of the places where the later Heidegger seems to be maintaining a position diverging from *Being and Time,* and yet claiming that this position corresponds to his original intention. In *Being and Time* "hermeneutic" investigates being in terms of an "interpretation of the being of *Dasein*," "an analysis of the existentiality of existence."[115] Now it is part of the turn in Heidegger's thought that hermeneutic in this sense disappears, and Heidegger concedes that the term "hermeneutic" has also disappeared.[116] Yet in precisely this context the term "hermeneutic" is revived in its connection with language. "The expression 'hermeneutical' is derived from the Greek verb *hermeneuein.* This verb is related to the substantive *hermeneus,* which one can connect with the name of the god Hermes, by a thought-play that is more binding than the rigor of science. Hermes is the messenger of the gods. He brings the message of fate. *Hermeneuein* is the presentation that brings news to the extent that it is itself able to hearken to a message. Such a presentation becomes the exposition of what has already been said by the poets, who, according to the saying of Socrates in Plato's discourse Ion (534e), are 'messengers of the gods'. . . . From all this it is clear that the hermeneutical does not primarily refer to exposition, but more basically to the bringing of the message and of news."[117] If hermeneutic both for the early and the later Heidegger has to do with interpreting being, the later Heidegger does this in terms of the path of language rather than in terms of the structures of *Dasein.* The ontological difference between being and

[114] *Unterwegs zur Sprache,* p. 96.
[115] *Sein und Zeit,* pp. 37 f. [*Being and Time,* p. 62.]
[116] *Unterwegs zur Sprache,* p. 98.
[117] *Unterwegs zur Sprache,* pp. 121 f.

beings lays its claim upon man, who corresponds to this claim with the response of his language.

This new correlation of hermeneutic to the later Heidegger's understanding of language provides the potentiality for a new correlation between God's word and man's understanding. If in the first half of this century the Barthians have tended to focus upon the one and Bultmannians upon the other, the possibility of a new theology which would take its point of departure in their unity seems to be possible. It is this possibility that is stated programmatically in Gerhard Ebeling's essay "Word of God and Hermeneutic,"[118] which provides the point of departure for the companion volume to the present volume in the series *New Frontiers in Theology*, entitled *The New Hermeneutic*.

Although Ott finished *Denken und Sein* before the publication of Heidegger's *Unterwegs zur Sprache*, he had access in unpublished form to some of the essays in that volume on language. And since the appearance of *Denken und Sein* he has himself entered into the new hermeneutical discussion with an unpublished essay of 1960 on "Language and Understanding as the Basic Problem of Contemporary Theology."[119] "The hermeneutical problem poses the question: What is understanding and how does a given text become understandable? The language problem poses the question: What is the nature of language and how does a given text speak to us? Yet both problems converge, indeed they are ultimately identical." From this correlation Ott derives the thesis that theology is essentially hermeneutic: "Theology is by its very nature the constant effort to eliminate empty talk from preaching, the incessant attempt to keep open or find ever anew access to the subject matter via authentic understanding. This effort takes place, however, in a twofold direction: toward the understanding of the Biblical texts on the one hand and

---

[118] "Wort Gottes und Hermeneutik," *ZThK*, LVI (1959) 224–251; *Wort und Glaube* (Tübingen: Mohr, 1960), pp. 319–348; English translation forthcoming in *Word and Faith* (Philadelphia: Muhlenberg Press, 1963) and in *The New Hermeneutic*.

[119] "Sprache und Verstehen als Grundproblem gegenwärtiger Theologie." Cf. also *Dogmatik und Verkündigung* (1961), pp. 10 f.

toward the understandability of the gospel in the present on the other."

This leads to the statement that hermeneutic is basically "trans-lation," meaning the trans-portation of the subject matter from then to now, as the event of language in the past speaks in our language today. Here again we have to do with an etymological reflection: The Greek verb *hermeneuein* means to bring to understanding, and from this focal meaning the verb was used in three specific but related senses: to speak, to interpret, and to translate.[120] The first two meanings (to speak and to interpret) suggest the close affinity of the problem of language and the problem of interpretation, since both are "hermeneutic" in the broad sense of bringing something to understanding. In a similar way the affinity of the last two meanings (to interpret and to translate) suggests the interrelatedness of exegesis and translation. At this point however a peculiarity of German usage is brought into play. The German word for "translate," *übersetzen*, retains in current usage a meaning that is perhaps rarer in English. To cross from one shore of a river to the other in a ferry is to *übersetzen*—much as in Christian legend a saint could be "translated" into the realm beyond, and his body could be "translated" into an earthly equivalent such as Westminster Abbey. This usage serves in the German discussion to point out that the task of interpretation is to "transport" the meaning of the text into the life of the modern congregation.

Biblical exegesis has not reached its goal in the historical-critical method, but should learn from new hermeneutical reflection to penetrate through to the subject matter, the revelation of God, and, led by the Biblical answer to the word of God, to answer to that word with the exegete's own words. Although Biblical language is not simply identified with God's revelation, but is rather an answer to God's word, it is the linguistic path to God's word, the linguistic "room" of the revelation, as Ott

[120] Cf. Gerhard Ebeling's article on "Hermeneutik," *Die Religion in Geschichte und Gegenwart* (3rd ed.), III (1959), 243.

puts it.[121] Just as one encounters being in this or that historic, fate-laden conceptualization, just so Christian language is not completely irrelevant or optional, but is rather the historic, fate-laden medium in which God's word speaks to us. Similarly our answer to God's word is not abstract, prior to or apart from our words, as if they were some optional or dispensable, secondary or incomplete expression of a response already made. Rather existence is itself essentially linguistic, and faith takes place within our language, which is our answer—not just a secondary *expression* of our answer—to God. The inadequacy of our linguistic response is the inadequacy of our response as a whole, and it would be to ignore our historicness to assume that the "accidents" of linguistic formulation were somewhere transcended in a truer "essential" response. The limits of our language are limits of our historic existence as such—and all the more so when language is understood to mean not just our vocabulary, but the encompassing medium for understanding and conveying meaning in which we exist. Thus language receives a more material relation to the theological enterprise than is often accorded it, by being freed from the stigma of being no more than an inevitably secondary, objectifying expression of a purer inner awareness.

Since it is basically language itself that speaks, Heidegger's study of language has taken the form of seeking to understand such concrete linguistic phenomena as poems. Ott infers that theological reflection upon language should not take place in the abstract, but rather in the concrete effort to understand the linguistic phenomena of theology's subject matter. Hence Ott accompanies his discussions with instances of "practical hermeneutic," the encounter with specific Biblical texts, to derive from such experience further clarification of the nature of the language with which theology has to do. It is in this sense that the two concrete examples in Ott's paper "What is Systematic Theology?" are to be seen in their methodological importance. Yet

---

[121] *Denken und Sein,* p. 190. Cf. the whole section on "The Word in Theology," pp. 188–192.

if this approach to hermeneutic by listening to Biblical language is to be carried out, it must become a task for Biblical scholarship as such. It is quite possible that Biblical scholarship will react to the new hermeneutic much as it did to Barth's *Romans,* by pointing pedantically to historical-critical inexactitudes, and missing the significance of what is happening. Certainly Heidegger's own interpretations of poetry are open to similar criticism, which has not been slow in emerging.[122] If, however, Biblical scholarship will join with philosophical thought in this enterprise, the gulf between the two disciplines may be bridged and a new access to theology achieved.[123]

D. *The World and the Saving Event*

One may recall that Ott's point of departure was his criticism of Bultmann's view of history, which in its distinction of *Historie* and *Geschichte* seemed to Ott to end in a dualism of two spheres of reality. Hence *Denken und Sein* defined its approach as follows: "The question that we bring with us is, generally speaking, the question as to the nature of the history in which we in faith know ourselves to be, the history between God and man."[124]

Ott consequently appended to his discussion of being in *Denken und Sein* a section on being as "historic room,"[125] to provide a basis for relating Heidegger's understanding of being to the theological problem of history. Of course the concept of

---

[122] Cf. the bibliography given by Löwith, *Heidegger. Denker in dürftiger Zeit* (2nd ed.), p. 13, n. 13. Walter Uhsadel's review of *Unterwegs zur Sprache,* in the *Theologische Literaturzeitung,* LXXXVI (1961), 217–221, is on this level. Of importance is the "Briefwechsel mit Martin Heidegger" with Emil Staiger published in the latter's *Die Kunst der Interpretation. Studien zur deutschen Literaturgeschichte* (Zürich: Atlantis Verlag, 1955, 2nd ed. 1957), pp. 34–49, and Staiger's article "Ein Rückblick" in the *Neue Zürcher Zeitung,* Sept. 27, 1959, Blatt 5, Nr. 2898(69).

[123] This proposal is made in detail in my essay "Heilsgeschichte und Lichtungsgeschichte," *Evangelische Theologie,* XXII (1962), 113–141, to appear in English under the title "The Historicality of Biblical Language" in *The Relevance of the Old Testament for Christian Faith,* edited by Bernhard W. Anderson.

[124] P. 27. Cf. also Ott's pamphlet *Die Frage nach dem historischen Jesus und die Ontologie der Geschichte (Theologische Studien,* Heft 62, Zürich: EVZ-Verlag, 1960).

[125] Pp. 152–157.

being as historic room does not mean simply a passive space where beings are placed ("in history"), but rather refers to being as providing "room" for beings. Heidegger can speak of being's "roominess," in that being makes it possible for beings to be. To speak of being as the historic room of beings calls attention to the essentially historic nature of beings, their historicness. Since the being of beings occurs as an event, it corresponds to the occurrence of history, and hence being's roominess is "historic room as a whole, the horizon and sum total of all occurrence."[126] If being is the bridge between thinking and beings, in that it is both the condition of the possibility of thinking and the being of beings, then historic room is the center for an all-embracing understanding of reality.

Ott's designation of being as historic room derives from the various historic aspects of being to which Heidegger has drawn attention. For being is not a static concept distinguished and set over against more historic factors such as becoming, appearance, thinking, ethical obligation. Instead, being includes them.[127] Hence Heidegger is concerned to understand as historic various categories previously conceived of in static fashion. *Wesen* is not static *essentia,* but rather a "taking-place"; truth is not a static correlation, but an unveiling; *physis* is not a static nature, but the being of beings as it comes forward, shows itself. (*The* Greek verb *phyein* means to put forth shoots, engender, grow.) Being is itself not a static "is-ness" (*Seiendheit*), but an unveiling. Even the ontological difference between being and the beings is not a fixed separation, but is itself the unveiling of being.

The outcome of this transformation of categories traditionally regarded as static into historic categories designating the event of being is that the word "event" is itself given a deeper significance in terms of Heidegger's philosophy. The German term *Ereignis,* "event," is etymologically related to the term *Auge,* "eye." From the root idea of catching sight of, Heidegger moves

---

[126] P. 153.

[127] *Was ist Metaphysik?* (8th ed.), p. 17. [*Existentialism from Dostoevsky to Sartre,* p. 215.]

to the idea of calling to oneself with a glance, and thus appropriating.[128] "Event" comes to mean "appropriation," and refers basically to being and man appropriating each other. Being is put in the trust of man as the shepherd of being, and man for his fulfillment must be given over to being. The unveiling of being to man's thought, the call of being to man's language, is this mutual appropriation. In this pre-eminent sense the unveiling of being is "event."

If being takes place as thinking and as speaking, a third dimension in which it takes place is called "world." Here "world" is not used in the common meaning of a place (the universe) in which things happen; rather world consists in the event of being, just as this event calls forth thinking and speaking. Nor are the three dimensions, thinking, speaking, and world, different events side by side; rather they are the structures of the one event of being, inseparable in occurrence, though having distinguishable *foci* of discussion.

If being is for Heidegger always the being of beings, world is always the world of things. World is the context of meaning that inheres in things. It is not an interpretation belatedly superimposed on things, but is the very way in which they are. Hence one gains access to Heidegger's understanding of world through his analysis of the essential nature of things.[129]

Heidegger takes his point of departure in the etymology of the word for "thing," *Ding.* The corresponding German verb *dingen* (cf. the Anglo-Saxon verb *thingan*) means to negotiate in court. Hence the noun *Ding* or "thing" means the issue at stake in such an assembly. One may note that other designations of real entities have much the same origin: German *Sache,* Latin *res* and *causa,* and Greek *rhema* all refer to the issue at stake at

---

[128] *Identität und Differenz,* pp. 28 f. [*Essays in Metaphysics,* p. 27.]
[129] Cf. esp. "Das Ding," *Vorträge und Aufsätze* (1950), pp. 163–185. In *Identität und Differenz,* p. 9 [*Essays in Metaphysics,* p. 9.] Heidegger says that the essay "Der Satz der Identität," *ibid.,* pp. 11–34 ["The Principle of Identity," *Essays in Metaphysics,* pp. 11–32], looks forward into the realm discussed in "Das Ding." The essay "Die Sprache" in *Unterwegs zur Sprache,* pp. 9–33, clearly presupposes the analysis in "Das Ding."

a court. Thus a thing is originally a meaning-laden issue at stake, and the common view of a thing as a completely neutral, objective entity is a secondary degeneration of the term.

Heidegger also explicates the primal meaning of "thing" by reference to the original use of the word to refer to the meeting or assembly itself at which an issue is at stake. The Anglo-Saxon name for an assembly, *thing,* is preserved in the Scandinavian designations for a parliament: *Althing* or *Storting.* Heidegger starts from the idea that a thing is a meeting, an assembling. There meet or are assembled in a thing the four sides of a square, which Heidegger characterizes as earth and heaven, the divine and the mortal. It is in this assembling that a thing has its being and its meaningfulness, its world.

A jug, for example, is not to be defined in terms of the technology of producing it, nor in terms of the material composing its bottom and walls, as if this were what it is. Rather a jug is to be understood in terms of its capacity for containing and pouring. This is the actual "essence" of the jug, what makes it a jug. For the scientist to say an empty jug is not actually empty since it is full of air is not to make a more accurate statement about the jug, but rather to lose sight of the jug's reality. A jug full of air is in the most meaningful sense empty, that is to say, it is ready for its contents. A jug is made for wine, not air. In terms of such a jug Heidegger reflects upon how a thing is a meeting, an assembling. In the wine the strength of the earth and the warmth of the sun meet to quench the thirst of the mortals and to present offerings to the divine. This thing, by assembling the square, constitutes world.

This is further developed in the essay on "Building, Dwelling, Thinking."[130] Here "building" (*bauen*) is traced etymologically to a basic meaning of inhabiting, dwelling. One may compare the English word "neighbor," which means etymologically "nigh-dweller." If building is for the sake of dwelling, then dwelling itself (*wohnen*), as the basic aspect of man's existence in the

[130] "Bauen Wohnen Denken," in *Vorträge und Aufsätze* (1951), pp. 145–162.

world, is in turn a "husbanding" (*schonen*) of the world, sparing it, letting it be itself; positively, caring or providing for it. This ultimate implication of "building" can be sensed for example in a bridge, which "assembles" the two shores at this point, provides passage for the flood water coming from the storm in the sky, provides the mortals passage on their way, and as it arches them over the stream points them up to the divine. The bridge assembles the square, makes place for it. Such a building is a dwelling since it husbands or provides for the earth.

This can also be described by Heidegger as saving the earth. For the verb for save (*retten*) means basically to "rid" something of what impedes it from being itself, to set it free to be what it is. In distinction from technology, which masters the earth, building saves the earth, lets it be. This relation of building and dwelling to the care of being is rooted in man's nature as ek-sistence, his standing out in or dwelling in the clearing of being, so that man is the "shepherd of being." This nature of man has previously been explicated by Heidegger in terms of thinking as the dimension in which man's nature takes place. Now building and dwelling are put alongside of thinking as basic structures of man.

Walter Schulz[131] locates in the new understanding of a thing the central element in the turn in Heidegger's thought. The Cartesian effort to make man the fixed point upon which all depends can be described as the desire to make man absolute or "unconditioned." The German word for unconditioned (*unbedingt*) contains the word for "thing," and means literally "not dependent on a thing." The later Heidegger, as the completion of his move toward understanding thought as given to man in a fate-laden way, accepts man's existence as conditioned (*bedingt*), dependent upon things to assemble the square which provides man with his world.[132] Thus the subjectivism of the metaphysical tradition is eliminated by renouncing the understanding of man as basically the subject of meaning in the uni-

---

[131] *PhR,* I (1953–54), 221 f.

[132] Cf. Heidegger, *Vorträge und Aufsätze,* p. 179: "We are—in the strict sense of the word—conditioned (die *Be-Dingten*). We have left behind us the presumption of all that is unconditioned (*Unbedingten*)."

verse. To be sure, this does not reduce man to a mere object upon which such meaning happens, for he is a side of the square which assembles when a thing happens. The thing is no longer a meaningless entity, but is the central meaningful occurrence, in which man as well as nature participates and finds his historicness. Things do not become symbols only when and if they are given meaning by man. Instead, meaning is constituted by things as they happen, and in this meaning man participates.

The Bultmannian use of the concept of the historicness of existence was a first step toward overcoming the subjectivism of the Cartesian epoch, in that it pointed out the basic relatedness of one's self-understanding to one's world. Yet this historicness was largely a matter of man's history in which the world partook, as when the tool or utensil partook in the purposefulness of the person who made it so as to have it at hand. The focus of meaning in *Being and Time* remained man. Ott argues that the later Heidegger's understanding of a thing as an assembling of the square provides a more balanced meaning-structure of the earth and heaven, the divine and mortal, and hence a more fitting correlation for the theologian's understanding of the saving event.[133]

This also implies that what is meaningful for man does not lie outside the world of things or only on the borderline, but rather in the simple everyday things, the jug, the bridge, a peasant's shoes. Thus the gnostic, a-cosmic overtone often attributed to existentialism would be replaced by a concrete corporeality of historic meaning. Dietrich Bonhoeffer's call for a Biblical down-to-earthness rather than a mystic other-worldliness in our doctrine of salvation would seem to find its concrete answer in terms of the later Heidegger. Ott envisages a doctrine of salvation that keeps its feet on the ground, yet, in terms of Heidegger's square, is open to the divine as one dimension of life on earth. With Heidegger's help he proposes to do justice to the eschatological understanding of salvation in the New Testament,

---

[133] "The World-Dimension of Revelation," *Denken und Sein,* pp. 222–225.

which is oriented to the bodily resurrection of Christ and the coming kingdom of God on earth.[134] This corporeality would also have its implications for doctrines of creation, the Lord's Supper, the church, providence, prayer.

To this Bultmann replies that the "corporeality"[135] Heidegger has in mind is not to be understood as physical materiality, but rather as an existential, much as Bultmann presented the Pauline concept of body in his *Theology of the New Testament*.[136] The mere physicality of things is rejected so as to make their corporeality in the true sense intelligible. Bultmann finds himself misunderstood when his position is taken to involve the irrelevance of existence in time and space. Rather he emphasizes that encounters and decisions are not merely between persons, but between persons and fate. Man's history cannot be cut off from what happens in nature. Bultmann fears that Ott's emphasis upon the material corporeality of theology would replace or obscure this existential corporeality.

Rather than the divine side of the square providing a dimension of transcendence, as Ott assumed, Bultmann argues that this is an "immanent transcendence,"[137] and that Ott has misunderstood this and fallen back into a metaphysical understanding of transcendence. The doctrines of creation, providence, and the final consummation do not find in Heidegger's square their structural foundation. Ernst Fuchs senses that Ott's use of the Heideggerian square to argue that man exists in constant confrontation with the divine, or transcendence, or an ultimate limit,

---

[134] Cf. Ott's booklet *Eschatologie: Versuch eines dogmatischen Grundrisses* (*Theologische Studien, Heft* 53; Zürich: EVZ-Verlag, 1958).

[135] Bultmann distinguishes between two terms for corporeality: *Körperlichkeit*, the physical body, and *Leiblichkeit*, corporeal existence.

[136] *Theology of the New Testament*, I, translated by Kendrich Grobel, (New York: Charles Scribner's Sons, 1951), pp. 192–203.

[137] In a conversation with R. Scherer, cited by Heinz-Horst Schrey, "Die Bedeutung der Philosophie Martin Heideggers für die Theologie," *Martin Heideggers Einfluss auf die Wissenschaften* (Heidegger *Festschrift*, Bern: A. Francke AG. Verlag, 1949), p. 16, Heidegger stated that philosophy cannot speak of God. Rather, what it calls God is a sublimated worldly concept, something immanent, everything else but the Christian concept of God.

is a return to natural theology,[138] in spite of the repeated denials on Ott's part.[139] Helmut Franz argues that Heideggerian thought is incompatible with Ott's interest in bodily resurrection, since for Heidegger corporeal existence is confronted with death, which would hardly be the case with the resurrected body, and for Heidegger a "thing" does not die, so cannot be used as a model for the body, which dies and rises.[140]

It is thus apparent that the relation of the later Heidegger's thought to the structure of theological doctrines is still in need of clarification. If Ott's *Denken und Sein* is only a first word rather than the last word as to the correlation of the later Heidegger and theology, it has nevertheless served the function of precipitating the discussion. It is not surprising that the theological debate about the later Heidegger has become acute only since the appearance of Ott's book, and has to a predominant extent taken the form of a debate with Ott.

III. THE LATER HEIDEGGER AND BULTMANNIAN THEOLOGY

The initial correlation of *Being and Time* with theology was worked out by Rudolf Bultmann and his pupils. It was to be expected that this school should be the first to take up the discussion of the relevance of the later Heidegger for theology. Not only are they equipped by long familiarity with Heidegger for such a debate; they are also directly challenged by Ott's presentation. Bultmann's own letter of reply to Ott is a defense of the superior theological relevance of the early Heidegger over the later Heidegger. Bultmann's pupils tend to concede that theology must work out a correlation with the later Heidegger, although they disagree basically with the correlation suggested by Ott. An

---

[138] *PhR*, VIII (1961), 107.

[139] *Denken und Sein,* p. 15 and *passim*. With regard to the square p. 224.

[140] "Das Denken Heideggers und die Theologie," *ZThK, Beiheft* 2 (1961), p. 84.

alternative correlation in terms of the tensions between law and gospel is beginning to emerge.

Bultmann begins his reply to Ott by acknowledging the value of *Denken und Sein* as an interpretation of the later Heidegger. Yet he challenges the validity of the relation between philosophy and theology envisaged by Ott. This relation cannot be that of a dialogue, since a dialogue presupposes a common seeking for truth made possible by a common relation to the truth. Yet theology based on faith believes that in distinction from philosophy it knows the truth. Theology does not even share its point of departure with philosophy, for, as Ott himself affirms, theology begins "consciously and strictly in faith in the revelation of God in Christ."[141] Nor can such a conversation be grounded, as Ott assumes,[142] in a common "problem of existence." For theology's problem of existence in distinction from that of philosophy is how man as sinner can exist before God.

The possibility and necessity of a relation of theology to philosophy is according to Bultmann rooted in the need to make Biblical statements intelligible to man if he is to appropriate them. They must be intelligible as statements about his existence. Now this necessity for "existentialist interpretation" presupposes the philosopher's clarification of what existence is. When he establishes for example that existence is what each person commits himself to, then room is left open for man's existence before God —but a "dialogue" with philosophy on this specific existence is not possible. Theology is dependent upon philosophy in that it must use current philosophy's analysis of man; it cannot ignore what the philosophers are saying and simply decide to prefer for example an idealistic or moralistic anthropology. If the theologian wishes to argue this anthropological point, he is functioning not as a theologian but as a philosopher, so that such a discussion would not be a dialogue between theology and philosophy, but a debate within philosophy.

Bultmann agrees that if theology is to remain related to

[141] *Denken und Sein*, p. 13.
[142] *Ibid.*, p. 15.

reality, it must be able to give account of itself to philosophy. This relation to philosophy is for Bultmann a dependence upon philosophy, for example upon its analysis of man, rather than a dialogue. Now it is this dependence of theology upon philosophy that Ott, as a Barthian, denies. Yet Bultmann asks how Ott can avoid the inference that Heidegger's philosophy formally determines theology, when theology to be understood must speak in terms of the historicness of existence worked out by Heidegger.[143]

Bultmann denies that philosophy can include the idea of God as Creator and of the world as creature. Philosophy does not go beyond the problem of the eternity or finitude of the world. To be sure, philosophy like science can correct traditional conceptualizations of creation. To this extent theology presupposes philosophy. But Christian theology cannot claim to be philosophy, as Ott assumes, since philosophy cannot recognize a revelation that is both a historical and an eschatological event. It is the relation of philosophy to this event that Ott has not clarified. If philosophical thinking has a history, the history of being, would not theological thinking have its own history, the history of revelation? To be sure philosophy can define what the *term* revelation or the *term* sin means, so that the nonbeliever can know what preaching is driving at. Philosophy can clarify ontologically the existentialist structure relevant to an ontic discussion of revelation or sin. For example, sin is a kind of guilt. Hence when theology expresses itself in the categories of existentialist anthropology, it has a positive relation to philosophy. Yet philosophy is not able to move beyond an ontological discussion about the categories into an ontic discussion about sin or revelation as such. Philosophy is not able to discuss theologically.[144]

---

[143] *Ibid.*, p. 157.

[144] Jüngel, "Der Schritt zurück," *ZThK*, LVIII (1961), 112 ff., criticizes Ott's interpretation of the relation of philosophy and theology in a way that is in general though not in all details like the criticism of Bultmann. Bultmann's position is like that of Heinz-Horst Schrey, "Die Bedeutung der Philosophie Martin Heideggers für die Theologie," *Martin Heideggers Einfluss auf die Wissenschaften* (Heidegger *Festschrift*, Bern: A. Francke AG. Verlag, 1949), pp. 9–21, esp. p. 14. Schrey states that this

Bultmann is not only dissatisfied with Ott's general position on the relation of philosophy to theology; he is especially dissatisfied with Ott's position on the relation of the later Heidegger to theology. Bultmann maintains that the theologian should be basically critical of the later Heidegger,[145] and he sketches the direction that such a criticism might take. In substance this sketch serves as a defense of Bultmann's use of the "existentialism" in the early Heidegger.

Bultmann begins by calling attention to the dialectic relation of being and beings: being does not occur apart from beings, and beings do not occur apart from being. Similarly, the relation between "primal" and "secondary" for Heidegger is not a chronological separation, but a material relation of possibilities that are present together. When Heidegger says that language's speaking is the condition of the possibility of man's speaking, this does not mean that language speaks before man can speak. Rather language speaks only in man's speaking. Now man's words always involve an objectifying element (although this is not necessarily that of scientific conceptualization), and yet man's speech is united with the primal language that calls it forth. Both belong together in a dialectic relationship. Similarly, the relation between language speaking and man expressing his experiences is dialectic rather than antithetic. A poem expresses an experience and as the poem "calls" or "tolls," it makes an impression corresponding to the experience it expresses. If language is the condition of the possibility of man speaking, man is the condition under which language becomes verbally articulate. Here one

position is that of Heidegger himself, presented in an unpublished address of 1927 on "Phenomenology and Theology." It is the position represented in the unauthorized but widely circulated student's notes of Heidegger's lecture in Marburg of Feb. 14, 1928 on "Theology and Philosophy."

[145] Although the Bultmannians have not shared Bultmann's basic reserve with regard to the later Heidegger, Ott has been consistently criticized for his uncritical stance toward Heidegger. Cf. Jüngel, "Der Schritt zurück," *ZThK*, LVIII (1961), 107; Fuchs, *PhR*, VIII (1961), 108; Franz, "Das Denken Heideggers und die Theologie," *ZThK, Beiheft* 2 (1961), p. 89. Gerhard Ebeling, "Verantworten des Glaubens in Begegnung mit dem Denken M. Heideggers," *ZThK, Beiheft* 2 (1961), p. 123, rejects a "global appropriation [of Heidegger's thought] and a neglect of critical debate."

catches sight of Bultmann's reason for emphasizing the dialectic nature of Heidegger's position: He is concerned to emphasize its inescapable relation to man, which Ott, in his reaction against existentialism, had minimized. Hence Bultmann asks why language addressed from man to man, in command or exhortation, is omitted from Ott's discussion of language.

Bultmann presses his point of the focal role of man by asking whether the historicness that Ott, with Heidegger, roots in things is not in fact derived from man's historicness. The jug, the peasant's shoes, the bridge, speak forth man's history and derive from him their historicness. The world they provide him is that of his own history. When a thing assembles the square and thus speaks, it is not the thing which is historic, but rather man who stands in the world of things. It is to man that things speak, and what they say is actually their relation to man's fate.

What Bultmann misses in Heidegger's treatment of things is the relation of person to person. Heidegger's analysis of the peasant's shoes neglected to state that they speak of the love with which one works to help another. Similarly with regard to the jug. It often speaks my history, the human relations in which I stand, as would be the case if I inherited it from my father or received it as a gift from a friend. This person-to-person relation characteristic of man is missing from the later Heidegger.[146] Good and evil, duty and responsibility, guilt and forgiveness are not treated. Yet things when they assemble *can* speak of these human relationships, and to this extent Heidegger's philosophy is only a limited analysis of reality.

Bultmann's criticism should not be misunderstood as if he were calling for philosophy to theologize. Rather it is the task of philosophy to provide philosophical analyses which theology presupposes. Guilt and responsibility, for example, are not theological doctrines, but rather dimensions of human existence as such. Theology needs philosophy to provide clarity with regard

---

[146] Gerhard Ebeling, "Verantworten des Glaubens in Begegnung mit dem Denken M. Heideggers," *ZThK, Beiheft* 2 (1961), p. 124, points out that the concrete place where language occurs, person-to-person relations, remains in need of clarification.

to just such dimensions. For example, theology is concerned with man as a person, and hence needs clarity as to what being a person means. If *Being and Time* understood historicness as that of each particular man, it thereby provided an understanding of man as a person. When now historicness is instead located in reality as such, the question of the nature of man as a person is left dangling. What is selfhood for the man who is at the disposal of the fate-laden occurrence of being? Where is man as responsible to God? To the extent that the later Heidegger does not provide structures for such theological concerns, his philosophy is of limited relevance to theology.

Ott's book was not only a critique of Bultmann's use of the early Heidegger, but also a debate with Ernst Fuchs over the use to be made of the later Heidegger. Hence it is not surprising that the debate with Ott has been carried on primarily by Fuchs and his pupils. Eberhard Jüngel was an assistant in the New Testament department of the *Kirchliche Hochschule* of Berlin when Fuchs was Professor there, and it is he who has published an article with the subtitle "A Debate with Heinrich Ott's Interpretation of Heidegger."[147] The essay is entitled "The Step Backwards," which is of course a play on Heidegger's term referring to the step back out of metaphysics into the ground of metaphysics. Jüngel means it as a criticism of Ott for falling back into metaphysics.[148]

Jüngel's charge that Ott has returned to metaphysics is based on Ott's use of traditional terminology whose roots are ultimately to be found in the subjectivism of the metaphysical tradition. Ott can speak of a "project of thought," whereas thought is not "projected" from the subject, but comes to him from the subject matter. Ott distinguishes between a formal and a material relation of philosophy to theology, whereas such Aristotelian categories as form and matter are to be replaced. Ott describes Heidegger's thought as "static" prior to the shift, "dynamic" after the shift,

---

[147] "Der Schritt zurück. Eine Auseinandersetzung mit der Heidegger-Deutung Heinrich Otts," *ZThK*, LVIII (1961), 104–122.
[148] *Ibid.*, p. 110.

and draws diagrams of it, whereas Heidegger regards thought as historic, as event. Jüngel most of all takes exception to Ott's defining Heidegger's approach as transcendental.[149] This suggests that the movement of thought comes from the thinker, as he moves step by step into the presup-*positions* of thought. But thinking is for Heidegger no longer what the thinker "posits" but that which comes to the thinker from being. Hence Heidegger should not be described as inquiring as to presuppositions of thought. Instead, he hearkens to what being bids him; his thinking corresponds to being. Thus Ott, in describing being as the presupposition of thought, is using a vocabulary which has not yet been brought into conformity to the subject matter of Heidegger's thought—an inconsistency frequently and perhaps unavoidably encountered in these initial stages of the discussion of the later Heidegger's thought.[150]

Ernst Fuchs' own review of Ott's book, although sharing quite decidedly in the general Bultmannian criticism of Ott, is primarily of relevance in that it sketches some of the outlines of his own current position. Fuchs meets Ott's criticism of him for not following Heidegger's path of thought[151] with the reply that he never intended to do so, since "faith is no path of thought." Fuchs understands Ott's talk of Heidegger's "path of thought" in the same way Jüngel understands Ott's description of Heidegger's method as transcendental: a "path of thought" suggests Cartesian subjectivism. Hence Fuchs sets up the antithesis: "If

---

[149] *Ibid.*, pp. 105 ff. Similarly Ernst Fuchs, *PhR*, VIII (1961), 108. Helmut Franz, "Das Denken Heideggers und die Theologie," *ZThK, Beiheft* 2, p. 85, criticizes Ott for trying to "reproduce Heidegger's thought in the language of German idealism."

[150] Jüngel appeals (*ZThK*, LVIII, 1961, 104 f.) to Helmut Franz' book *kerygma und kunst* as the proper use of the later Heidegger in relation to theology, by way of contrast to Ott's *Denken und Sein.* Yet Franz (*ZThK, Beiheft* 2, 1961, pp. 86, 100) uses the term "dynamic" as equivalent to "historic," and makes use (*ibid.*, p. 100) of diagrams like those of Ott. Cf. Heidegger's comment: "It belongs to the nature of such transitions that they to a certain extent must still speak the language of what they are helping to overcome." *Was ist Metaphysik?* (8th ed.), p. 43. [*Existence and Being,* pp. 380 f.; paperback ed., p. 350.]

[151] *Denken und Sein,* p. 186. Actually Ott is here criticizing Fuchs for not following Heidegger's understanding of language.

the 'path of thought' leads into the square, the *path of language* will lead again—to us." Man's efforts at thought are his works righteousness; thought is equivalent to law,[152] while language is equivalent to gospel. Being has its place not in thought but in language, for the hearing of the voice of being calls forth speech. Fuchs poses the "decisive" question to Heidegger: "When will the thinker finally give up thinking about being? If he has experienced that being speaks, then he will understand why I pose my question this way. The theologian, and Barth specifically, knows of being as 'being for . . .' "[153] Here Fuchs seems to identify being and God, an identification not made by Heidegger himself.

Another of Fuchs' former pupils, Helmut Franz, has moved via a critique of both Ott[154] and Fuchs[155] in their use of Heidegger to an independent position. Fuchs' rejection of Heideggerian thinking is for Franz a misunderstanding of what thinking means for Heidegger. Thinking is for Heidegger responding to being, and hence does not derive from man's initiative. Hence thinking is in this regard no more a works righteousness than is language. Nor is being understood as "being for . . ." only by the theologian. Heidegger himself understands being as "being for" beings, and so speaks of the favor of being.

---

[152] Gerhard Ebeling, "Verantworten des Glaubens in Begegnung mit dem Denken M. Heideggers," *ZThK, Beiheft* 2 (1961), p. 122 questions "whether faith in the sense of primal Christian living tolerates theology at all, that is to say, whether faith can be 'thought.' " He raises the question as to "whether theology is not essentially bound to metaphysical thinking." Yet, on p. 123, he describes theology since Luther as involved in the effort to overcome metaphysics. On p. 124, he wonders "whether the segregation of thinking from believing and the expectation that God could be promised to thought, together with the talk of the 'square,' may not be clinging to metaphysics."

[153] All quotations of Fuchs are from p. 108 of his review of Ott's book, *PhR,* VIII (1961). This review is significantly entitled "Thinking and Being?" ("Denken und Sein?"), which is both a play on the title of Ott's book and a suggestion of Fuchs' criticism.

[154] "Das Denken Heideggers und die Theologie," *ZThK, Beiheft* 2 (1961), pp. 83–85 and *passim.* He characterizes Ott's method as eclecticism.

[155] *ZThK, Beiheft* 2 (1961), pp. 89 f. Cf. also *kerygma und kunst* (Saarbrücken: Minerva-Verlag, 1959), p. 57.

Franz also presents a critique of Fuchs' earlier use of Heidegger in his *Hermeneutik*.[156] Here Fuchs had already interpreted Heidegger in terms of the latter's understanding of language almost a decade before the appearance of *Unterwegs zur Sprache*. He understands Heidegger to be presenting a complaint about the breakdown of language. Since for Fuchs authentic language is the word of God, he interprets Heidegger's complaint about the breakdown of language as posing the question of God. The question about God is then answered when Jesus' call of love responds as authentic language to the complaint and turns it into thanksgiving. Thus the unveiling of being as authentic language and the appearance of Jesus with his word tend to coincide. Franz suspects that theology here emerges simply as a dialectic transformation of complaint into its opposite. But most of all Franz expresses doubt that Heidegger can be correctly understood as the philosopher of man's collapse and complaint. That is to say, Franz sees in Fuchs' use of Heidegger the "existential misunderstanding" of Heidegger against which Ott argues.[157] Indeed, Ott's criticism of Fuchs' use of Heidegger consisted in asserting that Fuchs understood Heidegger to be interested in language in terms of its role in achieving authentic existence, rather than being interested in language "as language," as the voice of being.[158]

Franz himself advocates a clearer distinction between Heidegger's thought and Christian faith than was characteristic of the original positions of Fuchs and Ott. Indeed he interprets Heidegger as himself calling for a clear distinction not only between

---

[156] Bad Cannstatt: R. Müllerschön Verlag, 1954 (2nd ed. 1958). Cf. Chapter 5, "The Question about God (M. Heidegger)," pp. 62–72. In *PhR*, VIII (1961), 107, Fuchs states this chapter was written in 1950. Franz's discussion of Fuchs' *Hermeneutik* is scattered through *kerygma und kunst* and is summarized in *ZThK, Beiheft* 2 (1961), pp. 86–88.

[157] Franz, *ZThK, Beiheft* 2 (1961), pp. 82–83, makes the same criticism of Bultmann's use of Heidegger as he did of Fuchs. Heidegger's analysis of *Dasein* does not portray man's collapse as a pre-understanding for the gospel.

[158] *Denken und Sein,* pp. 185 f.

metaphysics and faith, but also between his own philosophy and faith.[159] Alongside remarks distinguishing *Being and Time* from existentialism occur remarks distancing it from theology, and specifically from dialectic theology.[160] Heidegger holds that his basic question as to why there are beings at all rather than nothing is stultified by faith, with its glib answer that God created them.[161] Actually, Heidegger argues, faith should regard his basic question as "foolishness," since it has no relation to faith's own concerns.[162] According to Heidegger, "the unconditionedness of faith and the questionableness of thinking are two different spheres separated by a chasm."[163] "Faith has no place in thinking."[164] Although in both these contexts "faith" refers to the authoritarianism and absolutism traditionally associated with religion, rather than to faith as the specific Christian self-understanding, Franz uses these quotations as support for his position that Christian faith in Heidegger's view requires a clear distinction from his philosophical thought.

When Franz comes to discuss the passages where Heidegger takes a more positive stance toward Christian faith, he defines such statements as only "on the fringe of his thought." He distinguishes Heidegger's experience in thinking from Heidegger's

---

159 *Kerygma und kunst*, pp. 62 ff. *ZThK, Beiheft* 2 (1961), pp. 92, 113 f., and *passim*.

160 *Vom Wesen des Grundes* (4th ed.), p. 42, n. 59.

161 *Einführung in die Metaphysik* (2nd ed., 1958), p. 5 [*An Introduction to Metaphysics*, p. 6 f.]

162 *Ibid.*, p. 6. [*Ibid.*, p. 7] Franz, *kerygma und kunst*, p. 64, draws attention to the diverging assumption of Bultmann, when in *Das Evangelium des Johannes* (originally published in the tenth edition of the Meyer commentaries, 1941, 16th edition; Göttingen: Vandenhoeck und Ruprecht, 1959, p. 18) Bultmann says: "The philosopher's question 'Why is there not nothing?' would also be answered by this sentence: 'In the beginning was the word.'" One may also cite Carl Michalson, *The Hinge of History* (New York: Charles Scribner's Sons, 1959), p. 126, where Heidegger is treated as an existentialist and his basic question translated "why am I something and not nothing?" Compare Heidegger, *ibid.*, p. 3 [*ibid.*, p. 4]: "If our question 'Why are there beings rather than nothing?' is taken in its fullest sense, we must avoid singling out any special, particular being, including man."

163 *Was heisst Denken?*, p. 110.

164 *Holzwege* (3rd ed., 1957), p. 343.

experience of Christianity and locates within the latter the statements that Ott uses to relate Heidegger's thinking to Christianity.[165] Thus Franz in his own way carries through a distinction —even within Heidegger—between thinking and believing, although not the same distinction Fuchs made,[166] and, like Fuchs, brings this distinction into correlation with the theological distinction between law and gospel.[167]

Franz explains the place of God in Heidegger's thought by clarifying Heidegger's answer to the question of how God entered metaphysics. The realm of being that calls forth thinking and language is the divine realm. In its own unveiling and calling, being does not present itself as God, for being is not a being. When, however, thinking ascends through logical processes toward that divine realm, it takes being for a supreme being, God. Now since this logical ascent of thought is a fate-laden occurrence of being (even though being veils itself thereby), the concept of God is just as inevitable as is metaphysics. Yet Heidegger's overcoming of metaphysics would involve a replacement of God with the divine realm, just as being as a supreme or universal being is replaced by being in its distinction from beings.

This analysis could suggest as one alternative the position taken by Walter Schulz in his address of 1956 on "The 'God of the Philosophers' in Modern Metaphysics."[168] Schulz argues that Heidegger has in his understanding of being achieved a kind of transcendence without God, and in the turn in his thought has gone through the equivalent of conversion. But rather than this suggesting that Heidegger has "found God," this suggests that modern man can get along even in his religious life without God

---

[165] Cf. Franz, *ZThK, Beiheft* 2 (1961), pp. 112 ff.

[166] In *kerygma und kunst*, p. 97, Franz explicitly rejects Fuchs's association of Jesus' word with Heidegger's language theory (*Hermeneutik*, p. 72), and associates the latter with the rest of Heidegger's philosophy as the world out of which Jesus calls us.

[167] Franz identifies thinking with the law and with works righteousness in the *ZThK, Beiheft* 2 (1961), p. 110.

[168] "Der 'Gott der Philosophen' in der neuzeitlichen Metaphysik," *Der Gott der neuzeitlichen Metaphysik* (Pfullingen: Günther Neske, 1957), (2nd ed., 1959), pp. 33–58.

or Christianity. This is the outcome that was feared by various theologians when *Being and Time* appeared.[169] Whether today Dietrich Bonhoeffer's program of a "nonreligious interpretation of Biblical categories" suited to a "world come of age"[170] opens an avenue to a positive reception of this alternative by theologians remains to be seen. There are some indications that point in this direction.[171]

Franz himself follows a different alternative.[172] When Heidegger on occasion speaks of the "divine God" in distinction from the metaphysical God,[173] Franz does not, like Ott, assume that this may be leading in the direction of the Christian God.[174] Instead, he identifies the realm of being as the "god-world," and the god emerging from it the "world-god." He points out that Heidegger derives his concept of the world from the New Testament, arguing that primitive Christianity, precisely in being

[169] Cf. Heinz-Horst Schrey, "Die Bedeutung der Philosophie Martin Heideggers für die Theologie," *Martin Heideggers Einfluss auf die Wissenschaften* (Bern: A. Francke AG. Verlag, 1949), p. 10, quoted in my review of Schubert M. Ogden, *Christ Without Myth*, in *Theology Today*, XIX (1962), 440.

[170] *Prisoner for God*, translated by R. H. Fuller (New York: The Macmillan Co., 1954).

[171] Gerhard Ebeling, "Elementare Besinnung auf verantwortliches Reden von Gott," *Wort und Glaube* (Tübingen: J. C. B. Mohr, 1960), p. 359: "A doctrine of God is today abstract speculation if the phenomenon of modern atheism is not present in it from the very beginning." With regard to Heidegger's thought Ebeling says (*ZThK, Beiheft* 2, 1961, p. 124) theology must speak of God nonmetaphysically, "and this means, according to the dominant theological tradition, godlessly." Herbert Braun's address at the meeting of old Marburgers in 1960, intended to present the exegetical aspect of the relation of Heidegger to theology as Ott's address presented the systematic aspect, presupposes a basic difference between New Testament times and our times in that God's existence can no longer be assumed. Hence his normative reinterpretation of God is an instance of such a "godless," that is to say, nonmetaphysical understanding: God is the dialectic of "you may" and "you ought" in inter-personal relations. Cf. "Die Problematik einer Theologie des Neuen Testaments," *ZThK, Beiheft* 2 (1961), pp. 3–18, esp. p. 3.

[172] *Kerygma und kunst*, p. 83, identifies Schulz's position as "an amazing misunderstanding." This would be true if Schulz really identifies being and God, as Hermann Diem assumes in his reply *Gott und die Metaphysik* (*Theologische Studien, Heft* 47, 1956).

[173] *Identität und Differenz*, p. 71 [*Essays in Metaphysics*, p. 65.]

[174] Gerhard Ebeling, *ZThK, Beiheft* 2 (1961), p. 124, identifies the "divine God" with the Christian God.

called out of the world, first clearly caught sight of "world."[175]
Then he quotes Heidegger with regard to the New Testament:
"A world separates all this from Heraclitus."[176] Hence we should
follow Heidegger's advice to take seriously the Christian subject
matter and regard philosophy as foolishness.[177] This Christian
subject matter is once defined by Heidegger as "the Christian life
that existed for a brief time before the writing of the gospels and
before the missionary propaganda of Paul."[178] From this Franz
argues that we should obey Jesus' call for repentance, his call out
of the world.[179] Such faith is freedom from the world as law.

Although Fuchs, Jüngel, and Franz have not agreed in all
respects, there does emerge from their presentations of the relation of theology to the later Heidegger a general direction, which
has been brought into focus by Gerhard Ebeling in the theses
with which he concludes the *Beiheft* of the *Zeitschrift für Theologie und Kirche* devoted to this debate.[180] While conceding that
the emergence of a philosophy that overcomes metaphysics and
that is consequently distinct from traditional Western philosophy
presents a "completely new situation" for the discussion between
philosophy and theology,[181] he argues that the distinction between
philosophy and theology remains clear. Since Protestant theology
is oriented to the distinction of law and gospel,[182] this pattern
is proposed for the definition of the distinction between the later
Heidegger and theology. Heidegger's thinking is an interpretation

---

[175] *Kerygma und kunst,* pp. 89 ff.

[176] *Einführung in die Metaphysik,* p. 103 [*An Introduction to Metaphysics,* p. 135.] *Kerygma und kunst,* pp. 80, 88 and *passim. ZThK, Beiheft*
2 (1961), p. 111.

[177] *Was ist Metaphysik?* (8th ed.), p. 20 [*Existentialism from Dostoevsky
to Sartre,* p. 218.]

[178] *Holzwege,* p. 202.

[179] *Kerygma und kunst,* pp. 88, 95 ff. *ZThK, Beiheft* 2 (1961), pp.
108 ff.

[180] "Verantworten des Glaubens in Begegnung mit dem Denken M. Heideggers. Thesen zum Verhältnis von Philosophie und Theologie," *ZThK,
Beiheft* 2 (1961), pp. 119–124.

[181] *Ibid.,* p. 121.

[182] Cf. Ebeling's programmatic essay "Die Notwendigkeit der Lehre von
den zwei Reichen," *Wort und Glaube* (Tübingen: J. C. B. Mohr, 1960),
pp. 407–428.

of the law, which corresponds to theology in that theology too interprets the law, but is in tension with theology in that Heidegger's thought does not understand itself as law. Since Heidegger, just as the law to a considerable extent, speaks what the times call for, faith is responsible to listen, since it is responsible for our times as they are. Yet it would be regression into metaphysical thinking to theologize about Heidegger's ontological difference between being and the beings. Instead, one could speak of a theological difference of God and creature. Yet, lest this be confused with a metaphysical difference between two worlds, such a theological distinction should be understood concretely. It is the difference between man the sinner and the God who justifies, a distinction which happens in the preaching of the word.

The analysis of the German debate concerning the relation of the later Heidegger to theology breaks off at this point, without having produced a conclusion or even a well-rounded picture. For that debate is itself still in full progress, and the situation is still quite fluid. Thus the American participation in that debate that takes place in this volume enters into an open discussion, and will, it is hoped, form a significant part of it.

2. What Is Systematic Theology?[1]

HEINRICH OTT
University of Basel

You have invited me to introduce our discussion of the nature of systematic theology. Consider my remarks merely as theses for a disputation. They are intended simply to open the necessary discussion. And yet, as was the rule with regard to the theses in medieval disputations, the discussion should keep to the course laid out in the theses, should grapple with the proposals made, and should give an answer to the questions posed.

I have chosen the simple title: "What is Systematic Theology?" I do not have in mind treating this theme historically, but intend to treat it exclusively with regard to the material issue itself—by which I do not mean to deny that historical research into this theological discipline and the history of its title could help to contribute elements essential to a well-rounded clarification of the material issue.

Martin Heidegger furnished the occasion for our discussion by the one-day seminar he held on the topic "Christian Faith and Thinking" at the last annual meeting of old Marburgers. I am acquainted with what took place at this seminar only through

[1] Paper presented as a basis for discussion at the annual meeting of old Marburgers in October, 1960. The notes reflect to a considerable extent the discussion following the presentation of Ott's paper. Since this discussion was introduced by a formal reply on the part of Wilhelm Anz, "Verkündigung und theologische Reflexion," which was published in the *ZThK, Beiheft* 2 (1961), pp. 47–80, the translator has added some allusions to that published reply in brackets in the notes in order to document the criticism to which the note addresses itself and thus to provide the reader with some impression of the course of the discussion.

a short summary. Nonetheless, I infer from it that essentially Heidegger did the following: 1) He proposed the statement: "Science does not think." In this connection he treated what he calls the "forgetfulness of being." 2) He posed the two questions: a) "What does 'thinking' mean, when we say: Science does not think?" b) "What is the nature of the thinking in which faith thinks?" The first question is the one with which he is incessantly grappling in his own work and on the path he has followed. The second question is directed to us theologians from that point of view. So far as I could see from the summary, the question was not answered. But it *was* picked up, and hence it continues to be posed to us today.

Thus we inquire as to the nature and the specific movement of the thinking in which faith thinks. There are two respects in which this inquiry must take place: in respect to exegetical theology and in respect to systematic theology. But in this inquiry the whole of theology is always at stake. For theology is a unity.

First of all, I wish to pursue the question: In reference to— and in distinction from—exegetical theology, what is so-called "systematic" theology? What is its specific place and its specific necessity in the one whole of theology? Then, in conclusion, I would like to return to our point of departure and place what has been said about the nature of systematic theology in relation to the thought of Martin Heidegger, who brought about our discussion.

I. The Nature of Theology as Hermeneutical

The nature of theology as a whole is hermeneutical. Theology is really hermeneutic, although not of course in the common meaning of hermeneutic as a general theory or "technique" of understanding. (In view of the subject matter, it is a question whether such a thing is even possible.) But yet theology, each time it is carried on, is *reflection on* the understanding of certain specific contents, and hence *effort toward* understanding these contents. It is a matter of understanding Biblical texts, of understanding the subject matter that comes to expression in them, and ultimately of the understandability of the witness to this subject matter in each present situation.

He who inquires as to the nature and the program of theology cannot avoid the problem of understanding, the hermeneutical problem. He must face up to the question of the nature of understanding. If the hermeneutical problem has been proposed for discussion with new urgency in our time, then this brings up for discussion again the nature of theology itself. This is an event whose significance—in this company I may say this without reservation and gratefully—can certainly not be overestimated! Perhaps we can say: What used to be treated in the system of orthodox dogmatics in the opening chapters entitled "De Theologia" and "De Scriptura Sacra" must be discussed today under the title of the hermeneutical problem.

Without being able to pursue here the question of the nature of understanding in its ramifications, I would still like, before going on, to present a twofold *first thesis* so as to be correctly understood as I proceed: 1) The nature of the understanding involved in theology is not to be definitely determined in advance without regard to theological themes. Rather, a contribution to this question is to be expected from reflection upon the specific themes of theology. 2) What will or will not be understandable becomes apparent only in the process of understanding itself, and no antecedent rules on this point can be set up.

Even though the question of understanding is developed in theology under three aspects (the understanding of the texts, the understanding of the subject matter coming to expression in the texts, and the understandability of the contemporary witness to this subject), the understanding involved is ultimately *one*. The unity can perhaps be expressed most readily by means of the term "kerygma." A single arch stretches from the Biblical texts to the contemporary preaching of the church. It is the arch of the kerygma and of the understanding of the kerygma. At each point, from the text to the sermon, it is the continuity of a single act of understanding, a single hermeneutical process. It is a matter of the same kerygma becoming audible today as then, that is, of the witness being trans-lated to our side of the shore. (The Greek verb from which "hermeneutic" is derived means to translate in the sense of trans-ferring, carrying, as it were, from one shore to the other. This trans-lating is what is meant by understanding!) One may not artificially isolate from one another the understanding of the text, the understanding of the subject matter, and the understanding of the contemporary sermon, as if these were three different things. No one of the three can live without the others. Preaching cannot be understandable if the text together with its "subject matter" is not understood. And the text cannot be understood without an understanding of its "subject matter", and this in turn is only understood when it comes to me as kerygma here and now, as a potential sermon. One might say that this is the point where the connection between "historical" and "theological" exegesis of the Biblical texts becomes apparent.

I am well aware that what has just been said was to a certain extent spoken unguardedly. For there is no final black-and-white distinction between "having understood" and "not having understood." Rather, it is probable that understanding by its very nature takes place at different levels. Yet this characteristic of understanding cannot be further pursued here. I would like to ask you, remembering this reservation, to consider what I have said about the unity of the act of understanding, the hermeneutical arch or process in theology, as my *second thesis*.[2]

[2] The figure of the "hermeneutical arch" should not be set in opposition to the more common figure of the "hermeneutical circle"! [The concept of a "hermeneutical circle" has a particular content in terms of the early Heidegger, in that it refers specifically to the interaction of one's own pre-understanding and the text's understanding of existence, and thus involves the interpreter's self-understanding directly in the hermeneutical process. Cf. Hans-Georg Gadamer, "Vom Zirkel des Verstehens," *Martin Heidegger zum siebzigsten Geburtstag (Festschrift)* (Pfullingen: Günther Neske, 1959), pp. 24–34. Hence Anz' criticism of Ott's concept of the "hermeneutical arch," *ZThK, Beiheft* 2, pp. 50 f., 59, is materially a criticism for ignoring the concept of hermeneutic of *Being and Time,* since the arch directs attention from the text to the preacher's language rather than to the preacher's existence, his faith.] The figure of the arch is intended to say that hermeneutic has to do with a single movement, a single

Incidentally, one could object at this point that all too much has been made of understanding as a purely human act, i.e., that the proper sequence of the questions has been reversed. One could argue that Biblical exegesis and preaching after all do not have to do primarily with human understanding, but rather with God speaking. Hence one could argue that one should not concern oneself so much about the problem of understanding, since the Holy Spirit surely sees to it that the message is understood. This "pious" objection, designed to make light of the hermeneutical problem, is quite popular. But on careful scrutiny it is seen to be the criticism of an inferior orthodoxy that either does not see or else obscures the problem, and in no sense carries us further. One should not degrade God to a *deus ex machina*. Actually, the contingency of God's speaking, the witness of the Spirit, is taken fully into account in the concept of understanding when this concept is itself correctly understood.

When we consider the unitary arch of understanding that constitutes the nature of theology, we can discern that the specific position of that activity of thought we are accustomed to call "systematic theology" belongs within the framework of and in continuity with the "hermeneutical process." Dogmatics is in its way a hermeneutical effort. The same is true of ethics.

Systematic theology finds its position, as it were, in the middle of the arch extending from the text to contemporary preaching. It stands between exegesis, which is primarily concerned with the text as such, and practical reflection, which is primarily concerned with the church's preaching. A discussion of its nature will have to keep this *"between"* in mind. This means remaining constantly aware that we have to do with a "between" within a *continuity*. Systematic theology, dogmatics or ethics, under-

---

continuous process of understanding. Hence, exegetical, systematic, and practical theology should not be artificially separated and isolated one from the other. They are in continuity one with the other. Only on the technical grounds of a division of labor did the various theological "disciplines" arise. Originally they were one. In my opinion, the figure of the hermeneutical circle interprets in more detail this arch of continuity. For example, the continuity comes to expression when dogmatics and exegesis illuminate each other in terms of the hermeneutical circle.

stood as "doctrine" standing in its own right, lifted out of the "hermeneutical arch", isolated on the one side from exegesis and on the other from preaching, immediately becomes an undertaking without foundation.

In this group's discussion last year the question was posed whether there can be such a thing as a Christian systematic theology at all. It was presumably in view of the hermeneutical nature of theology as a whole that the validity of systematic theology was contested or at least put in question. In any case it was assumed that the systematical contradicts the hermeneutical. This assumption must now be tested. In this we already presuppose that the nature of theology is hermeneutical. The discussion of systematic theology will then be able to show its legitimacy if it can indicate to what extent the specific function of systematic theology is indispensable for the hermeneutical transfer, that movement of trans-lating meaning.

Before we begin let me add yet a *third thesis:* This "translation" involved in understanding, when seen as movement, compels us to undertake systematic theology.

II. Systematic Theology as Reflection Upon the Hermeneutical in Theology as a Whole

First of all, I would like to conceive of a task or function being entrusted to systematic theology that, although it has not come to the fore so clearly in the history of this particular discipline, cannot be pushed aside, and can be done better by systematic than by exegetical or practical theology, precisely because of the former's in-between position. This function consists in reflection upon the whole of the unbroken "hermeneutical process," inquiry into the nature of the understanding that takes place in all theology. It is for systematic theology to reflect upon the understanding of the texts and upon the understanding of the sermon, insofar as it is a matter of the nature of the process of understanding itself. Here dogmatics and philosophy will meet, and yet, according to our first thesis, dogmatics cannot simply turn the solving of this task completely over to philosophy, that is, to a thinking not bound to revelation.

Martin Kähler says in one place in his "Der sogenannte historische Jesus und der geschichtliche, biblische Christus"[3]: "Surely no one detects the hidden dogmatician with such sure instinct as one who is himself a dogmatician. . . . And hence the dogmatician will have a right to set up a sign of warning in front of the historical scholarship that is supposedly free of presuppositions. . . ." These sentences are—*mutatis mutandis,* that is, taking into consideration the altered situation in exegetical research—valid today. What Kähler ultimately had in view still applies today: namely, some supervision by the systematician over the work of the exegete.

Let me now present my *fourth thesis:* The continuity and unity of the hermeneutical process (which constitutes the nature of theology) are confirmed in that the figure of the *hermeneutical circle* is preserved. There is no such thing as historical-critical results that stand unshakably, apart from theology's reflection upon its specific theme—results by which theology's reflection upon its subject matter would be absolutely bound. But there is also no such thing as fixed dogmas by which historical exegetical reflection would be absolutely directed. That is to say, dogmatics is no more absolutely and one-sidedly dependent upon exegesis than exegesis is absolutely and one-sidedly dependent upon dogmatics. Rather, dogmatics and exegesis stand in a relation of interaction with one another, as the figure of the hermeneutical circle indicates. They mutually illumine and explicate one another. And it is precisely because they stand in this relation to each other that their ultimately inseparable unity in the "hermeneutical process" of theology as a whole is demonstrated.

The dogmatician does not gain his insights without the exegete. This needs no further proof. But neither does the exegete gain his insights without the dogmatician. For the dogmatician reflects upon the hermeneutical presuppositions for thoughts that are involved—perhaps not explicitly, yet inescapably—in exegeti-

[3] Reprint in the *Theologische Bücherei*, vol. 2 (1953), p. 29.

cal work. He does not simply turn over this work to the philosopher (as has already been stated above). For the object of theological exegesis is a specific object, and it is to be expected that this specificity of the object could also result in a specific situation in hermeneutic.

To be sure, the objection could be raised at this point that exegesis, historical scholarship as a whole, is, at least to a considerable extent, in no need of critical accompaniment and supervision of its hermeneutical presuppositions because it is without presuppositions, or in any case is based on presuppositions that any rationally minded person would have to accept without hesitation. According to this view, then, the historian and thus also the Biblical exegete could make simple assertions that, even as the experiment of the natural scientist, can in principle always be tested objectively by anyone as to their correctness. Whoever argues this way—and all of us, thinking in the well-worn tradition of metaphysics, are at first simply conditioned to argue this way—has not yet become aware of the problem of language that here presses in upon us with great force. (Both with regard to the metaphysical background of our thought and also with regard to the problem of language I refer you to Heidegger's thought as a whole and to its main direction, about which I will have something to say again at the end of my lecture.) Even the simplest historical argument is after all basically a linguistic occurrence, an encounter with spoken or written utterances. Up to the present, no one has thought through the making of historical judgments in terms of the nature of language. (Perhaps this has not been possible; even today it may not be possible.) However, he who finds himself completely satisfied with the usual answer of historiography that it is without presuppositions and can as a matter of course control certain "objective" historical statements of fact—such a person has, without knowing it, already decided for a certain ("positivistic") interpretation of language and has already closed himself to the mystery of language and to the question with which it confronts us today.

With these comments I hope I have at least outlined and partially established one of the tasks of systematic theology: that as an aid to exegesis and preaching it has to reflect upon the hermeneutical situation in theology, upon the whole process of theological understanding. I am quite aware of the incompleteness and spottiness of my argument, which may have struck you. When one enters into virgin territory of reflection, one has no other alternative. For thought is a step-by-step experience. It requires patience and endurance, for the definitive formulations do not present themselves immediately. On such paths one must count on the good will and the co-operation of one's fellow thinkers and partners in discussion. May I here quote a saying of Heidegger's[4] that is a favorite of mine and that might be helpful for all our discussion: Real reflection, Heidegger says, "neither turns out contrary opinions nor tolerates easy agreement. Thinking steers straight into the wind of the issue."

Now I would like to move to the other task of systematic theology, which corresponds more to the traditional understanding of dogmatics. I strongly suspect that it is intimately related with the first task, although for the moment I cannot demonstrate it.

III. Systematic Theology and Exegesis

We now begin by asking, in view of the traditional form of systematic theology, as to the characteristic trait that distinguishes it from exegetical theology on the one hand and from practical theology or preaching itself on the other. What characterizes the specific "between" of systematic theology, in distinction from the two "ends" of theology's hermeneutical arch?

It is this: systematic theology is not directed in each case to a certain individual text. Exegesis has to do in each case with a given text. It inquires as to the text's meaning and origin, its historical "setting" (in the broadest sense). It inquires as to the connection of a number of isolated texts only insofar as it asks about their connection at the point of their historical origin (for example, one inquires as to the theology of Paul, as to the origin and the common "viewpoints" of the enthronement psalms, as to the *Sitz im Leben* of the hexateuch, etc.). Preaching in turn

---

4 *Aus der Erfahrung des Denkens,* p. 11.

proclaims for its part the witness of a given text to which it is bound and for which it is responsible. Systematic theology, however, does not hold itself to a single text, but rather looks out upon the whole horizon of all Biblical texts. (This need not involve putting all on the same level or attributing to all the same importance! Yet even where it makes a distinction and takes a stand, it still has the whole canon in view.)

This characteristic is due on the one hand to the situation of the church, and on the other to the nature of language. For the church does not in fact live with a single statement of its message, but rather with a whole number of witnesses, primary attestations of that reality and truth with which the faith constitutive of the church is concerned. These witnesses are brought together in the canon of Holy Scripture. They compose, as it were, the "linguistic room," the universe of discourse, the linguistic net of co-ordinates, in which the church has always resided and moved in its faith, its preaching, its prayer, and also its theology. The historic contingency of the canon belongs to the historic contingency of the church itself. Systematic theology reflects upon the "subject matter" with which the church has to do—upon this subject matter itself and as a whole; and it does this on the basis of the totality of the texts that are given to the church as the primary attestations of its subject matter. Thus systematic theology accommodates itself to the factual situation of the church.

On the other hand, the peculiarity of systematic theology, its moving beyond the individual text, becomes understandable in view of the nature of language. The individual text, and even connected texts such as the theology of Paul, John, Matthew, Luke, Hebrews, etc., are as linguistic utterance not already the subject matter itself. Rather they point to the subject matter, witness to it, name it, reflect upon it, call upon it to become present.

And the subject matter itself—where and what is it? Here two answers are possible, and perhaps, in terms of the nature of language, they are equally necessary.

The first is that the subject matter is the Christ event, the reality of revelation and of believing. This is no "fact" that can be "stated" and communicated in plain words, but rather a reality that makes itself heard in poetic and thinking speech and thus becomes present.

The second answer is that the subject matter is the gospel of Christ, the good news of the Christ event. This second answer alongside the first does not imply that the Christ event is simply identical with the gospel of Christ. The Christ event does not consist merely in the gospel of Christ. Christ is also at work where the gospel is not preached and heard. He has mercy also upon infants and the mentally diseased, the pagans, those who deny God, and the dead. Nevertheless the ambiguity of that double answer must be left standing. This dialectic belongs to the nature of language. To language belongs the area of the unspoken. The Christ event encounters us through the gospel of Christ, but the gospel is encountered through the Gospels and witnesses that are not yet and never will be the gospel itself. What is actually spoken is only the gospel *according to. . . .* , the gospel according to Matthew, according to Mark, according to Luke, according to John, but also according to Paul, and why not also, dependent on those and secondarily, the gospel according to Martin Luther, Calvin, Rudolf Bultmann, or Karl Barth? But the gospel itself —there is only one—remains unspoken. It is what is unspoken in all that is spoken in the Gospels and Christian witnesses in preaching, liturgy, and theology. This which is unspoken, the one gospel itself, is heard through all gospels and witnesses, if understanding takes place at all.

Permit me here a side reference to Martin Heidegger, whose reflection upon language is increasingly helpful for our own reflection. Heidegger says:[5] "Every great poet composed from only a single poem. . . . The poem of a poet remains unspoken. None of the individual poems, not even the total of them, says it all. Nevertheless, each poem speaks from the whole of the one poem and each time speaks it. Out of the poem's realm flows forth the wave that in each case arouses speaking as a poetic utterance."

The one gospel is thus, as it were, the unspoken poem of all

[5] "Die Sprache im Gedicht. Eine Erörterung von Georg Trakls Gedicht," *Unterwegs zur Sprache* (1959), pp. 37 f.

Biblical, at least all New Testament, witnesses, out of which they all compose.[6] What the situation is in the specific cases where previously Jewish texts are used, such as the Epistle of James, many parts of Revelation and also of the Gospels; how they as elements nonetheless fit, perhaps very much on the fringe, into the living and preaching process of the church, the composing on the basis of the one poem—this is a subject for reflection in its own right. So also is the question of the poem out of which the speaking of the Old Testament witnesses flow, and to what extent it is one with (not simply equal to) the gospel of the apostolic witnesses.

The factual, contingent situation of the church in relation to the canon makes it understandable that systematic theology looks beyond the individual text or historically connected texts to the totality of Biblical texts. Language's essential utterance, poetry (in the widest sense which also embraces the Biblical witnesses), is spoken out of and toward what is unspoken (the "poem"). This nature of language makes it understandable that systematic theology thinks through to what is unspoken, the subject matter itself, the gospel—much as Heidegger in his interpretations of Hölderlin and Trakl does not ask what Hölderlin or Trakl may have "meant," but rather thinks through to what was entrusted to them to say.

We said (in the second thesis) that systematic theology belongs within the hermeneutical continuum of the process of under-

---

[6] It may at first seem shocking that the gospel is here understood as "what is unspoken." After all, the gospel is kerygma, preaching, audible spoken word which "goes forth"! Yet one should recall that although God's word does come to expression in specific instances of audible human words, it is not exhausted in them. It can never be definitely captured in human words. Over against all human words it is again and again inexhaustibly new. Before a person lets himself be swept off his feet into making all too hasty objections about this, he should recall the basic state of affairs in all language, and the experiences that we all have with language: In all that is spoken there always remains something unspoken. And what is unspoken is the crucial thing. Without it, language would not be language. If that were not the case, we would not be able to understand the not infrequent occurrence that a person understands the words of a text or a speech word for word, and yet does not grasp what it is intended to say.

standing that is theology. We said further (in the third thesis) that the hermeneutical process, trans-lation, requires that systematic theology be undertaken. The *fifth thesis* is intended to elaborate this as follows: Looking beyond the individual text and looking toward the totality of Biblical texts, or, in other words, what is characteristic of systematic theology, is necessary in order that the hermeneutical arch that reaches from the text to the contemporary sermon be completed. Through this procedure the unity of the subject matter itself is verified, a subject matter that is common to all Biblical witnesses and the church in all its periods and in each of its contemporary preaching situations. The witnesses are many and varied. But the subject matter itself, the unspoken gospel, is one and indivisible.

At this point an explanation of the easily misunderstood title "systematic theology" should be inserted. The "systematic" aspect of theology as it has been presented is not the putting together of various doctrines into a doctrinal structure that may be readily surveyed, so that one is "well informed" about everything. (This would be the metaphysical understanding of systematic theology.) Rather, the systematic aspect consists in looking through the complexity of what is spoken to the indivisible unity of the unspoken, the subject matter itself that is called upon to be present in all that is spoken. This looking through what is spoken is necessary, moreover, for the sake of preaching. For while we preach in each case on a particular text, it is of little importance to comment on the individual text as such. Rather, what counts is to preach, together with the text and taking up its call, the one and whole gospel.

IV. The Procedure of Systematic Theology

In what follows we are to reflect upon systematic theology's movement around the arch, a movement which is hermeneutically so necessary. How, with what method, under what presuppositions, does this movement take place? What happens positively in such looking beyond the individual text, looking out upon the totality of the texts, and looking through to the subject matter itself? What is the structure of systematic theology's procedure of thinking?

In the following presentation we speak about the unity of believing, the thinking explication of this unity, and the method of this explication.

The Unity of Believing. It is hardly necessary to go into great detail on this point. For among us it is clear and undisputed that the Christian does not "believe" in a plurality of things, does not hold as true various saving facts. (Such a "faith" could only have the character of holding certain things to be true.) Rather, faith is a single and indivisible act, and correspondingly the subject matter, the "object" of faith is a single indivisible reality, namely God himself, who in his revelation is encountered as one who is gracious and righteous, as the limit and the supporting ground of existence and of his world. Faith is not "faith that . . ." but rather "faith in. . . ." It is the one and indivisible act of existence, which is grounded in its one and indivisible ground. Preaching does not inform about facts; rather, it speaks "from faith to faith," in attesting the one indivisible ground.

Theology is thinking in relation to believing. (I intentionally speak vaguely: "in relation to . . ." The question immediately arising as to just how this "in relation to . . ." is to be more closely defined will be answered later.) Theology is *fides quaerens intellectum,* "faith seeking understanding." This formulation from Anselm will also be developed later. Systematic theology has in view both faith and its "subject matter" in their totality.

Systematic theology—according to our *sixth thesis*—has to accommodate itself to the basic situation that faith is one and indivisible, and that its object too is one and indivisible. In the case of a Biblicistic or *Heilsgeschichte* theology in the narrower sense I am unable to see to what extent it does this. Hence it seems to me that such a theology stands in constant danger of bypassing its task and no longer serving preaching. On the one hand it seems to me that the dogmatics of Karl Barth, for example—who, by the way, has explicitly appropriated Anselm's formula—corresponds exactly to the maxim formulated in the sixth thesis. Barth's first steps toward his eschatology (which precisely does not have that *Heilsgeschichte* character) or his monism of grace over against Brunner seem to me to be symptoms of this. It is in *this* way that Barth should always have been understood. Many a fruitless misunderstanding from the "left wing" as well as from the "right wing" could then have been avoided. Another fine illustration for the decisive situation of the unity of faith and of its subject matter as the theme of systematic theology is presented by Gerhard Ebeling's *Nature of Faith*. Here even the arrangement and the chapter titles ("The Communication of Faith," "The I of Faith," "The Summons of Faith," "The Steadfastness of Faith," "The Future of Faith"—to name only a few) make it unmistakably clear that theology has to do with nothing other than the thinking explication of the one and indivisible faith according to the different structures that necessarily belong to it.

The Unfolding of Believing in Thinking. Theology is thinking in relation to believing. What faith is has been briefly formulated, to the extent that this was indispensable for the progression of the discussion. The theme itself is inexhaustible.

What, then, is the nature of thinking in relation to believing? It has been described pregnantly with the formula *Fides quaerens intellectum*. To be sure, this formula is in need of explication. Faith itself seeks intelligibility. It seeks the clarity of thinking, of thoughtful understanding. Now, to be sure, faith is as such always an understanding. Otherwise it would be a blind holding of things to be true, and not faith. Hence the question arises: Is the understanding faith seeks other, of a different kind, than the understanding it already is?

I would prefer to think of the understanding sought by faith as integrated into the understanding that faith already is. The concept *intellectus fidei*, "the understanding of faith," is not only to be understood as an objective genitive, but especially as a

subjective genitive. It is the "intelligibility," the clarity of understanding, which faith itself seeks, and which then, when found,
belongs to faith. Faith understands itself. To be sure, it is the
implicit presupposition of this train of thought that one must
then reckon with *levels of understanding.* We have already
touched briefly upon this phenomenon, but we cannot develop it
here thematically. Yet, let us at least say that theological understanding is a new level in the understanding of faith. It is not a
"higher" level (since the existential understanding of faith is in
any case the all-embracing, "comprehensive" entity, which also
embraces the new level and already contains it as a possibility
within itself!)—although it is in a certain sense a "clearer" level.
Faith presses toward presenting itself in the clarity of thought.
It is essentially *fides quaerens intellectum.* But then the movement
of "seeking understanding," that is, theology, is a movement of
faith itself.

The theological act of thinking is in a certain way an act of
believing. (Let this be said only quite tentatively. For we do not
yet know, we have not yet sufficiently explicated, what is meant
by an act of believing.) Here, too, one must avoid misunderstandings. That the theological act of thinking is an act of believing, a movement of faith itself, does not mean at all that only
the believer can understand theological thinking. For the subject
matter of faith and of theology, the gospel of Christ, is intelligible; it is intended for understanding; it is to be communicated
to him who does not yet believe. Neither does our statement mean
that one can simply infer from a theological thought that he who
thought it was a "believer." For faith is contingent and non-
demonstrable. As constantly exposed to temptation, as a constant "overcoming of disbelief," it has an inner dialectic, which
we cannot enter into fully here either. Yet these two reservations
do not invalidate our statement about the "thinking of believing."

The whole topic could be treated less laboriously if misunderstandings and false premises had not circulated among us. In
part they come from a sterile orthodoxy and neo-orthodoxy
(partly in the train of Karl Barth, yet contrary to the basic im-

petus of his own thinking!). Such a view closes itself to the nature of believing as understanding and even directly opposes the commission of theology to understand. For it claims to have the subject matter of faith and of theology definitely and without question at its disposal in the form of rigid formulae (be they fundamentalistic, confessional, in the form of "saving facts," or whatever), and it even counts this neglect of its duty as piety. But in part the misunderstandings come from those who rightly oppose that kind of orthodoxy, and yet bring into action presuppositions that obscure the nature of understanding. I have in mind the so-called "subject-object schema" and the view that all thinking and language to a very great extent necessarily have an objectifying character. According to this view faith and theology's thinking and speaking are to be basically distinguished, that is, one cannot at all speak of a believing thinking, since in this view all theological talking and thinking always take place from an objectifying distance. I shall refrain from going further into these misunderstandings. The thinking of Martin Heidegger performs the inestimable service of teaching us to see in a more primal way the nature of thinking, of language, and thus of understanding. If we listen to him and follow him even only a bit on his way, perhaps the day will dawn upon us when those obscuring premises will fall like scales from our eyes.[7]

[7] It is clear that the whole movement of theology's thought is brought about by faith's temptation in the world. Here I agree fully with Wilhelm Anz. [ZThK, Beiheft 2, pp. 57 ff.] Understanding directed toward clarification, to be discussed in what follows, is of course faith reassuring itself in the situation of temptation. Yet it is incomprehensible to me how faith is viewed as thereby carrying out a "movement of unbelief." [Anz, ZThK, Beiheft 2, pp. 58 ff., quoting Bultmann, Glauben und Verstehen, I, 312. Bultmann refers to theology carrying out a "movement of unbelief" when it makes use of a "movement of philosophy," namely the theologically neutral structures of Dasein worked out in Being and Time. Anz refers to faith carrying out a "movement of unbelief" when it brings the unbelieving pre-understanding into a circular movement with the text's understanding of existence. In moving through this hermeneutical circle one moves through the unbelieving pre-understanding and to this extent carries out a "movement of unbelief."] Does faith come and go in theology? Does it at times stop being faith? It is clear that faith constantly gains itself only by overcoming unbelief. But that belongs to the essential dialectic of faith and in my opinion is not present only in "theology."

I shall postpone the more detailed treatment of this topic to the end of my lecture and for the time being present you with my *seventh thesis.*

Theology, and at its special place systematic theology, is a movement of faith itself, in which faith unfolds the understanding that it itself essentially is in the clarity of thinking. Faith seeks this clarity, since it is directed toward preaching, communication, and attaining a common understanding. Systematic theology takes place in this sense as an unfolding of the structures of meaning of the one and indivisible meaning-content understood in believing.

The thesis in its first part summarizes what has already been said. But it then goes further and says, first, why the thinking explication of believing takes place, and, secondly, how it takes place.

To clarify the first point, the thesis brings together three terms: preaching, communication, and attaining a common understanding. This is the goal of faith. For, on the one hand, faith is not essentially a stance of the isolated individual, but is by its nature the faith of the *communio sanctorum;* and, on the other hand, this *communio sanctorum exists in the world.* The *communio sanctorum* is even to be regarded as a structural element in believing. Faith is aimed at communication and attaining a common understanding, or a communication that makes faith understandable. The vehicle of this communication and common understanding (the two are actually one!) is primarily preaching, and, inseparably connected with it, theology.

Communication and attaining a common understanding have a *triple direction:* They are directed toward the *communio sanctorum* itself, toward the world in which (and for which) it exists, and, finally, toward the individual believer.

In the *communio sanctorum* itself, a common understanding is reached; in the church the communication of the gospel occurs. For communion *consists* in the common understanding of the one "subject matter" of faith, in the living relatedness of all members to the common center. It is doubtless here also that the phenomenon of the symbols of faith basically belongs, the action of "confessing," the desire to keep the "doctrine" pure. The *communio sanctorum* confirms and manifests itself by saying, ever anew, as the situation and the necessity present themselves, what the common center is.[8]

A common understanding is reached, secondly, in relation to the world. The gospel should be proclaimed to the world, for God wills that all men should be helped and that all come to the knowledge of the truth. And the gospel is intelligible, it is basically understandable to all. *That* it is in a given instance understood and hence believed is, to be sure, a contingent event, *ubi et quando visum est Deo* ("Where and when it pleases God"). This characteristic of faith as event inheres in the last resort in all understanding. But that does not prevent us from holding the gospel to be basically understandable and to act accordingly. Rather it gives us the occasion to do precisely this. The concerted effort to make the gospel understandable may not be relaxed. And yet it may not take place except in the humility which knows that it can force nothing, and which says at the end: "Lord, we are unworthy servants; we have only done what was our duty." Faith as event and the basic intelligibility of the gospel are not mutually exclusive, but mutually inclusive.

In preaching and, in unity with it, in theology (primarily systematic theology, which has in view the whole of the content

---

[8] In this whole address I have intentionally avoided stating exactly what this common center, the one "subject matter" of all theology, actually is. The one subject matter of all theology is involved in the name Jesus Christ. But this name is not a theological formulation. Theology grapples with the appropriate formulation of this subject matter, in a never-ending discussion through the ages and across the frontiers of the separated confessions. This address is concerned with discussing the prolegomena to this common task. But the task itself is yet to be done, and its result should not be anticipated with some hasty formulation. Someone has tried to lead me to say that the one theme of all theology is "law and gospel" [cf. pp. 70–76 above]. I am quite decidedly unwilling to have myself bound in advance to this theological pattern of thought which is so powerful and prevalent and yet in its implications is still too little thought through. I would fear that this would impede and prejudice in a dangerous way the conversation, for example, with an Orthodox, a Roman Catholic, or even a Reformed theologian such as myself. Today more than ever we want to leave the room for ecumenical discussion wide open.

of faith), a constant courting of the world takes place, so that the gospel of Christ may become understandable and thus plausible to the "children of the world"; so that the world may know that the gospel places us under a genuine claim and before a real decision and is not a system of absurd doctrines that require blind assent. (It is in this connection that Bultmann's talk about the true scandal of faith belongs!) All this does not have the least to do with so-called "apologetics," for there is nothing at all here that can be proved. Nor is it a matter of leaning on the "subject matter" of theology to turn aside hostile errors of doctrine arising from the "world." Rather it is a matter of providing the gospel in the eyes of the world with that clarity which it already has in itself and which belongs to its very nature.

There is yet a final consideration, which brings us to the third direction of communication and common understanding, namely, the direction toward the individual believer. For in my efforts within the movement of *fides quaerens intellectum* to make faith and its subject matter understandable to brothers in faith and to the world, I am reaching an understanding with myself at the same time as to my faith. What I make clear to others becomes clear to myself, and I cannot make it clear to them in any better way than by really letting it first of all become clear to me. In giving account to others I give account to myself, and vice versa. For the situation of dialogue with the other person is a situation I have potentially in myself. Dialogue is not only a possible phenomenon, but rather a basic structure of all existence. Seeking after truth, after understanding, always takes place in dialogue, even when the thinker is alone. To the extent that he thinks, he is not alone but rather finds himself in discussion with humanity.

One more thing must be asserted here. The attempt to reach an understanding through communication is at the same time an attempt to reach understanding oneself. It is one and the same thing in all three directions. It is not a matter of three different activities, but rather of structural elements of one single activity.

We must keep in mind this characteristic of theology as an

attempt to make faith understandable to others that is at the same time an attempt to understand faith oneself. Unfortunately, there are all too many theological discussions that are no discussions at all, where one does not *think* but merely *argues,* and often not even that, but merely declaims. In this way theology loses its great inspiration and becomes a boring business. Then contributions to the theological discussion consist merely in presenting reservations intended to be pious, which clarify nothing and bring us no further. Theology's inspiration is the passionate struggle for clarity, for illuminating and expressing the depths of faith, so that in a compact and well thought through formulation basic words and themes of theology, such as sin, grace, justification, the office of the redeemer, the church, the Christian life, prayer, the consummation, begin, as it were, to shine, so that they—and through them and in them the "kernel" itself, the one subject matter of all theology—really becomes perceptible. Where this passionate struggle for clarity no longer takes place, where one instead is satisfied to dispute as pupil and master over minor divergences within the school, there theology becomes useless and hinders the preaching of the gospel instead of serving it.

Incidentally, I have no scruples, in this attempt to lay hold of the commission and the correct course for systematic theology, against appropriating positively the motivation that Anselm of Canterbury gives in *Cur Deus Homo?* as characteristic of his own theological thinking. Many had asked him, he writes at the beginning of that tractate, to formulate in writing his thoughts on the question of the incarnation of God. He yields to their request, for they had asked him, "not in order that they might attain to faith through reason, but rather that they might enjoy in their understanding and contemplation what they believed, and that they might be prepared as much as possible always to give satisfaction to all who ask them the reason for the hope that is in us." It could not be better said. Theology has to do with giving an account to others and to oneself. But at the same time and in unity with this, there takes place in theology the *joy* of faith beholding itself in the medium of thought.

The Method of Unfolding Believing in Thinking. We must now still reflect about *how* this unfolding and illumination of believing in thinking actually takes place. The seventh thesis gave us the guiding thread: Systematic theology unfolds the structures of meaning of the one and indivisible meaning-content that is understood in believing.

Of importance in this definition is on the one hand the unity of believing and of its subject matter and on the other hand the concept "structure of meaning." The former has already been explained: Faith does not have to do with a number of "saving facts," but rather is *one* in its relation to the *one* word of God. Hence systematic theology does not have to work at the systematization, the correct arrangement, of the "saving facts." A theology of saving facts is empty-headed thoughtlessness. For how could the theologian know something about saving facts if not through faith! But faith is falsified when it is understood as faith in facts. Faith is trust and thus is a disposition of existence as a whole; otherwise it is not faith. But then it is the exclusive horizon of theology, and not just a vehicle for producing the knowledge about saving facts that could not be arrived at otherwise—saving facts that then subsequently become the object of theology. But if faith is the exclusive horizon of theology, then theology has nothing other to do than to unfold in the clarity of thought what is "folded up" in faith as such. We do not believe in the cross and then again in the resurrection of Christ and in addition also in the ascension and the second coming. Rather, in believing, the Christian relates himself to the one saving act of God (which is not to be understood "punctually," but rather as the one event of the revelation of the gracious God, into which I would also like to conceive of the history of the Old Testament as integrated). Cross and resurrection, exaltation and second coming are structural elements of this one truth and reality. Otherwise they are not at all accessible to us, for they are accessible to us not prior to faith, but exclusively *in* faith. Hence I brand the theology of saving facts, which would like to be something other than exclusively the unfolding of believing, empty-headed thoughtlessness.

Thus the decisive point remains the *concept,* "structure of meaning." The subject matter of believing is an indivisible unity; it is a *meaning-laden,* significant unity, and precisely for this reason a historic unity. Structures of meaning are what I call the elements that constitute a meaning-laden, historic unity in its uniqueness as such and that belong indispensably to it. They are not parts of a sum that could be subtracted. For the meaning-laden unity is as such indivisible. Rather, they are structures, or more exactly structural elements, aspects of a total structure that comprise an unmistakable meaning. It seems to me that this concept and the kind of thinking in which it has its place are peculiarly suited to make understandable what dogmatics does.

Perhaps the concept "structure of meaning" can be made clearer with two illustrations of a non-theological kind.

A human relationship, for example, a friendship, composes a meaning-laden unity. It is no illusion, but rather historically lived reality. But as such it is also not merely an adding of facts and possibilities, but a genuine unity of meaning. Yet this its unity, the unmistakable uniqueness of its meaning, is again no monad, but in itself is variously ordered and arranged. It is an experiential process, which has its own basic direction and does not merely represent an accidental sequence of occurrences. Even though the chain of events may at first seem accidental, yet ultimately through the intertwining of significances everything rests in the one identical meaning that is complex and yet one: complex in its sources, and yet to be appropriated and answered for as one and whole and "holding together," as a totality of meaning, a connection of meaning. I can—and at times I doubtless must—unfold the meaning to make it clear to myself, to make certain of it, and this clarification doubtless also works back into my existential conduct. Thus I can bring to mind and reflect upon all that which belongs to this my friendship: recollection

and anticipation, the first meeting with the friend, the growth
of the friendship, common experiences, tests and crises lived
through together, common convictions and interests, points of
contact in certain aspects of life, plans and hopes, the view that
one has of the other, the particular way of appreciating each
other, the determination to be faithful to each other, etc. All
this can be spelled out as I reflect; and yet as I do so I am not
simply distant, "objectifying," beside the subject matter, but
rather I am thinking *as friend,* from within my friendship.[9] This
complex phenomenon that can be unfolded is what I call the
"elements of meaning" or "structures of meaning," which together make up the whole body of meaning. But in spite of the
structural complexity I must be responsible for my friendship
in each instance as one and a whole, as a single complex of
meaning.

As a second "secular" example we may use a poem. I need
not name any specific one. A poem speaks to us, lays claim upon
us in a particular way, has us encounter a certain meaning. In
the process, every stanza, every verse, perhaps even many a word
speaks distinctively, lays a claim upon us that is all its own.
An allusion, a single figure of speech, an evocation lets us meet
a whole world, opens up a horizon. A sentence, a few brief words,
confront us perhaps with a definitive attitude and answer. And
yet the poem speaks as a unity; it is experienced as a single
connection of meaning. And thus we have again the situation of
the complex structures and the indivisible meaning. A good interpretation of a poem will seek to direct one to the poem's
(unspoken) totality of meaning, by carefully touching upon and
pointing out the structure.

The situation thus described is not an exception; rather—
and this is my *eighth thesis* which explains the seventh—this is
the basic situation of all historic being. You will observe that
I use the concept of structure with regard to individual historic

[9] This is an instance of the possibility of my understanding of theology
as a movement of *faith!*

reality and not only with regard to recurrent situations (such as the structures of *Dasein* known as "existentials"). It seems to me that in the (extremely expressive) word and concept "structure" both possibilities of application are anticipated.

In the same sense, the historic reality of faith and of its subject matter is also a single, indivisible connection of meaning. It can and must be clarified, however, by unfolding its structures of meaning, which clarification takes place as an act of thinking from within the encounter that faith itself is.

Dogmatics is this explication. All the work of exegesis is directed toward dogmatics as its goal, and without dogmatics preaching cannot get by, since in each text and in each sermon it is a matter of the one whole of the subject matter of faith. Hence dogmatics is never a surveying, objectifying work of construction, but rather an *explicating understanding*. The structures that guide dogmatics in unfolding its theme, however, are to a certain extent always given. They are conditioned by the situation, that is, they are given by the unchanging *situation* and the unchanging *commission of the church* as the locus of faith and of preaching. I would like you to consider this and the following explanation as my *ninth thesis*.

The church of Jesus Christ is a brotherhood sharing a common fate, a common destiny, a common experience, namely, the revelation of the living God. Because of this destiny all who belong to the church stand in a common situation, without regard to all the differences of individuality and of time and place. It is in this factual situation of the *communio sanctorum* that the gospel, the subject matter of believing and preaching, must in certain respects be clarified, preached, explained, explicated. These are the continual problems, lines of thought, and assignments of a church dogmatics. There are such assignments for theological thought because preaching, as *the* assignment of the church, even when it takes its point of departure in the individual text, is always the preaching of the one whole gospel, and because preaching as such requires a clarification in such respects. However, this does not prevent certain themes from coming to the fore in the course of history, in the specific variations of the one situation of the church.

Dogmatics' unchanging assignments, in the order of the traditional list of dogmatic loci, are, for example, the following: The doctrine of God, the world (creation and providence), anthropology (the situation of all men in confrontation with God), the doctrine of sin, christology, the doctrine of faith and of justification. (To be sure, the last mentioned problem really belongs at the beginning together with theological hermeneutic, that is, with what one is accustomed to call prolegomena to dogmatics, and must also, in view of the subject matter, be represented in every dogmatic discussion, since, as we saw, faith is the exclusive horizon of all theological thinking.) Further, there are ethics; ecclesiology, pneumatology, and the theology of sacraments; eschatology; and finally prayer and mysticism. As one can see, there are about ten perennial problem areas and themes.[10] In conformity to these basic structures, systematic theology explicates its own theme. It sees itself in each epoch placed anew before the same assignment to think. It cannot dodge giving account to itself, for example, about the office of Christ, about the nature of faith, about prayer, about the nature of the church and the significance of the sacraments and about all the other themes. Here there is no basic distinction between dogmatics and ethics. Karl Barth's attempt to integrate ethics into dogmatics seems to me appropriate. For ethics is nothing other than a structure of meaning, an aspect of the unfolding of the one and indivisible theme of theology, of the subject matter of faith, which is such as to place a claim upon us, and hence requires explication and illumination in the sense of ethical reflection.

It is certainly the case that the individual concrete text, in

---

[10] It is so obvious as hardly to deserve mention, that the *loci* of dogmatics, its problems or "commissions," should not simply be taken over from the tradition, but rather must be *derived* from the subject matter itself, from preaching and its theme. [So the criticism of Anz, *ZThK, Beiheft* 2, p. 72.] But this cannot be developed further within the confines of this address.

order to complete the hermeneutical arch and to "strike home" in the individual concrete sermon, must pass through the stage of systematic reflection. Since the text points to the whole gospel as what is unspoken in it, and since the sermon has nothing other to proclaim as its one subject matter than this one whole gospel, there must be considered the totality of the gospel in the hermeneutical process which leads from the individual text to the individual sermon. This reflection upon the whole requires a clarification in accordance with the abiding fundamental structures of dogmatics, and the whole is confirmed in such a clarification. Doubtless a given individual text of the New as well as of the Old Testament—to the extent that it is understood not simply as the "opinion" of the author, but rather as an attestation of the one truth to be preached today, calling over to us—must direct us into the various lines of dogmatic thinking. This is so precisely because in the individual text, in its specific unique witness, still the integral whole, the complete subject matter of faith, comes into language. Thus, when a text is heard not only "historically," but rather as a text for preaching (and apparently according to Heidegger's understanding of language this is authentic hearing!), then the path via this "between" of dogmatics is unavoidable.

Two examples, a New Testament and an Old Testament text, may make this clear. Let us begin with Matthew 25. 31–46, the discourse about the last judgment. We assume that the discourse is of pre-Christian origin and that one only secondarily placed the name of Jesus or the Son of Man in the place of God. Nonetheless, the text, as we meet it now—and this would be the decisive factor for our understanding—occurs in the context of Matthew's witness to Christ. What is specific in the text—its picture, its situation, its statement—apparently seemed suited and offered itself, as it were, to be integrated into the preaching of Christ as an element for expressing it.

The specific element in the text is the encountering of the last judge and criterion in one's neighbor: "As you did it to one of the least of these my brethren, you did it to me." The hearing of this specific claim, to the extent that such hearing enters in upon the task of thoughtful illumination, requires clarification in various directions. For one thing, it requires clarification with regard to Christ himself. How is the basic fact of the revelation of God in Christ, the incarnation of the word, to be interpreted from the point of view that Jesus henceforth is encountered in the neighbor? Do we gain from the specific statement of the text deepened understanding of the incarnation itself? Further, what is the situation with regard to the eschatological or futuristic dimension of this specific statement? The text itself envisages a future unveiling of what is decided today in relation to the neighbor. Further, a clarification is called for in view of the problem of anthropology: How is the true "nature," the constitution of man's existence before God, to be interpreted from the point of view that apparently man, in the way stated by the text, can become "transparent" to God? Clarification is then especially important to the doctrine of faith and of justification: How does the statement of the text square with justification by faith alone? And with regard to the question of sanctification, to what extent do we encounter in the word of the text a (or the) "principle" of the Christian life? And how far does what is said by the text serve for a correct understanding of sin? Finally, what is the place and the function of the church within the procedure developed by the text? Is that criterion valid also outside the area of the church, and what is the difference, from the viewpoint of the text, between the church and the "world"?

All these questions or desiderata for clarification are still present even when one wishes to reduce all legitimate theological reflection about the text in question to the pure establishing of its claim as such, and hence excludes all further discussion as reflection unsuited to that claim. (I myself, buttressed by Heidegger, would like to regard such a reduction as ultimately an objectifying abstraction that does not correspond to the true nature of thinking and language.) But even in this case clarification by thinking in the indicated directions is called for, even if it is negative. In each case one would have to show to what extent further inquiry in these directions is not permissible.

As an Old Testament example we choose the First Psalm. Martin Buber devoted an impressive little study to it.[11] The psalm indicates two ways: the way of the righteous, which "the Lord knows" and which bears in it the promise of unfailing fruitfulness, and the way of the godless, which loses itself in emptiness. Simply in pointing out the two ways and opposing them to each other there lies a claim.

To the extent that we wish to hear the psalm as a word directed to us, as a witness to the God who is the Father of Jesus Christ, the legitimate concept of "righteousness" ("righteousness of faith" or "works righteousness") still remains to be clarified.[12] The psalm opens a view upon life in sanctification and in prayer. We must reflect upon the final basis in the Christ event of such fellowship with God as the psalm speaks about; we must reflect upon the interpretation of sin that results from the confrontation of the two ways; we must reflect upon the present and future of God's judgment that is carried out along the two ways; and upon the ecclesiological aspect of the text, whether the "way of the righteous" is bound to the church or actually comprises the church.

Thus a dogmatic discussion is unavoidable for the "understanding" and for the "striking home" of the text in the sermon. Clarification of the various motifs given with the situation of preaching itself is needed in order that the gospel in its wholeness may come into language in the specific voice of a text.

---

[11] "The Ways," in *Good and Evil: Two Interpretations* (New York: Charles Scribner's Sons, 1952). Part One, "Right and Wrong," translated by R. Gregor Smith, pp. 51–60.

[12] Whether such a Christian usage of the First Psalm is possible is a difficult exegetical and hermeneutical problem, which cannot be entered into here. A thorough reflection upon the nature of language would doubtless be indispensable for that task. In our example I take my point of departure in the hypothetical presupposition corresponding to my own assumption, to the effect that a Christian understanding of the text is possible. I am quite aware of the spectrum of exegetical problems implicit in this presupposition.

V. MARTIN HEIDEGGER'S THINKING AND THE SELF-UNDER-
STANDING OF DOGMATICS

With this, we return to Heidegger. I claim—and this is my *tenth thesis*—that the understanding of systematic theology developed here *corresponds* to the understanding of thinking and of language offered by Heidegger.

Heidegger maintains that science does not think and asks: In *that* case what is "thinking" and what is the kind of thinking involved in believing? He apparently visualizes thereby a thinking carried on by faith, a possibility of theology that is other than what he calls science. Theology would then in his sense no longer be a "science," and precisely for the reason that science "does not think." Expressed otherwise: Heidegger sees the possibility of theology truly *thinking*, that is, a theology beyond metaphysics.[13]

If we wish to try to follow him on this path we must above all clearly recognize what he understands by "metaphysics."

To explain his understanding, we may make use of the picture of the tree and the ground of the roots, which he develops in the Preface and Postscript added later to "What is Metaphysics?" "In what ground do the roots of the tree of metaphyiscs have their hold? . . . What is metaphysics, viewed from its ground? What is metaphysics itself, at bottom? It thinks beings as beings." It can do this since it already stands in the light of the truth of being (truth—a-letheia—unhiddenness—unveiling). "The truth of being may thus be called the ground in which metaphysics, as the root of the tree of philosophy, takes hold and from which it is

---

[13] I am quite aware that in his works Heidegger's position on Christian faith and theology is not unambiguous. Yet, in spite of the obscurities on this point that emerge when one surveys the complete work of Heidegger, I maintain that one can document unambiguously from Heidegger's writings the distinct thread of connection I seek to establish, the correspondence between Heidegger's thinking and the self-understanding of dogmatics. It cannot be denied that the aspect of importance to me has its basic lines set out in Heidegger's own work. [The alternate position, to the effect that Heidegger regards his own philosophy as "foolishness" for Christian faith, is presented by Helmut Franz. Cf. pp. 70–75 above.]

nourished. Since metaphysics investigates the beings as beings, it remains with the beings and does not turn to being as being." "Being is not thought in its unveiling essence, that is, in its truth." Metaphysics "says what beings are by formulating in a concept the beingness of the beings. In the beingness of the beings metaphysics thinks of being, but without being able in the way it thinks to think of the truth of being. Metaphysics everywhere moves in the sphere of the truth of being, which remains its unrecognized and ungrounded ground."[14]

If these statements had been considered more carefully, one would have probably better understood Heidegger's thinking as a whole! Moreover, there is in the same context an important comment of Heidegger's about *Being and Time,* which has been regarded as the work in terms of which he must primarily be understood. "If, as we unfold the question concerning the truth of being, we speak of overcoming metaphysics, this means: reflecting upon being itself. Such reflection goes beyond the customary lack of thought about the ground for the root of philosophy. The thinking attempted in *Being and Time* (1927) sets out on the way to prepare an overcoming of metaphysics, so understood."[15]

The way this works is simple and clear: Metaphysics (and with it all subjectivistic, objectifying, especially scientific thinking that grows out of it) confines itself to the beings. It thinks them as beings by formulating them in concepts and thus, as it were, fixating them. Metaphysics can do this only because it is grounded in the truth of being. But this truth as such it is no longer able to think.

Thus everything is concentrated in this question: What is the "truth of being," the unthought ground of metaphysics?

14 *Was ist Metaphysik?* (1929; 8th ed., Frankfurt a.M.: Vittorio Klostermann 1960), pp. 7 f., 44. Preface in *Existentialism from Dostoevsky to Sartre,* edited and translated by Walter Kaufmann (New York: Meridian Books, 1957), pp. 207 f. Postscript in *Existence and Being* (London: Vision Press, 1949), translated by R. F. C. Hull and Alan Crick, p. 382; paperback ed., p. 351.

15 *Was ist Metaphysik?* pp. 9 f. [*Existentialism from Dostoevsky to Sartre,* p. 209.]

From here it must become clear what "thinking" really means and what may be meant by "overcoming metaphysics." For Heidegger, truth is not the agreement of the intellect with the subject matter, but rather *a-letheia* is interpreted as unhiddenness. It is an unveiling, an occurrence. Only by means of unveiling is thinking possible. Thinking takes place insofar as what is to be thought unveils itself. This occurrence of unveiling is the truth of being. It is the ground of metaphysics. The latter thinks of beings as beings. It can do this because beings have unveiled themselves to it as beings. And because this happens, there is science, which is grounded in metaphysics. Metaphysics, however, closes itself to its own ground. *It thinks of beings as beings, but it does not think the truth of being, the occurrence of unveiling itself.* Thus it falls into the forgetfulness of being.

Hence metaphysics and everything deriving from it understand beings objectivistically and thinking subjectivistically. It assumes there are facts, and they can be established just as they are by means of the capacity to think, a capacity over which man as subject disposes. Metaphysics, and with it science, are no longer able to see that essential thinking is not man's disposing of the subject matter from a position of distance, but rather grows out of an occurrence that happens to him. Metaphysics and science want results. They want to "solve" the puzzles of the universe. But essential thinking does not arrive at results; it never arrives at a goal but always remains on the way. It is no establishing of facts from a distance but rather is experience, encounter. As such it is the essential act of man. It is a response to a claim. To be sure not every thinker and not every epoch stand under the same claim, but rather each great thinker has *his* path.

Heidegger does not reject science and its achievements, but rather shows that there is another kind of thinking, and that although metaphysics and science are ultimately grounded in this other thinking, they do not know it, since it belongs to their nature that they are no longer able to carry out this other kind of thinking.

From this insight of Heidegger's two essential inferences for theology are to be drawn:

1). Since essential thinking has experiential character and, as such, is the essential act of man, it is not permissible in the sphere of believing to distinguish strictly and in principle between believing as existential actuality and theology as thinking, and thus even to speak of "unbelieving theology." This does not keep us, however, from reflecting further on the difference between the act of believing and the theological act of thinking and on the dialectic of their converging and diverging.

2). Subjectivistic-objectivistic thinking is the thinking of metaphysics and science, which in the essential sense precisely does not "think." "Overcoming metaphysics" in the area of theology does not take place by defining all thinking as basically objectifying in nature, and then distinguishing from this thinking the contingent act of believing existence itself. Rather, it takes place by understanding thinking otherwise than as subjectivistic and objectifying thinking in the sense of metaphysics and science—namely, as experiential thinking. Moreover, the same thing holds true of language. There is such a thing as objectifying speaking. But each and every speaking about something may not be regarded *a priori* as objectifying. There is speech that is not objectifying expression.

Because I regard as compelling these inferences from Heidegger's understanding of thinking (and this is where the main emphasis of his whole work lies!), I am of the opinion that the conception of dogmatics developed above corresponds precisely to Heidegger's thinking. And this was the question that provided our point of departure.

In conclusion, I add an observation about the relation of dogmatics and philosophy. Philosophy—and this is my *eleventh thesis*—is not to be regarded as a presupposition and a basis for dogmatics, in the sense that it supplies a certain understanding of human existence as valid, which then delimits the area wherein the meaningfulness of the Biblical witnesses can first be shown.

I am bold enough to quote here a sentence that Martin Heidegger wrote me when my book *Denken und Sein* appeared: "As long as anthropological-sociological conceptualizing and the conceptualizing of existentialism are not overcome and pushed to the side, theology will never enter into the freedom of saying what is entrusted to it." We recall how Heidegger interpreted the function of his own book *Being and Time* for the whole context of the real intention of his path of thinking: The thinking attempted in *Being and Time* was on the way to preparing an overcoming of metaphysics as a "step back" into authentic thinking. For Heidegger, *Being and Time* does not have the intention of presenting definitive results about the nature of *Dasein,* but rather it forms the transition to the return to a thinking which no longer recognizes "results."

For this reason, I have proposed that dogmatics is simply to unfold thoughtfully without presupposing any philosophical schema the meaning-content experienced in believing from within the experience itself. In this way dogmatics will enter "into the freedom of saying what is entrusted to it." Its encounter with philosophy will take place "along the way," and indeed step by step, whenever dogmatic and philosophical trains of thought have the same theme. This will be especially the case with regard to the existentialist analyses found in *Being and Time.* In such cases the conversation with philosophy will without doubt be useful for the explicating, clarifying thought of dogmatics.

I would like to close this paper with an anecdote from Martin Buber's collected *Tales of the Hasidim,*[16] which gives us an example of the experiential character of thinking envisaged by Heidegger and of the experiential character of theological thinking in particular:

"What is Learned"

As Levi Yitzhak of Berditchev returned home from his first trip to Rabbi Shmelke of Nikolsburg, which he had undertaken against the will of his father-in-law, the latter jumped on him: "Now, what

[16] *Erzählungen der Chasidim* (Zürich: Manesse-Verlag, 1949), pp. 331 f. [Apparently this story is omitted in the English translation.]

did you learn from him?" "I learned," answered Levi Yitzhak, "that there is a Creator of the world." The old man called a servant and asked him: "Are you aware that there is a Creator of the world?" "Yes," said the servant. "Of course," cried Levi Yitzhak, "they all say so, but do they also learn it?"

II. American Discussion

3. Advocatus Dei—Advocatus
Hominis et Mundi

ARNOLD B. COME

San Francisco Theological Seminary

The question as to the relevance for theology of the later Heidegger is an example of the more general and perennial question concerning the relation of philosophy as such to a theology based on revelation. This general question is of special importance in relation to our particular example for two reasons. First, Heidegger claims to propose a program and method for philosophy in radical opposition to the whole process of philosophical thought from Plato to Hegel. Secondly, Ott argues that Heidegger has been misused by Bultmann, and that Heidegger's more radical position can be used to clarify and to stimulate a theology akin to that of Karl Barth! So a brief introductory statement on the general question is necessary as grounds for some of the positions here developed concerning our particular problem.

I

Heidegger asserts that Plato took Western philosophy off its track in his famous figure of the cave.[1] Plato's picture portrays man as separated from the eternal light of reality by an unbridgeable disjunction. All that man sees in actuality are the shadows cast by things of this world in the reflected light of that

[1] Cf. above, James M. Robinson, "The German Discussion of the Later Heidegger," p. 27.

eternal reality. In this context philosophy can be only the wholly subjective attempt by the mind of man to form concepts of reality by analyzing the shadows that are merely reflected appearances of the eternal ideas or reality. Reality for man consists of those objects of his thought and statement as are formed subjectively in his mind and conversation.[2] And for Aristotle *"logos* as statement becomes the abode of truth in the sense of correctness."[3]

Against this picture Heidegger portrays reality as having no transcendent being in itself but as occurring only in the existence of beings. Plato's insoluble problem of the mode of "participation" of eternal ideas in things is resolved by Heidegger when he asserts that the thinking of being is the self-unveiling of the miracle of the being of beings. The thinking activity of man, therefore, is not a self-initiated movement in which he futilely attempts to grasp at a wholly other object but is itself the occurrence of being in one of its forms.

On the basis of these and other views, Ott maintains that the Biblical doctrine of creation is on the same plane and moves in much the same direction as Heidegger's description of the relation between being and beings.[4] What does such an assertion mean for the general relation of theology to philosophy? Does it mean that Christian theology did lose its own soul by allowing the usage of Platonic and Aristotelian constructions (so that Nietzsche was right in saying that "Christianity is Platonism for the people"[5]), but that Biblical faith has now found in Heidegger its one truly congruent philosophy, the legitimately "Christian philosophy"? Does Ott mean that Heidegger's philosophy in its account of being points to the same reality that Biblical faith grasps, in its quite different way, as the personal God? Or would Ott suggest the extreme view that Heidegger's formulations are

[2] Martin Heidegger, *Einführung in die Metaphysik* (1957. 2nd ed.; Tübingen: Max Niemeyer Verlag, 1958), pp. 142 ff. [English translation by Ralph Manheim, *An Introduction to Metaphysics* (New Haven: Yale University Press, 1959), pp. 186 ff.]

[3] *Ibid.*, p. 142. [*Ibid.*, p. 186.]

[4] Cf. Heinrich Ott, *Denken und Sein* (Zürich: EVZ-Verlag, 1959), pp. 87–88.

[5] Heidegger, *op. cit.*, p. 80. [*Op. cit.*, p. 106.]

fresher, clearer, and therefore more effective indicators of the *same* truths that traditional Christian theology has been trying to express, and that therefore the former may replace or at least be combined with the latter in a common language and conceptuality?

I would like to suggest briefly an answer to the questions of the relation of theology to philosophy that I have developed at some length elsewhere.[6] The Biblical faith has not developed in its literary, historical, and theological expressions by means of a process of accretion and eclectic synthesis from a variety of alien sources. To be sure, the Judeo-Christian community has not been isolated from, nor impervious to, the cultures with which it has been in contact throughout its four thousand years of history. Rather, Biblical faith has maintained its own unique identity, while being profoundly stimulated by every aspect of its environment to plumb the as yet unsounded depths of its own professed revelation. Even Karl Barth has recently expressed a similar view. While seeing the attempt at a "Christian philosophy" as ending only in the confusion of a crypto-theology, he nevertheless defends the possibility, indeed, the necessity, of positive results from an encounter between theologian and philosopher.[7] This learning of the one from the other, he says, "can never mean that the one should ever step over onto the path of the other, but only this: that the one, without being untrue to his own responsibility, is guided to some further step, in some stage of his own path, through this or that element in the thinking and speaking of the other."[8] Moreover, the teacher should not expect that the element of his teaching will be understood according to his own intention, nor should he be annoyed when the one who has been taught takes what he wants and goes his own way. The philosopher and theologian simply walk two different paths. Yet they

---

[6] *Human Spirit and Holy Spirit* (Philadelphia: Westminster Press, 1959), pp. 12–24.

[7] "Philosophie und Theologie," in Gerhard Huber (ed.), *Philosophie und christliche Existenz, Festschrift* for Heinrich Barth (Basel and Stuttgart: Helbing und Lichtenhahn, 1960), pp. 98 f.

[8] *Ibid.,* p. 103.

must listen to each other because they both are ordinary human beings who find themselves in the same "room," taking their start from and being responsible to the one and the same and the only truth. They are co-humans who are called to different tasks by the same reality. So "pure" theology or "pure" philosophy would be an inhuman undertaking, because these two paths supplement and cut across one another.[9] And however the theologian may be stimulated or guided by the philosopher, the best thing he can do for the philosopher is to be a theologian, an explicator of the only theme theology has: Jesus Christ, given as the reconciliation and the light of the world by the God who is the creator of the world.[10]

With all this Heidegger himself seems to agree. He says, "A 'Christian philosophy' is a round square and a misunderstanding. There is, to be sure, a thinking and questioning elaboration of the world of Christian experience, that is, of faith. That is theology. Only epochs that no longer fully believe in the true greatness of the task of theology arrive at the disastrous notion that philosophy can help to provide a refurbished theology, if not a substitute for theology, which will satisfy the needs and tastes of the time. For the original Christian faith philosophy is foolishness."[11] That Heidegger still is of this mind came out in his remarks to the 1959 meeting of old Marburgers. After listening to their discussion, he took them to task because he had heard nothing but philosophical problems bruited. He wanted to know why a group of Christian theologians was not discussing the gospel. What else do Christians have to offer the world but the gospel, he asked.

Besides serving as a stimulus and guide for his own task, the theologian's openness to the philosopher serves another purpose. Granted, the theologian ought not to "step over onto the path of the philosopher" in the sense of smuggling theology into philosophy, is it not possible and desirable for the theologian to

9 *Ibid.*, p. 93.
10 *Ibid.*, pp. 104 f.
11 Heidegger, *op. cit.*, p. 5. [*Op. cit.*, p. 7.]

philosophize with the philosopher? To what point? The answer is that there are times when the Christian, before he can talk with a man about the gospel, must talk with him on his own terms. He must understand man-on-his-own and talk about reality as it appears to him, quite apart from the gospel. The Christian must know the world of unbelief before he can issue the call to belief. As Heidegger has put it, "a faith that does not perpetually expose itself to the possibility of unfaith is no faith but merely a convenience."[12]

This exposure of the Christian to the world of man-on-his-own is an absolute apologetic prerequisite for effective proclamation of the gospel. But it is something even more profound. It is, as Heidegger said, a condition for the continuance of faith itself. As Kierkegaard pointed out long ago, doubt is a permanent dimension of a life of faith. This is true because the Christian's participation in philosophy comprises not only an apologetic but also an existential preoccupation. The man for whose sake the Christian must understand man-on-his-own is *himself* as well as the unbeliever. If the Christian must live under the dictum, *simul justus et peccator,* he must also continue to acknowledge, *simul Christianus et paganus.* The Christian will mean and heed his own confession of faith aright only if simultaneously he will see that he remains a pagan in a pagan world, a pagan in the original sense of an outlander who has not yet moved in to the city of God, who therefore is still subject to the crushing hardships and threatening dangers of life in the "far country." It is the Christian who cries out, "I believe; help my unbelief."[13] And how is the Christian to remain sensitive to his pagan self? Not by his own doctrine of sin which assumes that he stands before God. Barth clearly answers this question by saying that the theologian ought to regard the philosopher not as the *advocatus diaboli* but as *advocatus hominis et mundi,*[14] i.e., not as the devil's advocate but as advocate of man and the world.

12 *Ibid.*
13 Mark 9.24.
14 "Philosophie und Theologie," in Huber, *op. cit.,* p. 105.

II

This present book is dedicated to the examination of Heinrich Ott's thesis that for theology today Martin Heidegger in his exploration of the being of beings is, *par excellence,* the advocate of man. Having set the limits and possibilities of such a service of Heidegger for theology, we turn now to a testing of Ott's thesis in regard to a few of his specific applications of it.

Ott's general proposal as to Heidegger's helpfulness for theology is quite overwhelming: if we but follow his lead, then contemporary rifts in theology will be healed because "obscuring premises will fall like scales from our eyes."[15] This will be accomplished by the "inestimable service" of clarifying for us the essential nature of being, of thinking, of language, of understanding, and of the world.[16] Ott proposes that these philosophical clarifications can suggest new theological departures in our concepts of God, revelation, the nature of theology, hermeneutic, and the saving event. However, although he has gone further than anyone else in discussing the full range of Heidegger's thought as a source of stimulation for the reconstruction of Christian theology, Ott has thus far succeeded only in pointing out some possible parallels in the structures of Heidegger's thought and Christian theology. His attempts at developing specific implications of the former for the latter have as yet been so tentative and incomplete as to make it difficult to judge the adequacy of his main contention.

One of the specific points at which Ott supposes Heidegger's philosophy offers assistance to Christian theology is on the subject of analogy. He affirms that Heidegger can help us to a new formulation of *analogia entis* which will bypass Barth's objections. Analysis of this thesis will facilitate evaluation of Ott's general program.

It was not Aquinas' own analogy of being that Barth attacked but a personal reformulation of it as found in Erich Przywara's

[15] Cf. above, Heinrich Ott, "What is Systematic Theology?" p. 93.
[16] *Ibid.*

Religionsphilosophie katholischer Theologie.[17] Barth believed the
same formulation to have been incorporated in the decrees of
the Vatican Council of 1870. Ott has correctly noted that Barth
opposed this formulation because it seems to assert an ontological
identity between God and man by subsuming them both under
the common category of "being." But Barth's opposition to this
analogy of being was even more directly concerned with the
epistemological implication that man can gain knowledge of God
simply by drawing an analogy from man's own being. Such a
possibility allows for a valid natural theology. Barth argued
against this that man's only valid knowledge of God is not to be
inferred from a relationship of *being,* but rather occurs in a
relationship of *action.* This action is the event of revelation, of
grace, of faith. Borrowing a phrase from Paul,[18] Barth opposed
to analogy of being an analogy of faith, or as he variously called
it, an analogy of grace or of revelation. Barth has described this
relationship as a correspondence, but he has also retained the
word "analogy" to emphasize the qualitative difference between
God and man while recognizing a vital oneness. At the same time
he asserted the active and reciprocal character of the relation by
the word, "faith," which assumes both God's initiative in his self-
revelation and man's response.

Against the ontological fusion of God and man that he perceived in the analogy of being, Barth proposed still another
formula, analogy of relationship. He felt this to be necessary because, on the basis of Przywara's formulation, he identified the
analogy of being as an analogy of intrinsic attribution.[19] Barth
insisted that man's likeness to God is not based upon some intrinsic attributes that man has in common with God. Rather,
man can be said to be like God because the relationship between
male and female is analogous to the relationship between the

[17] Müchen: R. Oldenbourg, 1927. Barth's *Church Dogmatics* shows re-
liance on Przywara's formulation of the analogy of being in two places: 1/1,
44, and 1/2, 144.
[18] Romans 12.6.
[19] Cf. "Analogy" in Bernard Wuellner, *Dictionary of Scholastic Philosophy*
(Milwaukee: Bruce Publishing Company, 1956).

Father and the Son of the Trinity. And these two relationships do not stand in a static similarity, because the relationship between Father and Son also finds dynamic expression in an analogous relationship between God and man. In this way Barth hopes to assert a dynamic ontological likeness between God and man, yet preserve a qualitative difference between them, and also leave the whole initiative with God. In 1950 Barth was persuaded by von Balthazar that both his complex *analogia relationis* and Aquinas' original *analogia entis* are examples of analogy of proportionality and so do not conflict.

Be that as it may, Barth could hardly agree with Ott that Heidegger's cor-respondence of being is a helpful and more adequate formulation of his analogy of relationship, or of his analogy of faith. Heidegger does preserve an ontological difference between being and beings. For him being also has the initiative in man's thinking of being, and their cor-respondence does demand an element of human responsiveness. But any application of these terms to the faith relationship between Creator and creature becomes inappropriate when it is noted that the members of this relationship are not the same as those of Heidegger's cor-respondence.

For Heidegger, being is not God. Heidegger does not pretend to be a theologian, so he does not undertake to affirm or to deny the reality and the knowability of God. As Ott has made clear, Heidegger's rejection of the metaphysics that has made its way into some Christian doctrine does not mean that he is categorically atheistic. Indeed, he seems to want to leave open the real possibility of knowing God. But he conscientiously confines himself to his own province and job as a philosopher. He remains advocate of man and the world.

In his first writings he sought to be the advocate of man through a thorough analysis of that one peculiar being, man. Now Ott has shown us conclusively that this analysis of human existence was not an end in itself but just a deliberate preparation for Heidegger's real concern, the analysis of the being of beings. Through this analysis he tries to determine the "ontological difference" between beings and the being of beings. In this later phase, Heidegger adopts the role of which Barth speaks as "advocate of the world." By "the world" we mean here not Heidegger's technical use of the term but the whole sphere of beings and the being of beings. This is the sphere to which Christian theology refers as "creation," which has the character of being an "other" alongside or over against the Creator. It has its own peculiar, mysterious kind and way of being, even while it is utterly dependent upon the Creator as its source and sustainer. It has a "givenness" that never occurs as a thing itself, nor is to be perceived or apprehended as such by man. But this givenness occurs in all things and events, and it takes a unique conscious form in man.

It is this dimension of the world that Heidegger calls being and which he conceives to be the true subject matter for philosophic inquiry. He thinks it tragic that human thinking has forsaken this primary task, and either has become bogged down in the classification and control of the secondary entities with which the sciences (pure and natural) are concerned or has sought to construct a pseudo-theology in the guise of philosophical ideologies. He proposes that man is true man only when he turns his attention and concern to that level of his experience where his thinking and understanding can be flooded with the calling and the unveiling of the being of man and of all existing things. This event calls upon man to think and to speak poetically, nonconceptually at a pre-logical level.

When the two factors of the relationship are being and man so conceived, then it is requisite to drop the term "analogy" and to use only "cor-respondence." Then it is proper to describe human thinking as a "clearing" of the path of history in which the light of being shines forth. In such a relationship the distinction of subject and object does become meaningless, even a block to the occurrence of meaning. Because of the unbroken immanence of being and beings, being cannot be treated as an object to be manipulated by an autonomous subject, nor does man need the ladder of reason's dialectic to climb up to some supra-mundane sphere of truth. It is inevitable also that being can be described only in most general terms, namely, "permanent, always identical, already-there, given—all meaning fundamentally the same: enduring presence."[20]

While all of these statements are valid concerning the relation between being and man, none of them are valid, but rather are extremely misleading, if applied to the relation between God and man. It is true that theology cannot avoid the question of God's being, along with the question of the world's being and of man's being.[21] But this does not mean that God and the world can be classified under any common heading. Rather, the being of the world is a derived, dependent, and determined being. And it is God's being in his absolute originality and freedom that makes his being ultimately undefinable and so only describable in terms of his action. The attempt, therefore, to use insight concerning the responsiveness of man to the call of the general being of the world as an aid to understanding (by analogy? or by identity?) the faith-theological response of man to the calling of the word of God can only lead to confusion and error. One aspect of the being of the world is that it is always already-there, *given*. But God is the Giver of this givenness. And there is no giver of the Giver, because God is precisely the ultimate, eternal and self-determining One. Nor is he just the first cause at the head of the whole chain of causes that runs throughout the history of the given world. The relation of Giver to given as creation is *sui generis* and is not to be compared, either in analogy or in identity, with the relation between being and beings or with the relation between the general and the particular as explicated by science and philosophy.

It is, of course, good and necessary that man be sensitive and responsive to the being of the world, that he respond to the allusive character of the things of his world so as to penetrate deeper into the mystery of the pre-logical immanence between

---

[20] Heidegger, *op. cit.*, p. 154. [*Op. cit.*, p. 202.]
[21] Barth, *Church Dogmatics*, translated by T. H. L. Parker, *et al.* (Edinburgh: T & T Clark, 1957), II/1, 259.

himself and the rest of the world, so that he may find his place in the history of the world. But this level of experience is not the one that is ultimately definitive of human nature. Man quite properly heeds the calling of his biological needs and drives. He does distinguish himself by the possibility of being conscious of the voice of being and of responding by "speaking" being. But man is ultimately characterized by the fact that God himself, the Giver of being, enters the realm of being and addresses man and calls man into fellowship with himself. The nature of this relationship between God and man, in comparison with the relationship between being and man, comprises the heart of the problem and dilemma of modern theology. It is this problem which Barth has sought to resolve by his principles of *analogia relationis* and *analogia fidei*. It is a gross misunderstanding of Barth (and of Heidegger, also!) to suggest that his position and intent might be better stated along the lines of Heidegger's principle of cor-respondence between being and man. At least Barth and Heidegger themselves, as theologian and philosopher, seem to be quite aware that they are talking about two quite different relationships between man and "the one and only and same Truth."[22]

III

At this point the question might be asked whether at least Heidegger's analysis of the character of thinking might not help theology in that the theologian thinks, and surely all thinking of man must be of the same basic nature, whatever the subject matter of thought may be. But now it must be recognized that Heidegger's view of cor-respondence is not just an epistemological statement. One's view on the limits and possibilities of knowing are rooted in and revelatory of one's view on the nature of reality. For Heidegger, thinking comes from its subject matter.[23] The subject matter of real or primal thinking is the "ontological dif-

[22] Cf. Barth, "Philosophie und Theologie," in Huber, *op. cit.,* p. 94.
[23] Cf. above, "The German Discussion of the Later Heidegger," p. 44.

ference" between being and beings. This difference comes to light in thinking; so the event of real thinking and the being of beings tend to become identified with each other. Yet being is never caught and objectified in thought as a concept. Since being happens in the event of real thinking, the thinker is aware that there is "that which is not thought," that the difference is never fully or perfectly thought, that the event of thinking is not an autonomous act on the part of man. He sees rather that the event of thinking is made possible by the power of thinking which is the power of being-that-is-not-thought to give itself to be thought and to call man responsively into the event of thinking. Hence Heidegger invites us to take a step backward from scientific and metaphysical thinking which tries to objectify and to control being, into that kind of thinking with that which is given to be thought and where the language of thinking therefore becomes more fluid and allusive, poetic.

Ott seems to be suggesting that theology will be helped if it is able to see the following analogy of proportionality. Philosophic thinking is to being as faith's thinking is to God. Now real thinking arises out of its subject matter. And the subject matter that Heidegger is concerned about is the fact that things not only *are* in a kind of dead, inert meaninglessness, but that things have being or are the happening of being, that is, have meaning that is intentional and knowable. But this is not the same subject matter as that out of which theology arises. Heidegger wants to distinguish the secondary thinking of science and metaphysics from his real thinking on the grounds that the subject matter is different. Must not the thinking of theology also be distinguished from that of Heidegger's philosophy just because its subject matter is unique? There may be some parallels between theological and Heideggerian thinking. Both subject matters may be said to be knowable only as they give themselves to be known, to demand the active response of man, and to be to a degree ineffable.

But how does all this really help the theologian when the *mode* of knowing, the *kind* of response demanded of man, and the *reason* for the ineffability are all very different in the case of God

than in the case of being? The convergence of being as that
which is given to be thought with the event of thinking, in Heidegger, seems to mark his position still as an idealism, in the
form of an aesthetic intuitionism rather than a logical concep-
tualism. In the Christian faith-event the knowing, the response,
and the ineffability are all to be understood in light of the fact
that God relates himself to man as Person to person *in act*. This
act calls into play the whole being of the Creator and of the
creature, including the thinking dimension. But thinking is a
function at the service of the total act, not an end in itself. Inter-
personal language when used by Heidegger (the voice of being
calling to man, the initiative of being in unveiling, man as the
shepherd of being, man entrusting himself to being's care and
favor) must be taken in a purely figurative sense. If it were taken
substantively, then we would have to conclude that being is his
God and that he is constructing a mystical religion of a panthe-
istic variety.

These considerations bring us to a specific and basic point of
disagreement with Ott's proposed application of Heideggerian
principles to Christian theology. As Heidegger has proposed for
the field of philosophy, so Ott proposes for theology, that the
great *bête noire* of the modern mind is the so-called "subject-
object schema." Of course Heidegger is right in asserting that the
schema does not apply at the level of primal thinking where man
is simply open to the unveiling of the being of beings. Man is one
expression of being among many. He is continuous with being
and in cor-respondence with being. So in his fundamental relation with being, man cannot act as an autonomous subject who
manipulates, at will, reality as an object. In order to plumb the
depths of being, which is not an object among others but that
which only occurs in all beings and events, man must resort to
pre-logical, nonconceptual thinking, to poetic and aesthetic expression in general. He must take a step backwards from abstract
thought carefully controlled by means of categories and allow
being to unveil itself in unpredictable and unconditional ways.

Heidegger asserts, and Ott agrees, that such objectivist (or subjectivist) thinking has invaded much traditional theology. Granted. And it is wrong, because God certainly does not exist as a being exists, nor as the sum total of beings exist. God cannot be subjected to conceptual formulation and definition as one more object of human attention and analysis. Nevertheless, it is quite a different thing for Ott to propose that Heidegger's analysis of the relation between being and thinking may help clarify the relations between God and faith's thinking and between revelation and theology as well as the whole hermeneutical problem. The relationship is simply of a different order. God is not an objective thing but neither is he simply the ground out of which human thinking arises. Man is not an autonomous subject but neither is he simply an expression or an occurrence of the divine. There is a sense in which God is objectively over against man, and a sense in which man has his own objectivity of being under God. However indestructible the continuity is between God and his creation, there is nevertheless an irreducible discontinuity between God and man, precisely as subject-to-subject, that has no parallel in the relation of man to the general being of all creation. And to interpret the former in the terms of the latter can only lead to distortion.

Of course, emphasis on the distinction between these two different relationships must not lead to a reversion to what Bonhoeffer branded as "thinking in terms of two spheres,"[24] thinking in terms of "pairs of concepts as secular and Christian, natural and supernatural, profane and sacred, and rational and revelational, as though they were ultimate static antitheses."[25] God does come to encounter man in the midst and through the structures and events of the being of creation of which man is an expression and form. Therefore, revelational events do share in the characteristics of events of being. God reveals himself finally "incarnate." But in an event of being that is also an event of the revelation of God, there is an added dimension which is not pres-

[24] *Ethics*, edited by Eberhard Bethge, translated by Neville Horton Smith (New York: The Macmillan Company, 1955), p. 62.
[25] *Ibid.*, p. 64.

ent in any other event of being. The event of real human encounter between man and man is an analogy of the God-to-man
encounter. But, even that is not the *same* as being encountered
by the One who is the Giver of being, encountered in a way that
demands the response of man-as-subject to the sovereign Subject.
For all his use of the language of "calling," "unveiling," and
"cor-respondence," Heidegger cannot describe the relation of
being and man in terms of subject-to-subject encounter, love, and
fellowship. The latter *must* be the language of the Christian
theologian as he speaks of revelation.

IV

The results of applying to theology patterns derived from the
later Heidegger are not as novel as Ott seems to think. Heidegger's program of taking a step backward from science and metaphysical doctrine to a pre-logical level of experience, of thinking,
and of speaking is obviously reminiscent of Schleiermacher. One
could hardly hope for a more imaginative and creative attempt
than Schleiermacher's to explicate every facet of Christian faith
in terms of a center consisting of a human feeling of God-con-
sciousness as utter dependence upon the Whole which is neither
a thing nor the sum total of things but that out of which, by
which, and to which everything exists. Or again, the insistence
upon the total rejection of the subject-object distinction in our
speaking of man and God, and the results thereof, were clearly
and fully stated by Rudolf Bultmann as long ago as 1925, before
the publication of Heidegger's *Being and Time* but after the beginning of his conversations with Heidegger at Marburg in
1922.[26] This distinction, he said, involves us in the "arch decep-
tion . . . in that we see ourselves from the outside as the object
of self-orienting thinking. . . . And the case is not improved
at all by having a theistic or a Christian ideology, based on the
view that our existence is grounded in God. . . . For in this too

[26] Cf. his "What Sense Is There to Speak of God?" in *The Christian
Scholar*, XLIII, No. 3 (1960), 213–222.

God is viewed as an object just as man."[27] The solution proposed was Bultmann's original, thoroughgoing existentialism. He tells us that the only reality that the human self and God have lies in the event of God's word and act in which he gives us our existence by changing us from sinners to righteous men. Therefore, "we *know* nothing of God; we *know* nothing of our own reality; we have both only in faith in God's grace."[28] "We cannot talk about our existence because we can not talk about God; and we can not talk about God because we can not talk about our existence. . . . If we can talk about God *in* God, then we could talk about our existence, and vice versa. . . . Thus it remains true: if it be asked how it is possible to speak of God, then it must be answered, only by speaking of us."[29]

These lines of Schleiermacherian and Bultmannian thinking have landed contemporary theology in an impasse not yet resolved. Barth has progressively withdrawn from his original existential, dialectic formulation of the nature and content of Christian faith. Bultmann has stayed consistently with such a formulation.[30] What this means for our present topic is this: for Heidegger, being itself remains the shadowy reality that can never be surprised in a human vision and knowledge of being itself, but that can only be described in most general terms by implication, or better yet, can be received in pre-logical thinking. Being unveils itself. The being of beings happens in the primal thinking of man. Between being and thinking-man there is an unbroken continuity and identity, no matter how being transcends men. In a similar fashion, Schleiermacher sees the revelation of God as identical with man's sense of dependence. And Bultmann sees revelation as taking its primary form in man's new self-understanding. So, rightly or wrongly, Schleiermacher

27 *Ibid.*, p. 217.
28 *Ibid.*, p. 221.
29 *Ibid.*, pp. 218 f.
30 Cf. Schubert M. Ogden (ed.) in his "Introduction" to *Existence and Faith: Shorter Writings of Rudolf Bultmann* (New York: Meridian Books, Inc., 1960), p. 14.

has been accused of pantheism, and Bultmann of reducing theology to anthropology.

What else could result from Ott's proposal to explicate the relation of revelation and faith in terms of Heidegger's description of the relation between being and man? As Heidegger says of being, so Schleiermacher and Bultmann say of God: of course he is there—behind, in, under, through everything and especially the event of forgiveness, that is, the event of man's self-fulfillment. But we can say and know almost nothing of God as such, or even of *God* as he unveils himself because this unveiling takes the form purely of the transformation of *man's* own consciousness and self-consciousness. But at this point, Bultmann is too much of a Biblical theologian (and believer!) to stay completely with Heidegger's schema. In another early essay (1930), Bultmann sensed a real tension between Heidegger and Gogarten concerning the grounds and nature of man's decision about his existence. Heidegger held that man's historicity (self-realization) is constituted by his resolution in the face of death. Gogarten saw this resolution as occurring decisively in the face of the thou of another man, and ultimately in the face of the supreme Thou of God in Jesus Christ, because only in the situation of the latter does there become possible that *love* which fulfills man's being.[31] Bultmann sought a way to unite these two forms of human decision but, as Schubert Ogden has pointed out, he has not developed a Christology adequate to the resolution of this tension.[32]

Karl Barth also adopted the whole I-thou schema, and the existentialism involved therein, as the most adequate contemporary conceptuality for interpreting the revelatory situation. But Barth maintains that in God's address to man as a thou the divine I who speaks does actually unveil his own Self and so becomes known by man, even as man comes to know his own true self for the first time through this encounter. Barth would insist

---

[31] Cf. "The Historicity of Man and Faith," in Ogden (ed.), *op. cit.,* pp. 102–110.

[32] "Introduction" in Ogden (ed.), *op. cit.,* pp. 20 f.

that in the faith event a real relationship is established *between two,* the one and the other. This relationship of faith has the peculiar power to establish the objectivity of each over against the other *in* and *through* their communion in love and knowledge. This communion is the third dimension of a trinitarian revelation and knowledge of God, that is, the Holy Spirit. It is this factor in Barth's theology which preserves the essentially existential (ontic) character of faith and yet allows for the development of a legitimate, though limited, objectivity (ontology) in speaking about both God and man.

Strictly speaking, Barth would agree with Bultmann that "we *know* nothing of God, we *know* nothing of our own reality; we have both only in faith and in God's grace."[33] But, Barth would insist, we do have *both.* So if it is legitimate to use a "scientific interpretation of Scripture" in order to pursue an "inquiry into the understanding of human existence which finds expression in Scripture,"[34] then it is also legitimate and necessary to make a corresponding inquiry into the understanding of *God's* being as the other factor in the faith event. Hence, if a formulated Christian *anthropology* is permissible, so also is a *theology.* The latter is no more abstract and speculative than the former, *if* God truly speaks as I to man as thou, *and if* God gives himself to man in the communion of love and knowledge.

The vital weakness in Schleiermacher and Bultmann, and in any theology that would strictly apply Heideggerian concepts, lies in their posing the problem of human existence before God in binitarian instead of trinitarian terms. They pose the whole problem in terms of transcendence and immanence, God's otherness and omnipotence, man as over the abyss of nothing and as participating in being, the hidden Father and the personal Word. Without the third factor of *communion,* which simultaneously unites while preserving the one and the other, man is limited to talking about his accepting the miracle of his being accepted

[33] As quoted above.
[34] Bultmann, "The Problem of Hermeneutics," in *Essays, Philosophical and Theological,* translated by J. C. G. Greig (London: S C M Press Ltd., 1955), p. 258.

without knowing the someone or the something that accepts him.[35] Even Barth in his early theology thought in these dialectical terms. But he finally sensed that something was lacking and in his *Church Dogmatics* he made the doctrine of the Trinity, if not normative, at least integral to his whole theology. Even in the early volumes of the *Church Dogmatics* the *logos* tended to swallow up the meaning and function of the Holy Spirit, but in the later volumes the peculiar role of the Holy Spirit in the event of *reconciliation* has delivered him from a dualism in the epistemological problem of *revelation*. This was inevitable as a development of the principle of *analogia relationis* which takes the trinitarian structure *within* God as normative for the structure of the relation of God *ad extra* with the world of man. The *analogia fidei*, on the other hand, still left the whole God-man relationship posed in a dialectical form concerning the problem of knowledge.[36]

V

What service, then, can a study of Heidegger perform for Christian theology? This service cannot be isolated and described if we go on the assumption that he is talking about the same subject matter, the same factors in reality, and the same relationships as is theology. At the same time, there will be no answer either if we assume that Heidegger and theology are talking about two mutually exclusive subject matters. Man, other beings, and the being of both, which are Heidegger's concern, are also factors in theology's concern. Heidegger clearly and consciously excludes from his consideration the other factor of Christian concern: God.

Does this mean, then, that the so-called "Christian doctrine of man" incorporates and transcends all the insights of Heidegger's philosophy and so makes a consideration of the latter unneces-

---

[35] Paul Tillich, *The Courage to Be* (New Haven: Yale University Press, 1952), p. 185.
[36] Cf. *Church Dogmatics*, II/1, 279.

sary? Some theologians have taken this attitude, but the fact is that every formulation of the Christian doctrine of man shows evidence of the stimulus and imprint of some form of non-Christian thinking, from Plato and Aristotle to Whitehead and Heidegger. In fact, for the Christian a kind of independent doctrine of man is impossible, because for theology man and his world are defined by and in their living, dynamic relationship with God. In faith this relationship is fulfilled and made explicit. So man as such, by himself, does not exist for faith and its theology. Nevertheless, even in faith, man remains *simul justus et peccator,* and sin is precisely un-faith. So man remains *simul Christianus et paganus.* I live by faith, but I also live as one who has not yet heard the gospel, and I live in a world which goes its way as if Christ had not lived, died, and risen again—a world which does not really go its way without Christ, but *as if.*

The real confusion comes when the Christian, assuming that his doctrine of man includes and replaces all pagan knowledge of man, goes on to three further assumptions: (1) that his understanding of man by faith is built into the structure of man's existence in this world and can be seen there, and, therefore, that (2) the world can be expected to order itself and treat the Christian according to this Christian doctrine of man, and, finally, that (3) Christian faith can determine beforehand the content of pagan knowledge of man and his world. When paganism then reasserts itself—in history, or in society, or within one's own personal existence—it appears to this Christian that the very ground of his faith has been destroyed. Against all of these false assumptions, the Christian must remember that his very doctrine of creation does give man and his world a relatively objective character of scientific investigation and knowledge. It is also the basis of the possibility of paganism, of man's attempt to live apart from God. Therefore, really to understand the infinite possibilities for good and for evil that reside in creation, it behooves the righteous Christian, who is also sinful pagan, to listen to all the voices of man and his world as they attempt to unveil their nature as such. He must listen to them as advocates of man and the world. These voices, even in the deep pathos of their incompleteness and perversion, are deeply revealing, both of God's creation as such and of depths of meaning in God's redemption in Christ. In an ultimate perspective, they must be viewed as another voice of the same God who speaks in Jesus Christ. As we know ourselves to be pagans, we must always turn and listen to the voice of Jesus Christ, the advocate of God. As we know ourselves to be Christians, we must turn and listen to the voice of worldly wisdom, the advocates of man and the world.

Heidegger is not the first such advocate to whom Christian faith has listened with profit, nor will he be the last. But profit there is in listening to him, *if* the nature and limits of his service are clearly understood to begin with. Our present task has been only to try to set the limits, and therefore to reduce the dangers, of a conversation between theology and Heidegger.

4. Theology as Ontology and as History

CARL MICHALSON

Drew University

A picture of the later Heidegger is important for its double exposure of the contemporary theological scene. The foreground brings to light the shape that theology is taking at present. More importantly, although indistinctly and in the background, there appears a defensive reaction to the threat to systematic theology that the hermeneutic of the earlier Heidegger inspired. Rudolf Bultmann, in employing the existential insights which Heidegger's *Being and Time* developed, advanced a method of interpreting the Scriptures that so thoroughly articulates the Christian faith that it has put in question the need for systematic theology. Meanwhile, however, Heidegger has elevated other elements in his position than those which Bultmann found useful. May there not be some basis in this later, non-Bultmannian Heidegger for countering the threat to systematic theology that Bultmann's position represents?

I

The theologians who profited by dialogue with the early Heidegger were primarily influenced by his understanding of what history is. In classically conceived philosophy, thinking was always in some direct relationship with being. Reason always had some immediate rapport with ultimate reality. Immanuel Kant was the first major philosopher to separate thought and being. That separation was the end of ontology in its classical form.

But Kant nevertheless allowed man's reason to stand in harmony with man's own being. That thesis was the open door to ontology in its modern, anthropological form. Hegel subsequently revealed a separation within the nature of man, showing phenomenologically that reason is not simply alienated from reality; it is alienated within itself. The only cure for this alienation, according to Hegel, is to be found in history. One cannot relate to "being itself" without historical mediation. Hegel's phenomenology, then, is the source both of modern historicism and of existentialism. To historicism, truth appears in history alone. But, to existentialism, history appears as an *aporia,* that is, a reality upon which man depends for his reconciliation to ultimate reality, yet a reality that records only alienation.

The early Heidegger was existentialist, phenomenologist, and historicist. Søren Kierkegaard supplied the basic existential formula, largely through the inspiration of Hegel: "existence separates thought and being," so that nothing of being can be in thought without the mediation of existence. Edmund Husserl's phenomenology supplied the logical rigor for working philosophically within that formula: man must live by what appears in human existence. Wilhelm Dilthey supplied the cultural materials, the specifically human substance of history, in his historical science of hermeneutic. Heidegger's *Being and Time* drew these three rays into focus, and Rudolf Bultmann and Friedrich Gogarten, pre-eminently, have done their theology within that focus.

For Bultmann, the focus revealed why one could read the New Testament as history. But the term "history" no longer meant what it had before the days of Kant and Hegel. History was now the sole medium in which reality appeared and in which thought struggled to overcome its emptiness. In that setting, the New Testament was no longer a record of first-century facts that one had only to interpret in twentieth-century language. The New Testament was history's way of submitting what reality there is in it as the basis for the meaningful life of the existing man.

Probably Gogarten among contemporary dogmatic theologians best saw the implications of this method for systematic theology, for he is the only major dogmatician who, on principle, has not attempted a system. As early as 1921 Ernst Troeltsch anticipated this future for Gogarten when he called him "an apple from the tree of Kierkegaard."[1] When one understands history as the medium in which reality appears, concedes that one's own rationality is fully historical, and appreciates the Bible as the history of the appearance of reality in its ultimacy, dogmatic theology seems to have nothing to add to the exegesis of the Scriptures. Dogmatic theology could even be said to be a distraction, for it treats its statements about reality as if these statements were true independently of the history in which reality appears.

Meanwhile Heidegger seems to have effected one of the most stunning shifts of emphasis in the history of philosophy. Where classical philosophy from Socrates to Descartes had operated on the assumption that thought and being are always in continuity, and where modern philosophy had held that it is history which mediates being to thought, the later Heidegger has been promoting a third possibility. It is a matter of indifference to theology that this position was already present in his early work, because it has only come to prominence and thus begun to influence theology through his later works.

In the later emphasis of Heidegger, questions of history surrender their primacy to questions of being. But they do not do so in the classical way, where being is in continuity with thought. Being now becomes the unthought but necessary mediator between thought and existence.

For Heidegger's phenomenology, this new position was no radical change, since being is still encountered only as it appears in existence. For his historicism, the shift was quite significant, since he no longer looks for being *as history,* but only for being *as historic,* that is, for being *as the possibility of history.* For his existentialism, it was calamitous, for two reasons. First, one no longer thinks in the face of death, which is the rudimentary *aporia* of historical existence. One thinks in the presence of the

[1] "Ein Apfel vom Baume Kierkegaards," in *Die Christliche Welt,* Vol. 35 (1921), 186–190.

something without which history would mean encounter with nothing, that is, in the presence of being. Thus, in the later Heidegger, poetic calm and rational ineffability supplant existential anguish and the quest for a concrete historical articulation of meaning.

The second notable occasion for Heidegger's retreat from existentialism was his suppression of subjectivity in the determination of meaning. Hence, where the early Heidegger emphasized the mediation of man in the realization of meaning, the later Heidegger criticizes this emphasis as a remnant of idealism, of Nietzschean self-assertion, holding it responsible for subjectivistic fragmentation and for manipulation of the wholeness of reality. In the later, more ontologically disposed position, the self has learned submission to being, which is revealed without the self's transforming activity. One sign of Heidegger's resoluteness in this turn away from subjectivity is his restoration of *things* to a place of centrality.

This turn in Heidegger's philosophical development, like a flare above the battle, clearly exposed the relative positions of the main theological strategists of Europe today. Ordinary information, of course, already gave the general picture. It was widely known through the ranks that Barth lay to the right and Bultmann to the left, and that to the right of Barth were flanked his cautious codifiers, like Otto Weber and Hermann Diem, and to the left of Bultmann his incautious advance patrol, like Ernst Fuchs and Gerhard Ebeling. The Barthians were identifiable by their concern for the priority of the being of God in himself and the Bultmann contingent was known for its existential interpretation. But a large body of theologians eager to see service found it difficult to join forces with either side. The Barthian dogmatics was held to be too traditional, too easy to reduce to orthodox patterns, too trinitarian to be adequately cruciform. The Bultmannian method of interpretation was held to be too indifferent to the broader demands of theology as a systematic science, remaining silent about anything that did not have meaning for man as man, and being satisfied to substitute expositions of Biblical texts for comprehensive outlines of Christian belief.

The value of the sudden illumination from the Heidegger turn was not that it exposed these positions but that it disclosed a corridor between them. On the basis of his own reconnaissance in the light of the later Heidegger, Heinrich Ott for one has called for a third front in the development of systematic theology. It is based neither upon the *being* of God, which is the Barthian trend, nor upon *hermeneutic* as the analysis of human existence, which is the trend of Bultmann, but upon *hermeneutic* as the analysis of being.

Systematic theology as the hermeneutical analysis of being means two things above all. First, systematic theology is not a science in the customary modern understanding of the word. According to Heidegger, "science does not think," because it does not know what it *means* by what it does. Systematic theology is a non-scientific form of thinking as a discipline that is oriented to the question of fundamental meaning. If it is a science in any sense, it is a hermeneutical science, which by definition must know what it means in what it does. It is thinking, disciplined for the purpose of interpreting meaning, to the end that being itself, and thus God with respect to his being, may be revealed. Thinking in this sense is not proving but pointing. That kind of thinking, as Ott believes, classifies systematic theology more closely with prayer than with science.

In the second place, systematic theology is necessary as one phase of the generally accepted hermeneutical circle. According to the strategy of the hermeneutical circle, before one can understand a reality—a work of art, a writing, a conversation—he must bring some understanding to it, even though only in the form of a question. Systematic theology in Ott's view has the function of helping the exegete interpret the text of the Bible by supplying him with the proper questions to ask of the text. Hereafter, what systematic theology intends by its outline of doctrines—incarnation, atonement, eschatology, and the like— is not a description of reality, and least of all a body of right teaching that is synonymous with faith, but a series of right questions to be asked of the text. The doctrinal framework of systematic theology is the handmaiden to the interpretation of the Scriptures, a deductive moment in theological reflection which facilitates the more inductive process of exegesis. Systematic theology is a unity of vision in a discipline that might otherwise be content with fragmentation. It is a trans-scientific thinking without which Biblical interpretation might never rise beyond the scientific level, the level of philology and textual criticism, not knowing what it means by what it does.

When Ott's paper was originally presented, his audience was composed largely of Biblical scholars. Their immediate reaction was that Ott had made exegesis an auxiliary science to systematic theology. Whatever Ott's intention, quite the opposite is implied. Ott is a systematic theologian who, after encountering Rudolf Bultmann's exegetical method, was left wondering what work was left for him. This twofold proposal for a systematic theology is not the ostentatious and indulgent offer of succor from a queen of sciences. Rather, systematic theology is now in the position of being required to supply a reason for its existence. It is in the process of being kidnapped by New Testament theology and of offering a ransom for its life. Ott believes the ransom is subscribed by the later Heidegger.

If this analysis of the situation is accurate, two questions need to be answered: (1) What is there about the historical hermeneutic of Bultmann that makes it such a threat to systematic theology? (2) Is Ott's alternative of ontological hermeneutic able to achieve what he projects?

II

Bultmann has always contended that the interpretation of a Biblical text is not only exegesis but dogmatics, preaching, and apologetics as well. No one has ever paid much attention to this claim. In one way, it was too obvious. These four operations have always been able to occur in any single individual, successively. In another way, it was too unrealistic. These four functions are already structured into theological institutions today. Is it not enough that they interact without having to deny them some measure of autonomy? However, either of these ways of looking at the matter has misjudged the rigor in Bultmann's method. The four theological functions do not occur successively, whether in the same person or in four different departments of theology. They occur simultaneously when one exegetes the Scriptures properly. A proper exegetical contact with a text will *be* dogmatics, preaching and apologetics because it will *do* what every one of these disciplines is designed to do. The act of understanding a text (exegesis) is the act in which the significance of the faith appears (systematic theology) in such a way as to become significant for the interpreter (preaching), despite all his prior resistances (apologetics).

How can exegesis bear so heavy a burden? The key to that is in what Bultmann has meant by hermeneutic as a historical science. Traditionally it has been supposed that the exegete is a historian oriented to the past. He will determine, for instance, what the apostles believed. The systematic theologian is oriented to the present. He must say what we can mean by what the apostles believed. In the hermeneutic influenced by existentialism, however, historical science stands in the present. It is absolutely cut off from the materials of the past unless they are addressing questions that the man of the present is asking. The capacity for the past to survive in the present is a direct attribute of the interest the past holds for the present. One does not seek in ancient manuscripts what does not interest one. Therefore, the old understanding of history as a river flowing out of the past into the present is misleading and false. In hermeneutic as a historical science, the systematic theologian is no longer needed to bring the Biblical faith up to date. The exegete, for whom nothing can be delivered from the past which does not present itself meaningfully, is already engaged in that operation, and within the general procedures of historical method.

Again, traditionally the preacher has been the one who takes the results of Biblical scholarship and makes them edifying to the hearer, appealing to the hearer to believe this faith. According to Bultmann, faith is a historical reality. That means faith is part of the structure of history itself. One does not hear a meaningful statement, then decide to accept it. Believing is ingredient in the structure of meaning. Thus, the exegete asks of the text those questions the text is asking which are also the questions he as an existing man is asking. When the text answers these questions, to say the exegete understands the answers is to say he finds them answering his questions. In that moment, exegesis is identical with preaching. Preaching is primarily the hearing of the word and only secondarily the declaring of the word. The act of preaching presupposes that a word that has been heard will make possible the hearing of the word. Hearing implies that the word has been received as the answer to the question of one's existence as a man.

Now it can be understood why exegesis, seen in this thoroughly historical way, also absorbs the functions of apologetics. Traditionally, apologetics was a way of convincing the incredulous of the rightness of the faith. Bultmann knows no way of doing apologetics which is not simply preaching, and thus exegesis. The faith, being history, carries its own power to convince. There is nothing magic in this liaison. History occurs when an event which was meaningful for others becomes meaningful for me. There is no way of establishing a meaningful connection with an event from outside the event. Yet, when the event does become meaningful through one's interior connection with it, it does so with a suddenness and illumination that dispel resistance and thus dispense with apologetics.

Considering this omnicompetent exegetical procedure, is there anything distinctive left for systematic theology to do? For Ott, two things remain: (1) an interpretation in which *being* and not *human existence* is the horizon for hermeneutical interrogation; and (2) a deduction of the relevant questions to which being will reveal its secrets in the exegetical moment. In the face of Bultmann's historical hermeneutic, are Ott's proposals really able to save the relevance of systematic theology?

III

The issue between Ott and Bultmann is not whether systematic theology will be a hermeneutical science but whether its hermeneutic will finally be oriented to ontological questions or to historical questions. Because of his preoccupation with historical questions, Bultmann found the early Heidegger's existential concerns helpful to theology but declined to give his ontological concerns the kind of priority that Heidegger sought for them. In the later Heidegger references to history have virtually dropped out of his language, and the materials upon which he exercises his hermeneutical analysis of being are not historical materials but the verbal medium often considered to be the furthest removed from history, namely, poetry. Ott now proposes to develop theological hermeneutic as an ontological enterprise. The suggestion is ingenious, because New Testament scholarship, bound as it is to historical method, could not employ this form of hermeneutic without in some sense becoming ancillary to a discipline other than historiography. Thus, Ott appears to have come upon an invulnerable method of saving a place for systematic theology among the theological disciplines.

The struggle between ontology and historiography as bases for a theological hermeneutic is reflected in every one of the major questions suggested by Ott's proposal. Three such questions deserve examination.

a. *Is the analysis of being properly a pre-understanding that delivers the meaning of an historical text such as the Bible, or is it a prejudgment that thwarts the emergence of such meaning?*

Paul Tillich, for instance, long ago decided that the question about "Being itself" was the fundamental question, because he believed "Being itself" to be the only non-symbolic way one has of referring to God. Tillich learned this title for God when he was Heidegger's colleague at Marburg. Meanwhile Heidegger has insisted that "being" is not "God" just as Samuel Beckett has insisted Godot is not. While he is willing to entertain the possibility that there is some analogy between theological thinking and ontological thinking, Heidegger has not endorsed what medieval theology called the analogy of being, which is the method of arriving at the truth of God by asking the question about being. Yet, in his book on the later Heidegger, Ott has made the point several times that in view of Heidegger's ontology, Barth's objection to the "analogy of being" is overcome. By that he meant that being, for Heidegger, is not an ultimate reality accessible to human reason, as it was in pre-Kantian, scholastic theology. Being makes itself accessible in an unthinkable language.

Should Barth be satisfied with analogy of being done on this basis? Quite to the contrary, the revision in ontology which Heidegger sponsors has not affected the grounds of Barth's objection. Barth was not interested in denying either God's power to reveal himself or man's power to intuit God's nature. He was interested in availing himself of the concrete understanding which the triune God chose to make available in history, in Jesus of Nazareth. *Analogia entis* for Barth is not countered by *analogia fidei* of the sort where the truth of God can only be revealed to a modest and receptive intellect. *Analogia fidei*, Barth's alternate to *analogia entis*, means *analogia relationis*, the relation of faith. The relation of faith is man's relation to God's self-relation, to God as trinity. But this relation is mediated by Jesus Christ, who is the form in which the trinity communicates itself in history. Hence, the *analogia relationis* involves the relation of the concretely existing man to the concrete history of Jesus of Nazareth. This analogy of relation is currently being conserved in the "new quest of the historical Jesus" where faith is illumined not by the question about ultimate being but by the question about the historical form in which God has made himself present in human history. That quest is in the tradition of historicism where historical questions are prior to ontological questions. The discussion that followed the oral delivery of Ott's paper was so preoccupied with references to being that Heidegger himself took the floor to ask, "What has all this to do with Jesus Christ?" He was not being pious. He was suggesting that for a theologian there may be only one thing worse than forgetfulness of being, and that is forgetfulness of history.

Theologians oriented to ontological hermeneutic are fond of saying that if there is such a thing as being, theology must deal with it. Since the days of Edmund Husserl and the advent of phenomenology, that simply does not follow. Husserl showed how it is possible to bracket out the question of being in order to give the question of meaning priority. In that sense Husserl's phenomenology is closer to the historical science of hermeneutic than it is to the later Heidegger's phenomenological ontology, for as Dilthey said, "Man is there not to be but to act." Heidegger, in putting his kind of ontology-as-a-discipline beyond history-as-a-discipline, classifies history as a descriptive enterprise. The subject-matter of history is thought to be merely a qualification of man's being. For him, the methods of history do not determine one's relation to history but presuppose such a relation, which is ontological and therefore best explored and renewed by ontology.

If that were the whole truth about history, it would be convincing to observe that ontology, transcending adjectival qualification, is necessarily prior to the methods of history. That attitude toward history is quite appropriate with reference to historical positivism, but it tends to bypass modern historiographical gains. History in contemporary thinking is man existing in his acts, not simply describing them. In contemporary historicism, man is his history, and where he has no history, he has no being. History is both the creation and the revelation of man's being. Therefore, ontology, while it may well be a kind of pre-philosophy, as Heidegger claims, is itself dependent upon historiography, which defines man where he really is.

Two things of importance follow for theology in relation to the later Heidegger. First, history cannot be treated, as Heidegger treats it, simply as one more regional ontology. History is not one among several areas but the horizon of every area of investigation. From this the second thing follows. Historicism, the philosophical position which orients all questions to the question of history, ought not be classed as a species of ontology just because it happens to define being as historic. In asking the question about the meaning of reality through the medium of history, historicism constitutes a way of being which does not emerge when the question of being is raised. History is an horizon so inescapable that being is itself a derivative of history.

The Bible, for instance, does not ask the question of being but of historic meaning and act. To be sure, Exodus names God the "I am who I am." But the Hebrew expression "to be" (*hāyā*) embraces the connotations given it not by ontology but by the history of Israel's responses to the acts of God. Thus the Hebrew Scriptures respond not to ontology but to what the Japanese theologian, Tetsutarō Ariga, calls "hayatology," or what the Western world knows as historiography. The question of being raised from the standpoint of the question of meaning for man (historiography) is a completely different question from the question of meaning raised from the standpoint of the question of being (ontology). Does the New Testament raise the ontological question when it cites Jesus as saying, "Before Abraham was, I am?" To say that this is a question of being is to attempt to go behind what for the New Testament is final, namely, eschatology —the redemptive presence of God in Jesus of Nazareth. In the eschatological faith of the New Testament, being cannot qualify history because it is history which qualifies being, giving it its end. Therefore, to ask the question about being is to engage in a hermeneutic of prejudgment, bringing to the text concerns which are not prior for it.

New Testament faith is eschatological and not ontological. That is, it is an *answer* to the question of the meaning of history where the answer is given within history *as* history and not at the horizon of history as being. Even if being were identical with God, one would have to say that the New Testament is not oriented to God in his being but God in his act of self-revelation, God giving history its end in the form of Jesus of Nazareth. The ontological theology of Paul Tillich is innocent compared to

Ott's project because Tillich has not attempted systematic theology as the deductive phase of Biblical hermeneutic, as Ott has. In Ott, however, the deductive pre-understanding collides with the nature of the text. If put into operation, it would convert his proposed hermeneutical system into a system of pre-judgments.

b. *Is there sufficient guarantee in Ott's method that the doctrinal questions by which he proposes to inform exegetical work will be continually subject to revision from the initiative of the text itself?*

Implicit in a hermeneutical circle is the subordination of the deductive phase (the question of the interrogator) to the inductive phase (the question of the text). Ott's fondness for such traditional, ontologically weighted questions as doctrine of God, Christology, sin, and justification inspires skepticism regarding his outcome. In Europe more than in America, of course, dogmatic theology is built upon the ecumenical creeds and particular church confessions. For instance, when Karl Barth left the pastorate to teach theology at Göttingen (in the pay of American Presbyterians), he was forbidden to name his course "Dogmatics," for the only dogmatics admissible there at the time was Lutheran. That condition existed in the twentieth century.

Biblical theology, however, originated as long ago as the seventeenth century as a reform within dogmatic theology itself. The reform was brought on by the necessity for historical method in handling the Bible, combined with the unwillingness of systematic studies to accommodate to the same necessity. Exegetes ought never let dogmaticians forget that day of their liberation from dogmatics. Exegesis as a New Testament science that, thanks to the rise of the historical consciousness in the modern world, has so recently won the right to allow the Bible to speak for itself, is justifiably cautious about entering into liaisons with a discipline that does not usually submit itself to the same kind of historical dialectic.

There are evidences in Ott's discussion that he is not prepared to protect the gains that have been made by Biblical studies in their independence from dogmatics. One is that he seems willing to give the Bible as canon priority over the Bible as history. In so doing he supports a medieval position which the Reformers denied by their willingness to change the canon. Ott clings to the canon because on this basis systematic theology can be to Protestantism what the *magisterium* is to Roman Catholicism, the agency that interprets the intention of the church in holding the Bible as its constitution. Thus Ott claims that theology must integrate the Old Testament into its consideration, but, consistent with the official dogma of the church up to the present time, he does not give a rationale to support his demand.

As an illustration of how his method would work, he offers an exegesis of Psalm 1. But his hermeneutical presuppositions are New Testament presuppositions, as Wilhelm Vischer's are when he looks for Christ in the psalms. Presumably that would be possible on the basis of a hermeneutic of being if being were a continuous reality within all its historical manifestations, bridging the gap between the Testaments. But the Biblical faith testifies to a God who binds his people through historical covenants. Now that the new covenant has occurred in Jesus Christ, is it historically justifiable to interpolate that covenant into the record of God's old covenant? Theology is unwarranted in affirming that the God we meet in the Old Testament is the same God we meet in the New Testament. That is not to say there are two Gods but only that the Testaments are conceived not on the basis of one being of God but on the basis of two historically distinct modes of relationship to God. Inasmuch as Christians are those related to God on the basis of his covenant in Christ, the Old Testament does not have the same status as revelation as the New Testament, the analysis of being notwithstanding.

Ontological presuppositions are also employed by Ott to provide unity within the New Testament. It is true that the New Testament is a highly diversified account of the meaning of Jesus Christ and of his impact upon the early church. However, such diversity is utterly characteristic of historical reality. To go beneath it is to jeopardize its status as history. To attempt to smooth over its ruggedness by ontological unities that exist only at the limit of history, as does Ott's use of Heidegger's being, is alien to history's intrinsic structure. A historical science ought to win its sense of unity and continuity by thoroughly historical means. The variety in the accounts of the resurrection, for instance, must not be unified, as Ott proposes, by participation in what he calls the Christ-being. But, then, what is the alternative? What the resurrection means ought to be found in the historical materials themselves, inclusive of the records of the witness of the pre-Easter Jesus to his own mission.

Ott's illustration of unity in variety, taken from the experience of friendship, is very misleading and tends to make ontological gains on the basis of unreflective piety. Friendship, he says, is a silent being beneath all friendly conversations. Analogically, is the God-relation a continuous reality beneath all verbal witness to it? Is the God-relation reflected, like Martin Kähler's morning sun, in every scattered dew-drop of historical witness, giving the diverse witness a common being? Tempting as the analogy is, it depreciates the historical character of faith for which the God-relation of a Christian is always mediated by a historical word— the word God speaks in Christ and renews in the witness of the church. Beings are related not on the basis of their being but on the basis of their acts, their covenants—uttered, remembered, and renewed.

c. *Is it theologically justifiable to separate the Christ event from the message about the Christ event?*

Ott's desire to do so shares the fundamentally positivistic and common-sense drive which operates to some extent in every Christian thinker. The difference for Ott is simply that he illuminates his conviction by Heidegger's very sensitive and sophisticated ontology. His explicit justification manifests two main concerns.

1. *Christ is at work even where he is not preached.* What does that mean? Presumably for Ott it means that the preaching of the church like the apostolic witness derives its validity from its participation in the Christ-being, which is the ontological event

continuous in all historical witness to the Christ. The Christ-being is there, *extra nos,* independent of the contingencies of witness. In historical hermeneutic, on the other hand, exegesis is not a reflective relation to an event which is there without that relation. As Ernst Fuchs has said, exegesis is standing in the event. Heidegger prepared for that understanding in paragraph forty-four of *Being and Time,* where he asserted that before the laws of Newton were discovered, they were not true. But he did not add that once the laws were discovered, one had only to re-late reflectively to their truth. Truth, he said, "is in the dis-closure." One might ask, "Where is the Christ now?" just as one might ask, "Where is Beethoven's Ninth Symphony?" In the light of the earlier Heidegger he might answer, as indeed the late Maurice Merleau-Ponty did, that the Ninth Symphony ap-pears only in the different renditions one gives of it, although the symphony is not reducible to the rendition.[2]

The theological significance of this phenomenological sugges-tion is patent. Heidegger knows that in the phenomenological method of Husserl and in the historical method of Dilthey sub-jectivity is not a distortion of reality but an aspect of its structure, an aspect that does not emerge without one's deliberate sub-jective penetration into that subjective structure. Yet, even with that subjective initiative in the discernment of who Christ is, Christ remains a reality *extra nos.* Subjectivity does not reduce him to a psychological state of other men. He is significant *extra nos,* yet only in his disclosures. His disclosures occur in the wit-ness that is made to him. But the witness is always an inter-pretation that is made of him. Disclosure is an event of historical mediation, mediation through human existence, in which a man's life is embraced by God's meaningful claim.

The urgency of the theological task is directly related to this historicity of the Christ event. What is in history survives in the witness that is made to it. What is in being, on the other hand, can be said to happen, but if it happens without such witness, it does not happen meaningfully, that is, historically. To suppress

[2] *Les Sciences de l'Homme et la Phénoménologie* (Paris: 1961), p. 13.

subjectivity in hermeneutical work, as Heidegger and Ott now do, is hazardous, for nothing happens meaningfully which does not involve a human interpreter. Not that meaning originates with human understanding, but that the question of meaning is nowhere raised nor the answer given except as mediated by the historical form of existence.

Does not that claim tend to bypass nature as a meaningful reality? Ott believes that the ontology of Heidegger could overcome the dichotomy between nature and history which seems so prevalent in existentially influenced theological thought. He will probably evoke the appreciation of sacramentalists and devotees of natural theology, as Tillich has with his ontological version of these concerns. But there will be an equivocation at the base of this achievement. Nature for historical hermeneutic is the structure of reality where the question of meaning for man is not asked. History, on the contrary, is the structure of reality where the question of meaning for man is asked.

The equivocation of the ontologists appears in their saying that Christ is at work in nature, especially when they invoke the Johannine *logos* doctrine of creation in support of their claim. When the prologue to the Gospel of John identifies the Christ as a participant in the act of creation, it is not saying that nature has the word of God hidden in it. Nature is reality where such humanly meaningful questions are not raised, as they are not in the scientific measurement of the exterior world, or in the historical (*historisch*) effort to establish facts without regard to their fundamentally human (*geschichtlich*) significance. Creation, therefore, cannot be confused with nature, inasmuch as creation is the act in which man receives the world from God as man's own responsibility. Sacrament cannot be confused with nature inasmuch as a sacrament is the seal of God's promise that the world is there redemptively, that is, in the best interests of man. In this definition of terms, if one treats the world as nature, one ceases to regard it as creation and it becomes demonic, as Paul said to those who made the world their object rather than their responsibility. If one treats a sacrament as nature, that is, without participating in its fundamental intention, one receives it unworthily, and ceasing to be a sacrament, it becomes an instrument of wrath.

Ontology in Heidegger's sense does not support the naturalizing of creation and sacrament. However, it does give courage to such efforts, because it allows one to refer to what is real in being without relating to the historic frame of reference out of which such realities are founded. This danger is revealed in Heidegger's equivocal response to attacks upon the a-historical character (*Geschichtslosigkeit*) of poetry. Ott's discussion feeds upon this equivocation. Heidegger claims that poetry—in this case the poetry of Trakl—"does not need historical 'objects' [*historische 'Gegenstände*']. Why not? Because his poetry is in the highest sense historical [*geschichtlich*]."[3]

When *Being and Time* was written, this comment would have meant that scientific history (*Historie*), which looks for objects in history as if they were objects in nature without raising the question about their meaning for man, is not the sufficient cause of the history man lives (*Geschichte*). Appearing as it does twenty-six years later, however, the comment means that a truly historical (*geschichtlich*) event manifests the power of destiny (*Geschick*). The poet pre-eminently expresses that power found in events, but he does so without reference to any event in particular. This view was already expressed by Heidegger in his essay on "The Origin of the Work of Art" in which he developed the position that historic truth comes into existence through art. "All art is in essence poetry," he said; and "whenever art occurs . . . only then does history begin."[4] This creativity of a poet, as of any artist, makes him a threat to all cultural structures that are oriented to prior historical manifestations of destiny. But this same creativity is also the reason why poets, and ontologists as well, can be called a-historical (*geschichtslos*)

[3] "Die Sprache im Gedicht," in *Unterwegs zur Sprache* (2nd ed.; Pfullingen: Günther Neske, 1960), p. 80. This essay first appeared in 1953 under the title "Georg Trakl: Eine Erörterung seines Gedichtes."

[4] *Holzwege* (Frankfurt a.M.: Vittorio Klostermann, 1950), pp. 59, 64, 65. The essay was first presented in lectures delivered in 1935–36.

without meaning simply to imply that they do not do history as a natural science (*unhistorisch*). Insofar as poetry and ontology find meaning which is not an attribute of some event or events in particular, they are a-historical "in the highest sense" of the term "historical." Preaching does not enjoy the luxury of poetic creativity, for while it creates "new being," it always does so "in Christ," that is, by reminiscence of God's historical act.

2. *There is a silence in faith which is deeper than expression.* One might say of the later Heidegger what Hegel once said of the German idealists, that their favorite text is Acts 17.23, "to an Unknown God."[5] Heidegger's being reveals itself as the "unthought." This suits the mystic mentality. And it is significant that in his early career Heidegger announced he would some day write a large study of the mystic, Meister Eckhart. It also suits the Counter-Reformation mentality. I refer to the decision of Trent affirming, against the rising Protestant theology of the word, the hermeneutical inaccessibility of the Bible: and it is significant that Heidegger began his schooling in a Jesuit seminary in Freiburg, preparing for the priesthood. Medieval theology was a theology of grace which emphasized the prevenience of God's activity. Protestant theology is a theology of the Holy Spirit which, without de-emphasizing prevenience, always holds God's activity in equilibrium with his word. Grace operates effectively in silence, without being understood. The Holy Spirit works when the church interprets the gospel in such a way as to be understood. That circumstance is not a proscription upon God's action but a promise of his action. Beyond that, the Protestant expression of the faith is not simply to be identified as a reality primarily verbal, as Heidegger and Ott are willing to do, with their accent on language as the house of being. It specifies that language is constitutive of meanings that can be linguistically articulated without loss of meaning and without resort to the esotericism of poetry—that is, in the medium of history. The later Heidegger's emphasis on ineffability is edifying,

---

[5] *The Logic of Hegel,* translated by William Wallace (2nd rev. ed.; Oxford: Clarendon Press, 1892), p. 136.

inspiring one with a sense of the holy. But the Protestant faith is unimpressed by signs of holiness that do not interpret themselves in continuity with the word in which God has expressed his intention for the world, which is a word inextricably historical.

Protestant faith is a religion of maturity in which man is oriented toward the world through the mediation of an historically illuminating word. Ott, with Heidegger, tends to draw faith back into the days of silent meditation on mysteries deeper than words. Heidegger's early writing expressed a certain sadness about man without God in the world. His later writing has overcome this sadness through a sense of the hiddenness of an unnamed being at the horizon of existence. Theologies such as those of Bonhoeffer and Gogarten have no need to take this step with Heidegger into his later thought because the early Heidegger had already expressed in a secular way what the eschatological faith of the New Testament was saying. Man must learn precisely to get along without God in the world and to cease living in religious wistfulness for a silent mystery on the horizon. The good news of the gospel includes God's act of making man his heir, turning the world over to him as his responsibility. The poetic mystification and ineffability of the later Heidegger is a wholesome corrective where philosophical and theological language claims too much. However, it courts the danger of gratifying modern man's immature religiousness rather than calling him to responsibility, because it fosters quests for the unknown even after those quests are terminated by the revelation, however modest, in which the unknown God is named.

What, then, is to be gained by turning to the later Heidegger? Ontological hermeneutic is unsuited to a radically historical faith. Theologians who are still being called "younger" do not enjoy resisting new possibilities, especially when these are proposed by still younger theologians. But there is some relief from that strain in the realization that the younger proposal is based upon the older Heidegger. One hundred years of Protestant stumbling in theology might have been averted if the older

Schleiermacher had not compromised the freshness of his younger position. In his earliest writings he had said, ". . . religion begins and ends with history."[6] Contemporary theology is just discovering the truth in that early claim, and, with the help of the younger Heidegger, it has seen how the claim can be implemented for theology, as Schleiermacher apparently had not seen. It would be a pity if an older Heidegger were now to lead us away from that possibility even before it has had a chance fully to be understood and developed. When it is developed, so that systematic theology does continue to exist as an independent discipline, it should take the shape not of an ontological but of an historical hermeneutic. That will mean that in theology the question of the historical form of God's word will be given priority over the question of its being.

---

[6] *On Religion; Speeches to Its Cultured Despisers,* translated by John Oman with an introduction by Rudolf Otto (New York and Evanston: Harper & Row, Publishers, 1958), p. 80.

5. The Understanding of Theology in Ott and Bultmann

Southern Methodist University

Professor Ott's general theological position seems to me to be defined by two basic characteristics, toward which my own attitude is essentially positive.

First, it affirms as possible a genuine discussion between Christian theology and secular philosophy and, in particular, attempts to enter into such discussion with the philosophy of the later Martin Heidegger.[1] Unlike most other theologians whose primary indebtedness is to the work of Karl Barth, Ott insists that the theologian has no reason to mistrust or reject the aid of philosophical concepts and that any such mistrust or rejection inevitably works against the precision and understandability of theological thinking and speaking.[2] To this extent, his position strongly resembles that of his other theological mentor, Rudolf Bultmann, who for over a generation has resisted Barth's demand for a purely Biblical or "church" theology by also insisting on the theologian's proper dependence on the work of the secular philosopher. Ott, however, relates theology and philosophy even more closely than Bultmann. Whereas Bultmann clearly distinguishes the two disciplines by limiting philosophy to the task of

[1] Cf. *Denken und Sein* (Zürich: EVZ-Verlag, 1959), pp. 13–26.

[2] Cf. "Objektivierendes und existentielles Denken," in H. W. Bartsch (ed.), *Kerygma und Mythos* (Hamburg: Herbert Reich-Evangelischer Verlag, 1955), IV, 120 f.

a purely formal ontological analysis and reserving to theology the clarification of the material or ontic possibility of Christian existence, Ott is suspicious of such a sharp distinction. Indeed, he even goes so far as to say that there is finally but *one* truth that theology and philosophy alike are obligated to tell and that each discipline is responsible to the other in its attempts to tell this truth. How he can say this while apparently maintaining a Barthian (and Bultmannian!) type of exclusivistic christocentrism, is, to be sure, a serious question. But one of the most striking characteristics of his view is its insistence on the possibility of a real discussion between theology and philosophy, and this is solid gain.

I am also largely sympathetic with the second basic characteristic of Ott's position. He is convinced that Bultmann's theology as it presently stands is less than fully adequate primarily because of its questionable philosophical foundations. Bultmann, he argues, is too exclusively dependent on the philosophy of the early Heidegger, the Heidegger who can be too easily misinterpreted as an atheistic existentialist. The result is that Bultmann's theology is restrictively existentialist, in the sense that, according to Ott, Bultmann cannot speak of God directly, but only indirectly by speaking of man and his possibilities of existential self-understanding.[3]

My own view is that this criticism of Bultmann, which has been made by many others besides Ott, is essentially correct. I would question whether Bultmann is as restrictively existentialist as Ott alleges and I would argue that both in theory and practice he has never been bound to any narrow existentialism. But I agree with Ott that the philosophy of the early Heidegger, taken solely in itself, cannot provide an adequate conceptuality for Christian theology. Therefore, I look with favor on his attempt to show that the somewhat ampler philosophy of the later Heidegger offers real resources for overcoming the limitations of

[3] Cf. *ibid.*, p. 121; also Ott, *Geschichte und Heilsgeschichte in der Theologie Rudolf Bultmanns* (Tübingen: J. C. B. Mohr, 1955), esp. pp. 194–203.

Bultmann's position. My enthusiasm for the later Heidegger is not as unrestrained as Ott's, since I see in the work of process philosophers like Alfred North Whitehead and Charles Hartshorne even more significant resources for completing and supplementing Bultmann's basic theological program. But with Ott's concern to go beyond Bultmann by making Heidegger's later work as fruitful for theology as possible I have the greatest sympathy.

I

Turning now to Ott's essay on the nature of systematic theology, I do not propose to consider his particular theses, with many of which I am in agreement. Rather, I want to concentrate on what he himself evidently regards as the heart of his argument, namely, the twofold claim that his understanding of theology corresponds with the later Heidegger's analysis of thinking and speaking and that, as such, it represents a more adequate alternative than the position of Bultmann, which is severely handicapped by its too exclusive dependence on a certain understanding of Heidegger's early work.

The key to Ott's argument is Heidegger's analysis of thinking. Primal thinking, Heidegger claims, is something different from what passes for thinking in traditional metaphysics and the special sciences. Whereas the latter kind of thinking is detached and objectifying, abstracting altogether from the concrete object of thought in the truth of its concreteness, genuine thinking is existential or has experiential character and thus occurs as immediate encounter between the mind and the concrete reality as such. According to Ott, Heidegger's analysis provides a model for also reconceiving the character of the thinking appropriate to Christian theology. Because thinking in the proper sense is not the subject-object thinking of metaphysics and science, but rather is itself existential or experiential, it is illegitimate to distinguish as sharply as Bultmann does between faith as existential self-understanding and theology as the explication of faith by a necessarily detached and objectifying kind of thought. Properly understood, theology shares in the immediate encounter or experience of faith and is, in fact, "a movement of faith itself," faith seeking understanding.[4]

Thus, Ott concludes, the way to overcome metaphysics in theology is quite different from that followed by Bultmann and other existentialist theologians. Instead of assuming that all thinking, and thus the thinking of theology also, is necessarily objective and is overcome solely in immediate experience or in the existential understanding of faith, we must recognize that theological thinking need not be objective at all, but is properly interpretable after the paradigm of Heidegger's analysis of primal thinking. Likewise, Ott argues, Heidegger's interpretation of language or speaking can free us from the prejudice that theological statements must necessarily objectify the reality to which they refer. Just as there can be a theological thinking that is nonmetaphysical, that does not objectify the reality of faith and God's revelation, so also can there be a theological speaking that is not objective in the manner of metaphysics and the sciences.

At first glance, it would appear that Ott is justified in regarding this understanding of theology in relation to faith as significantly different from Bultmann's. Bultmann does emphasize the difference between theology and faith and, at least in many of his statements, he takes for granted that theological thinking and speaking necessarily objectify the existential understanding of faith itself. In one place, for instance, he speaks of "the paradox of theology" as the fact that "like all science, theology can speak of faith only by objectifying it, and yet does so in the knowledge that all such speaking finds its meaning only in a transcendence [Aufhebung] of objectification."[5] That this transcendence is one effected not by theology itself, but solely by the existential decision of faith, would seem sufficiently clear from the context of the statement. Therefore, in this instance at least, Ott's charac-

[4] Cf. above, Ott, "What is Systematic Theology?" pp. 92, 94.

[5] H. W. Bartsch (ed.), *Kerygma und Mythos,* III (Hamburg: Herbert Reich-Evangelischer Verlag, 1954), 58.

terization of Bultmann's position would seem confirmed. Even so, he overstates the differences between Bultmann's view and his own.

In the first place, for all of his emphasis on the close connection between faith and theology, he does not simply identify them. On the contrary, he states quite explicitly that there is a "diverging" as well as a "converging" between them and that their relation is not one of simple identity, but constitutes a "dialectic" of identity *and* difference.[6] His reasons for taking this position become evident earlier in the essay when he disavows the consequences that follow if faith and theology are too closely identified, namely, that the man of faith alone can understand theological thinking and that the theologian *qua* theologian can be presumed to be such a faithful man.[7]

It must be admitted that Ott nowhere makes clear just how his position manages to avoid these consequences. In fact, one of the great weaknesses of his argument is that he takes Bultmann to task for too sharply distinguishing between faith and theology without in the least explaining how he can qualify this distinction and yet not fall into the dangers that Bultmann presumably wishes to avoid by making it. Nevertheless, he himself also makes some such distinction and apparently intends it to be sufficiently sharp to enable him to escape from these dangers.

Just how he can do this, while remaining within the framework of thought of the later Heidegger, is, however, something of a problem. For it is not at all apparent that the later Heidegger's conceptuality allows for such a distinction. If Heidegger's concept of thinking is the proper parallel to what Ott means by theology, then which of the later Heidegger's concepts can be properly appealed to for clarifying what Ott understands by faith?

When Heidegger says thinking is the essential act of man and that it has a character that Ott presumably describes accurately by such words as "experience" and "encounter," he seems to be

[6] Cf. above, "What is Systematic Theology?" p. 109.
[7] Cf. *ibid.*, p. 92.

speaking of something at least formally similar to what he spoke of in *Being and Time* as existential understanding, that is, the kind of cognitive act that involves man's entire existence and is a matter of free historic decision. In other words, what the later Heidegger means by primal thinking seems to be closer to faith than to theology, insofar as theology is distinguished from faith.

Ott could reply, of course, that both faith and theology can be appropriately clarified by Heidegger's single concept of primal thinking, that they represent different levels of such thinking. Indeed, he introduces the notion of levels by speaking of faith and theology as different "levels of understanding."[8] However, he nowhere speaks of them as levels of *thinking,* and he almost invariably has recourse to the terminology of the *early* Heidegger and Bultmann (employing such terms as "existential understanding" and "existential actuality") when he wants to clarify faith in its distinction from theology. Hence the question remains whether he can sustain the claim that his understanding of theology corresponds with and fits into the *later* Heidegger's analysis of primal thinking.

Be this as it may, Ott does not intend simply to identify faith and theology, but rather, like Bultmann, he also wants to acknowledge a distinction between them. Because, however, he largely neglects their distinction in so emphasizing their convergence, Ott's difference from Bultmann is made to appear greater than it is.

A second reason for claiming that Ott overstates his difference from Bultmann is that Bultmann recognizes the close relation between faith and theology to a degree obscured by Ott's one-sided presentation of his position. This does not mean that Ott is simply mistaken when he claims that Bultmann distinguishes between theology and faith. Bultmann ordinarily does precisely this, and there can be little question that his intention, even where he seems to speak otherwise, is to make such a distinction. But when Ott points this out without taking into account the

[8] Cf. *ibid.,* p. 92.

other things that must be noted along with it, Bultmann's position is misrepresented.

Thus, for example, it is not Ott but Bultmann who first speaks of theology as a movement of faith itself and argues that theology is neither speculative nor scientific in an objectifying sense, but rather is existential, that is, a mode of thought in which, in the formula of Adolf Schlatter, the "act of thinking" remains inseparably connected with the "act of living."[9] How Bultmann can argue in this way and yet also say that the paradox of theology is that it necessarily objectifies faith is, admittedly, a question. I would suggest that what he probably means (hence the point of the word "paradox") is that, while theological thinking and speaking must indeed be objective, their intention is not to grasp and communicate information to the intellect, but rather to address man as an existing self by confronting him with a possibility for understanding his existence. In any case, the very fact that Bultmann speaks of theology as in some sense existential is sufficient indication of the one-sidedness of Ott's interpretation of his position. Bultmann makes it quite clear that, although theology and faith are by no means simply the same, their relation also is not one of simple difference, but rather is dialectical. In fact, he insists that theology indirectly shares in the existential character of faith and preaching and therefore can be quite properly thought of as *"indirect* address."[10]

There are other evidences that might be adduced to this same effect, especially some of Bultmann's statements about the character of religious and theological language, which closely parallel Ott's own statements.[11] But enough has been said to indicate

---

[9] Cf. Schubert M. Ogden (ed.), *op. cit.*, p. 97; and Rudolf Bultmann, *Theologie des Neuen Testaments* (3rd ed.; Tübingen: J. C. B. Mohr, 1958), pp. 586, 588, 594, 599. English translation by Kendrick Grobel in *Theology of the New Testament*, II (New York: Charles Scribner's Sons, 1955), 237, 240, 246, 251.

[10] Cf. Ogden (ed.), *op. cit.*, p. 88; also Bultmann, *Glauben und Verstehen* I, (2nd ed.; Tübingen: J. C. B. Mohr, 1954), 114–118, 186 f.

[11] Cf. e.g., H. W. Bartsch (ed.), *Kerygma und Mythos*, II (Hamburg: Herbert Reich-Evangelischer Verlag, 1952), 187.

that Ott's representation of Bultmann's view is subject to important qualifications. When these qualifications are considered alongside the first reason for holding his difference from Bultmann to be overstated, his claim that his understanding of theology represents a real alternative to Bultmann's is called in question. Since he himself affirms the difference of theology and faith as well as their identity, and Bultmann insists on their identity as well as their difference, the two positions appear to be essentially the same and their differences merely verbal.

To be sure, there does seem to be *one* point at which the two positions are genuinely different, namely, where Bultmann affirms and Ott denies that theological thinking and speaking unavoidably objectify the existential actuality of faith and revelation. But it is far from evident that Ott's denial at this point is justified.

I stated earlier that one of the weaknesses of Ott's argument is that he never adequately explains how he can qualify Bultmann's distinction between faith and theology without simply identifying them and thus becoming involved in the consequences that follow from such identification. My point now is that there is another and correlative weakness that also impairs Ott's argument. He equally fails to make clear how he can concede that theology and faith are not simply identical without also allowing the consequence that Bultmann holds to follow from such a concession, namely, that the difference of theology from faith lies in its being unavoidably objectifying. Ott asserts, of course, that this consequence does not necessarily follow because Heidegger's concept of thinking enables one to avoid it. But it is questionable whether what Heidegger conceives of as thinking can be legitimately appealed to in this way. If, as seems evident, what Heidegger means by thinking is closer in meaning to what Ott refers to as faith than to what he distinguishes as theology, the consequence is avoided only verbally. On the other hand, if thinking can be appealed to for clarifying both faith *and* theology, he still is faced with the problem of explaining how the difference between the two levels can be understood otherwise than as Bultmann understands it. That Ott nowhere solves this problem strongly suggests that Bultmann is correct in insisting it is insolvable.

In his discussion with Karl Jaspers, Bultmann argues that thinking, whether philosophical or theological, necessarily objectifies its subject matter. As reflection on, or conceptual explication of, its subject matter, thinking is something different from immediate experience or existential understanding because it is able to deal with its subject matter only mediately or indirectly through the use of universal concepts. Thus Bultmann insists that "Jaspers cannot help explicating what he calls 'clarification of existence' in such a way that it becomes universally understandable, i.e., he must present it in the form of objective doctrine."[12] Bultmann's point is that Jaspers can clarify existence only by means of universal concepts and therefore cannot guarantee that his clarification will be understood as an existential communication rather than misunderstood as simply so much information to be appropriated by the intellect.

This point has relevance also to the later Heidegger's concept of thinking, insofar as Ott is correct in claiming it can be legitimately used to clarify what he means by theology as distinguished from faith. Formally, at least, Heidegger's "thinking," as Ott uses it, and Jaspers's "clarification of existence" seem to be closely parallel. Both refer to a level of understanding different from immediate existential understanding, and yet not objectifying in the manner of philosophical and scientific reflection. Therefore, the question must be raised whether thinking does not of necessity involve the same kind of objectification to which Bultmann calls attention in his discussion of Jaspers's "clarification of existence." If theology as thinking is really distinct from faith and is, as Ott says, the attempt to reflect on faith and to explicate it in the clarity of thought, then theology can hardly help making use of universal concepts that abstract from the concrete actuality of the event of faith itself. Theology unavoidably runs the risk of what Heidegger apparently means by the forgetfulness of being

[12] *Kerygma und Mythos*, III, 54.

(or what, in Whitehead's phrase, one could speak of as "the fallacy of misplaced concreteness").

In sum, Ott's argument as it now stands fails to justify the claim he makes for it. It doubtfully fits into the later Heidegger's analysis of thinking and speaking, and, so far from establishing a genuine alternative to Bultmann's position, it appears to be impaled on the horns of a dilemma. If Ott insists that theology is different from faith, and is different from it precisely as reflection on it or as its conceptual explication, he seems all but verbally committed to Bultmann's view that theology is unavoidably objective. If, on the other hand, Ott presses his point that theological thinking can be non-objective and therefore nonmetaphysical, he seems to deny any basis for distinguishing it from faith and thus is forced against his intention to accept the consequences that follow from such a denial.

I would emphasize that my criticism is not that Ott's argument is actually caught in this dilemma, but that he does not satisfactorily show how he escapes from it. As in his criticisms of Bultmann generally, he fails to establish as genuinely possible the alternative constructive position from which alone his criticism can be made and supported. He himself often stresses the tentativeness of his constructive thinking and nowhere advances the claim that his position is securely established. My point, however, is that it is even less secure than his criticisms of Bultmann imply.

II

The reader will perhaps have surmised that my own position on this matter is quite close to Bultmann's. Bultmann is correct when he insists that theological thinking and speaking are necessarily objective insofar as, by their very nature, they cannot but employ universal concepts or abstractions and therefore are only indirectly related to the existential actuality of faith and revelation. At the same time, he is also right in holding that the primary *intention* of theological thinking and speaking is a different one than characterizes the thinking and speaking of philosophy and the sciences. Unlike the latter, theology intends to be an existential communication. Its primary purpose is not to communicate information to the intellect—although it does that, too—but to facilitate actual existential encounter between God's word in Jesus Christ and man as the one who must continually decide how he is to understand his existence. Nevertheless, Bultmann correctly maintains that theological thinking and speaking are quite distinct from the actuality of faith itself. Although they originate in faith and are mainly concerned to clarify and communicate it, they still share in the same objectifying character that distinguishes the thinking and speaking of metaphysics and science.

Does this mean that theology is unavoidably metaphysical and that Ott's concern to overcome metaphysics in theology is illegitimate? In one sense it means precisely that. Insofar as all objective thinking and speaking are metaphysical and theology is necessarily objective, there can hardly be any such thing as a nonmetaphysical theology.

Even so, this conclusion in no way sacrifices the legitimate motive behind Ott's concern. The logic of Bultmann's position in no way requires an understanding of theology in which its primary existential intention is obscured. Bultmann himself constantly stresses the dialectical or paradoxical character of theology and thus leaves no doubt that its *intention,* regardless of its objective form, is very different from that of philosophy and the sciences.

Furthermore, Bultmann has also helped us to understand that, although all theological thinking is necessarily objective, there can be certain forms of such thinking that are more appropriate to theology's intention than others. For example, the concepts of Heidegger's existentialist analysis are better adapted to explicating the Christian understanding of man than the mythological concepts employed by the writers of the New Testament. The reason for this is not that Heidegger's concepts somehow avoid objectifying man (although Bultmann, unfortunately, sometimes speaks as if this were the reason), but that they objectify him more appropriately than, say, the anthropological concepts of gnosticism. Unlike the latter, they explicate man's being as precisely that of a free historic subject and thus make clear that his actual concrete existence transcends objectification. Likewise, the reason Bultmann can allow an analogical speaking of God, while at the same time calling for radical demythologizing, is that, although analogy objectifies God, it does so without the inappropriateness attaching to mythology. Whereas myth speaks of God in concepts that properly apply only to the world, analogy makes use of the very different concepts of existentialist analysis. The result is that it can appropriately represent God as the eminent subject, whose concrete acts transcend objectification and can be encountered solely through the existential decision of faith.

In short, Bultmann points to a more adequate way than Ott's of overcoming metaphysics in theological thinking and speaking. By employing the more appropriate concepts of existentialist philosophy, rather than those of mythology or of the classical philosophical tradition, Bultmann makes clear not only that faith as self-understanding is qualitatively different from theology, but also that the God of faith is not the impassive absolute of traditional metaphysics, but the living, personal God witnessed to by the Old and New Testaments. He fails to clarify this second point adequately because, in spite of his theory and practice of analogy, he insufficiently develops the specifically theological elements in his position. Because of his understandable concern that God not be falsely objectified, he presents faith predominantly in the form of anthropology and thus opens himself to the criticism of Ott and others that his theology is restrictively existentialist. Even so, Bultmann's theory of analogy, and even more his actual practice, point beyond a one-sided existentialism to a more adequate conceptuality for Christian theology.

In this context, I would also raise the question whether Ott properly understands the importance of Heidegger's work for contemporary theology. When he constantly reiterates that Heidegger overcomes metaphysics and does not intend to develop a new philosophical "system" or "theory"[13] so that Heidegger's is the kind of thinking that no longer knows any "results,"[14] he seems to be caught in the same confusion about the nature of philosophical thinking that haunts so much of existentialism.

Beginning with Kierkegaard, the existentialists' polemic against the objectifying systems of traditional Western idealism has tended to take the form of a rejection of systematic philosophy as such. Kierkegaard's famous dictum that "an existential system is impossible"[15] has been widely understood not only as a criticism of Platonic and Hegelian idealism, but also as excluding the very kind of systematic existentialist philosophy that Kierkegaard himself more or less adequately developed. Thus it is hardly surprising that the existentialist thinkers have so often been interpreted as antitheoretical in their basic motivation and that one of the most popular and influential of the English-speaking studies of their work has appeared under the title, *Irrational Man*.[16]

The careful student is aware, however, of the gross misunderstanding of existentialist philosophy that such an interpretation involves. However much the existentialists themselves may have contributed to this misunderstanding (and one of the strengths of the *early* Heidegger is that he emphatically did not contribute to it!), the real significance of their work is not to have put an end to systematic philosophy, but to have helped lay the foundations for a more adequate system than any that has heretofore been developed in the Western world. By focusing on the concrete existent or actuality as what *is* in the primary and full sense of the term, they have radically called in question the tendency of Western philosophers so to overestimate the importance of abstract philosophical thinking as to commit what Whitehead speaks of as the "fallacy of misplaced concreteness," i.e., the fallacy of regarding the abstract essence or universal grasped in con-

---

[13] Cf. *Denken und Sein*, p. 104.

[14] Cf. above "What is Systematic Theology?" p. 110.

[15] *Concluding Unscientific Postscript*, translated by David F. Swenson (Princeton: Princeton University Press, 1941), pp. 107–113.

[16] Cf. William Barrett, *Irrational Man: A Study in Existentialist Philosophy* (New York: Doubleday & Company, Inc., 1958).

cepts as the primary metaphysical reality. The result is that the existentialists have made clear that being no longer need be understood as the fixed or static being of the classical tradition, but can be interpreted more historically as dynamic and self-creative event or process. Correlative with this, they have also shown that thinking should be understood primarily as experience or existential encounter, rather than as the abstract and detached contemplation of universal essences.

In showing this, however, the existentialists themselves have made very thorough and exhaustive use of just such abstract and detached thinking. Their work represents, not an abandonment of theory, but "a triumph of theoretical analysis."[17] Precisely by engaging in a more sensitive theoretical thinking than most of their predecessors, they have worked out a philosophical system in which both the rights and the limits of theory are more adequately defined.

I believe it is against this background that the significance of the work of the later Heidegger also has to be assessed. Ott may be correct in claiming that Heidegger's later work moves sufficiently beyond that of the existentialists to overcome their restrictive absorption with human existence and to point toward the truly general ontology and epistemology that they (and the early Heidegger himself) barely more than imply. But I cannot agree with him that Heidegger accomplishes this by somehow transcending the limitations that adhere to *all* philosophical thinking. It seems evident that one can overcome metaphysics, at least in the realm of thought, only by developing another metaphysics, and that this is true even if the new metaphysical system is more adequate than its predecessors precisely because it clearly focuses the limits of all metaphysical systems. Heidegger succeeds in relativizing the subject-object schema and the kind of epistemology and ontology based on it only by working out a more adequate understanding of thinking and being that, in its own way, constitutes a philosophical system and thus does not com-

---

[17] John Wild, *The Challenge of Existentialism* (Bloomington: Indiana University Press, 1955), p. 181.

pletely escape from the objectifying character of all abstract thinking.

Unfortunately, like Ott, the later Heidegger fails to distinguish adequately the levels of thinking in his own thought. He obscures the point that his transcendental thinking of thinking is by its very nature something different, something more abstract and objectifying, than the immediate experiential kind of thinking it seeks to think. The failure to distinguish these levels seems to underlie the turn in his recent writings to a much more oracular and poetic style, as compared with the relatively rigorous and "scientific" style of *Being and Time*. Thus Ott's insistence that Heidegger escapes from the perils of system-building and does not regard his work as issuing in results reflects confusions in Heidegger's own thought.

This means that we must take special care in assessing the significance of the later Heidegger for Christian theology. The import of his work (and, *a fortiori,* of the work of American thinkers like Whitehead and Hartshorne) is not that it somehow ceases to be abstract conceptual thinking. Rather, it is precisely by a sensitive employment of such abstract conceptual thinking that Heidegger shows that our primal encounter with reality, our primal thinking of concrete actuality in the truth of its concreteness is something quite different from the abstract thinking by which alone this can be shown.

To some extent Ott recognizes this, for he is eager to claim that Heidegger's concepts—and what are concepts but "results"? —provide a way of conceptualizing reality that overcomes the inadequacies of traditional philosophy. Thus Heidegger's concept of being, for instance, is not the traditional concept of fixed, static being, but the concept of a reality that is by its very nature historic, dynamic, and becoming, embracing essentially the features also focused by Whitehead's "creativity" or Hartshorne's "process."[18] Ott quite properly suggests that such a concept promises to be of the utmost importance not only in reconceiving the Christian understanding of God, but also in achieving a more

[18] Cf. *Denken und Sein,* pp. 152–157.

adequate view of the world or of created being. But because this is so, I fail to see why he must so often indulge in the gratuitous denial that Heidegger's thought has results or that it offers a system (at least in outline) that, in the questions it asks, as distinct from its answers, is directly comparable with the great philosophical systems of the past.

I am convinced that Heidegger's provocative analysis of thinking and being will not be free to bear its most important theological fruits until it is seen in its continuity, as well as its discontinuity, with the classical philosophical tradition. Only then can it be taken together with the other and, in my judgment, generally more adequate resources provided by the parallel work of Whitehead and Hartshorne and make its full contribution to developing the ampler conceptuality that theology requires. *This* use of Heidegger's work, however, will in no way alter the basic logic of Bultmann's position. Metaphysics will be overcome only by developing a more adequate metaphysics, and theological thinking and speaking will still be understood to have the dialectical character that Bultmann rightly attributes to them.

I would add one further word in support of this position. The genius of Bultmann's view is that he attempts to apply also to the realm of knowledge, and thus to the problem of theological methodology, the Pauline-Lutheran doctrine of righteousness by faith alone without the works of the law.[19] Therefore, what is ultimately at stake in his insistence on the dialectical relation between theology and faith is the general dialectic of works and faith and, beyond this, the "infinite qualitative difference" between time and eternity that is Bultmann's overriding major premise. Significantly, however, it is just this major premise of which Ott is most critical. From his study of Bultmann on, he has consistently called for a more synthetic conception that can overcome what he speaks of as Bultmann's "eschatological-paradoxical dualism . . . which probably has its final basis in the

[19] Cf. *Kerygma und Mythos,* II, 207. English translation by R. H. Fuller in H. W. Bartsch (ed.), *Kerygma and Myth* (New York and Evanston: Harper & Row, Publishers, 1961), pp. 210 f.

dualism of law and gospel."[20] It is hardly surprising, then, that he is also critical of Bultmann's understanding of theology and wants to replace it with a view in which theology and faith are regarded as somehow more continuous than Bultmann is willing to regard them.

But it is precisely at this point that Ott's program poses for me the deepest problem. To the extent that what he proposes obscures the qualitative difference between theology and faith, his view is, however unintentionally, reactionary. Instead of pointing beyond Bultmann to a more adequate alternative, it really points behind him. It threatens to involve us once again in the fatal confusion of faith and works in the realm of knowledge that Bultmann, as much as any other, has helped us to overcome.

[20] *Denken und Sein,* p. 8; italics deleted.

III. Reappraisal and Response

6. Is the Later Heidegger Relevant for Theology?

JOHN B. COBB, JR.

Southern California School of Theology

Robinson's essay, with which this volume begins, presents essential elements in the philosophy of the later Heidegger and summarizes the German discussion as to their relevance for theology. Heinrich Ott has played the leading role in clarifying the views of the later Heidegger in relation to those of the Heidegger of *Being and Time* and was asked to give leadership to the discussion of the relevance of the later Heidegger for theology at the 1960 meeting of old Marburgers. The essay presented by Ott on that occasion has been used to focus the discussion for American critics.

The minimum thesis to the discussion of which this volume is dedicated is that the later Heidegger does have important distinctive relevance for contemporary theology. Specifically, Ott's lead essay suggests that the later Heidegger can assist theology to achieve a new and clearer understanding of its own function and method. This thesis is criticized in divergent ways by Come, Michalson, and Ogden. In the light of these criticisms, a new assessment is required.

The point of view from which this essay is written may be summarized as follows. The critical essays have shown that there are dangers in the use of the later Heidegger by theology and that Ott does not protect himself with sufficient care or clarity against these dangers. Major aspects of Ott's thesis can still be sustained by careful and moderate formulation. A formulation somewhat different from that of Ott will better follow the analogies suggested by Heidegger's thought and can be more adequately defended against criticism. Such a formulation raises again the question of the function and method of systematic theology that Ott supposes he has at least partially answered.

The procedure of this essay is as follows. First, it discusses the basic understanding of thinking proposed as a model for theological thinking by Heidegger and Ott. Next it explains and criticizes the manner in which Ott draws his conclusions as to the function and method of theology, and it proposes a more Heideggerian alternative. Finally, it tests against the arguments of the critics the basic thesis that the later Heidegger does provide a model by which theology can in part understand itself.

Even if it is shown that theology *can* understand itself in analogy to the later Heidegger's understanding of philosophy and poetry, the *importance* of this fact remains in question. The proposed self-understanding of theology may be but little different from that already operative. Furthermore, there may be more fruitful ways for theology to understand itself, i.e., the possibility of one mode of understanding theology does not in itself deny the equal possibility of other modes. Much of the critical discussion of Ott's thesis in the preceding essays focuses quite properly on these questions of the originality and desirability of his proposal rather than on the question of its possibility. The present essay, however, is largely restricted to the one question of possibility.

I

Heidegger's later philosophy has been primarily a thinking about thinking. Its novel significance for theology must be seen first of all in its implications as to the kind of thinking that theology is. The systematic treatment of the general question as to whether the later Heidegger is relevant for theology must begin by determining what Heidegger understands by thinking.

Much has been done by Robinson and the other contributors to this volume to illuminate Heidegger's important and original thinking about thinking. The attempt here is to state his position as simply as possible in quite different words and thought patterns. By translating Heidegger's thought into another language one inevitably distorts it, but just such appropriating translation seems to be demanded by Heidegger himself. One can only hope that the total understanding to which one's words point is in crucial respects closely parallel to that of Heidegger.

The central clue to the nature of primal thinking is offered us in the example of the poet. That is by no means a random example, for Heidegger takes poetry as one of the few expressions of such thinking. (The others are philosophy and perhaps theology.) Heidegger sees the poet as one who is grasped or formed by being and in whose language being reveals itself.

The crucial concept here is that of "grasped by being." In all human experience there is both the relatively passive reception of impressions and the formative activity of the mind. This formative activity is directed by received patterns of interpretation and by present interests and purposes. To some degree it is always a distorting of what is received. In our own day experience has become so conventionalized that it is almost wholly divorced from its roots in the self-revelation of being.

To some men, however, there come moments in which the incrustations of inherited culture and pragmatic concerns are broken through and exposed in all their artificiality. Being commands attention in itself. Openness to being as it is can be cultivated by the philosopher through the discipline of phenomenology. This openness is spontaneous to the poet. His poetry is thus the self-revelation of being as it grasps him. We may even say that his poetry is the opposite of art, if art is understood as the imposition of form.

Heidegger applies these ideas specifically to words. In ideal poetry the words are not self-conscious creations of the poet but direct expressions of the way in which being appears for him. Words thus formed have a long history of corruption through use in contexts where there is little or no openness to being. But the possibility remains of tracing them back to their origins and so of recovering something of the authentic openness to being in which they arose.

It is important to note that the being to which the poet is open is not static but dynamic. Being is always being as it appears prior to all artificial structuring. This appearing of being is itself specific to each generation and even to each poet. Therefore, *the* poem of each poet, as the appearing of being to him, is different, although each poet has only a single poem.[1]

The approach to poetry governed by this view of its nature is that of attempting to stand where the poet stands so as to be grasped by being as it appears to him. This is not a matter of asking the psychological question as to the poet's intention but of re-living the encounter with being that generated both the intention and the poem. Insofar as we succeed, the understanding of one of his poems is the understanding of all of them, since *the* poem that constitutes the meaning of all is the same. Of course, any attempt to verbalize *the* poem and thus to inform others as to what it is, can at best be another poem alongside the others and dependent upon them.

This account indicates that Heidegger's thinking about thinking seems to point to a duality even in such primal thinking as poetry. There is, on the one hand, the poet's own openness to being by which *the* poem is formed in him and from which his poems proceed. There is, on the other hand, the thinking of the reader of the poem who stands *with* the poet experiencing being with him and thus sharing *the* poem with him. Whatever he may say properly about the poem flows from this experience and becomes another poem expressing the same *one* poem.

We may assume that what Heidegger speaks of here as the proper response to poetry is a real possibility for man, at least as an ideal. Heidegger is by no means alone in suggesting that a poem expresses a vision (*the* poem) given to the poet and that

[1] Cf. above, Ott, "What is Systematic Theology?" p. 87.

through reading the poem the reader may hope to receive some share in that vision.

Heidegger knows, of course, that there are many other things that may be said about poems. One may talk about the opinions and purposes of the poet, the circumstances of the writing, the ideas that influenced him, and the forces in his unconscious that gain expression through the poem. One may talk also about the formal properties of the poem and the use of special devices to achieve particular effects. Although Heidegger brushes all this aside, there is no necessary reason to deny that information of these sorts may assist some readers in gaining a real understanding of the poem.

With this summary outline in mind of how primal thinking operates in poetry, we must now ask whether theology also can be a form of primal thinking. On the assumption that this is possible, we must inquire further whether the theologian should think as the poet thinks or as the reader of poetry thinks.

The former alternative, although thoroughly out of fashion today, is not wholly absurd. Schleiermacher's *Speeches on Religion* points to it as does the thought of the more radical Quakers and Christian mystics. But in terms of the contemporary theological discussion only the second alternative is relevant.

The assumption, then, is that Christians see the canonical writings as the poems about which the theologian is to think. Information about the Bible afforded by historians, philologians, and psychologists may be helpful to the theologian, but such information must be sharply distinguished from the primal theological response to the texts. This primal response to the writings is so to stand *with* the writers that one is grasped by the same vision of saving reality that grasped them. Sharing this experience with them, the theologian can proceed to articulate in his own way that reality which has grasped him as it grasped them.

This brief summary may leave the impression that looking *with* instead of *at* a poet or religious writer is some simple act upon which we may decide at a moment's notice. Nothing could be farther from the truth. Heidegger's own writings express and illuminate the extremely deeply rooted obstacles to attaining the kind of openness required. No better preparation for achieving this openness can be found than thinking painfully and laboriously with Heidegger about thinking.

The exposition thus far has been limited to the one central aspect of the Heidegger-Ott proposal that seems to stand in the face of all criticisms. Theology *could* understand itself in these terms, and such understanding would cure some of the recognized limitations of other approaches. This may not mean that all aspects of the theological enterprise can be conducted in this way. For example, Ott's essay in this volume is a responsible piece of theological writing that is still objectifying in Ott's own sense. But such exceptions could be handled as propaedeutic without basically disturbing the thesis that the work of theology proper is a kind of primal thinking. Ott may agree that in what he calls the first task of systematic theology, i.e., reflection on the hermeneutical as a whole, there is an inescapably objectifying element.

II

Ott's thesis that theology should understand itself after the model of Heidegger's interpretation of poetry is weakened by the way in which he applies his thesis in his theory of systematic theology. Ott proposes that systematic theology stands to exegetical theology as the interpretation of *the* poem of a poet stands to the interpretations of his poems severally. Just as Heidegger holds that all the poems of the poet express *the* poem, so Ott holds that all the writings of the Bible express *the* gospel.[2] This doctrine introduces an element into the whole discussion not derived from Heidegger and in considerable tension with the more natural implications to be drawn from him.

On the surface, at least, a much better parallel between Scrip-

2 *Ibid.*, p. 87.

ture and poetry could be made if the poetry of a whole school of poets over a period of centuries were considered. In such a school there are some common elements in the vision of all the poets so that the reading of some of them will enable us better to understand others. But if we approach them all on the assumption that only *one* poem underlies all their poems, we are likely to falsify and to respond poorly to much that we read.

Ott has indicated some uncertainty as to whether he should not allow a difference between *the* poem of the Old Testament and of the New.[3] But this advance would be only a beginning toward allowing the Biblical records really to speak for themselves as the Heideggerian principle demands. The principle that we should look *with* rather than *at* the New Testament writers means that we should look with Paul, with John, with James, and with Luke. We are not really looking with any of them if we bring to bear the prior conviction that we must see the same thing in each case.

Ott's reasoning in opposition to this is that each of the Biblical writers understands himself as a witness to God's acting. This acting is the Christ event or God's gracious presence to man. Hence the appearing of God constitutes the vision in every case, and since it is the one God who appears, the reality that grasps each witness is the same. To stand with any witness is to be grasped by that same reality. Even if we should acknowledge a difference in the appearing of God in the two Testaments, at least in the New Testament all writers witness to the one appearing of God in Jesus Christ.

Clearly Ott brings to this discussion a dogmatic conviction not derived from Heidegger. He holds that the understanding of the witnesses that they are witnessing to the act of God is valid. It is on this basis alone that he can affirm the unity of *the* poem in the New Testament. But to reject in general the genuineness of the witnesses is to stand outside the circle of faith, and further criticism of Ott's position would then be wholly untheological. The

[3] *Ibid.*, pp. 87–88.

relevant question, therefore, is whether the acceptance of this conviction necessarily implies the conclusions Ott draws from it. Again the parallel with poetry should help.

Two poets viewing the same human situation as focused in the same event may nevertheless write very different poetry. Heidegger would not say that because the same event inspired both poems therefore *the* poem of each of the two poets is the same. Whether they are the same could only be decided by responding to each in a primal way in independence of the other. The identity of the event and the shared experience of the event as illuminating the human situation as a whole does not guarantee *a priori* an identity of visions.

To argue that the Christ event constitutes an exception requires special argument not fully developed in Ott. However, in view of the influence of Barth upon his thought, such argument may be briefly indicated. The Christ event is the self-presenting of God to man. The witness is one for whom personally this event constitutes such a self-presenting by God. Since the initiative here is with God, and since God's act is not conditioned by the personality or prior experience of the receiver, it must be always self-identical.

That this Barthian approach can function as the basis for a very impressive theology has long since been amply demonstrated. In the present context we can note only two points in criticism. The first point is that the understanding of the Christ event that we are required to bring to the reading of the New Testament has arisen in a specific twentieth-century context and cannot safely be assumed to be that of all the witnesses. If we are to employ the model of Heidegger's primal thinking for the understanding of the New Testament, we cannot bring to our reading so heavy a burden of theological freight.

The second point is that we can clearly affirm that it is the one God who reveals himself to man in the one Christ event without supposing that each recipient of the revelation has the same vision, gospel, or poem. This can be shown best in the terminology of Whitehead.

In Whiteheadian terms the presence or appearing of God must be understood as the prehension of God by man. This language does not imply any denial of God's initiative in this event. Tò make this clear we could say instead that God has been causally efficacious for man in the specific ways reported in the Bible. But the language of prehension is required for adequate analysis.

Every prehension has an initial datum. This initial datum is exactly what it is however it is prehended. That is, the multiplicity of ways in which it is prehended from diverse perspectives does not affect its own concrete self-identity in and for itself. Hence we may certainly say that what appears or is prehended, in Old and New Testaments, is one and the same. Thus far the argument holds.

However, the identity of the initial datum does not determine an identity of prehension. Every prehension abstracts from the totality of that which is prehended and from diverse perspectives different abstractions occur in terms of diverse subjective aims. There may, of course, be identical elements in these diverse prehensions, but whether these exist and how important they may be are questions to be answered empirically or ontically, not deductively or ontologically.

This means that the way in which the one selfsame God is present to different persons differs, and that the extent and importance of this difference is to be determined by examination of their experience. This does not preclude the possibility that God was prehended in essentially the same way by all the Biblical witnesses, or at least by all the New Testament witnesses, but it does deny the legitimacy of assuming such identity *a priori* simply on the grounds that it is the same God. The question should be dealt with in purely exegetical terms. The contemporary situation of such exegesis suggests that when this problem is approached in these terms differences appear of considerable magnitude and importance. Furthermore, these differences are found not only between the Old and the New Testaments but also within each Testament.

The foregoing criticism of Ott's doctrine that *the* poem of all the witnesses is identical may appear somewhat labored in view of Ott's limited discussion of the point. However, his entire view of systematic theology in distinction from exegetical theology rests upon this doctrine. This can be shown if we return to the parallel of the reading of poetry.

In attempting to understand Hölderlin's poems in a primal way one is attempting to grasp or be grasped by *the* poem underlying all the particular poems. One can only begin by reading the individual poems, but one soon finds that each must be read not only in itself but also in the light of all the others. Thus there develops a body of understanding of *the* poem informed by the understanding of each of the poems but not identical with the sum of such understandings. Having achieved this partially autonomous understanding, one then brings it with him for the further illumination of the poems from which it arose. The re-reading of these poems in its turn reacts upon the comprehensive understanding.

Ott proposes that we think of exegetical and systematic theology after the analogy of the understanding of the individual poems and *the* poem of the great poet. Our understanding of *the* gospel can only arise out of the understanding of the many gospel texts, but when it has arisen it can illuminate further study of all the texts. Hence, systematic theology can arise only out of exegetical theology, but insofar as it emerges it can in its turn contribute to exegesis.

This analysis is unexceptionable in itself. But clearly it bears an importance for Ott that depends upon the doctrine that *the* gospel of all the New Testament writers is the same. That is, one may agree that in the study of one Pauline text our total understanding of Paul is relevant. There is, in other words, a Pauline theology which is something other than the sum total of exegesis of individual texts. But Ott wants us to believe that systematic theology bears to the whole of Scriptural exegesis the relation that Pauline theology bears to the exegesis of Pauline texts. This assumes that all the writers bear witness to *the* gospel in the manner discussed above.

The importance of this issue for theology is great. If the New Testament can be treated as having a single theology, then that theology can be regarded quite simply as normative for Christian belief. If, on the other hand, we must acknowledge diversity in the primitive witness as reflecting diversity in the primitive apprehension of saving reality, then the theologian cannot avoid a critical function. It has been argued above that he can and should attempt to stand with each witness unencumbered by prior commitments as to that which is witnessed.[4] This is the natural implication for the theologian of the later Heidegger's profound analysis of primal thinking. But just because of this we cannot escape the relativism introduced by the variety of the witnesses. This relativism must constitute the peculiar problem for systematic theology.

Furthermore, we must distinguish between sharing the vision of a writer with him and finally committing ourselves to that vision. This distinction can best be made in reference to the third mode of primal thinking—philosophy. Heidegger in his "dismantling" of the history of Western philosophy makes this distinction clear. He does not overcome Hegel by looking at Hegel and measuring him against ideas existing in his own mind. Rather he tries to look with Hegel at the "unthought"—being as it revealed itself to Hegel—and then through immanent criticism to transcend the limits of Hegel's thought. This encounter with Hegel leaves an indelible impression on the thinker who thus thinks with him, but it does not involve commitment to Hegel's vision. The assumption throughout is that the thought of Hegel, in common with that of all the great thinkers of the West, has been formed by the unveiling of being, even though this unveiling may also have been a concealing. The history of those fateful unveilings poses—it does not answer—the philosophical question for our own day.

Once we acknowledge diversity in the Christian witness, we are placed as theologians in a situation closely parallel to that of the philosopher. We are convinced as Christians that God has

[4] Cf. above, p. 181.

disclosed himself to Christian faith throughout Christian history. But the diversity in the historic witness implies that in God's disclosure there is a concealing as well as an unveiling. Hence the thought even of the canonical witnesses is not beyond valid theological criticism. Such criticism must consist in viewing with them the "unthought" that revealed itself to them, thereby discovering also the limits of their thought. The history of Christian witness poses—it does not answer—the theological question for our own day.

In Heidegger's view of the history of philosophy the relativity is not absolute. He is clear that in the first awakening of the Greek mind to wonder at being there was a purity of appearing of being that has been clouded in the subsequent history of the West. In a similar way the Protestant surely believes that the primitive Christian community was apprehended by God's self-revelation with a purity that has been clouded in the subsequent history of the church. But Heidegger does not suppose that there is some way of returning to the primitive Greek vision without dismantling the philosophical history that has formed us, and we too should not suppose that we can overleap the centuries and simply recover the vision of some primitive Christian writer as our own. Genuine philosophy must arise in a renewed openness to being like that of the primitive Greeks, an openness we can only achieve as we free ourselves from the distorting conceptualizations imposed on our vision by our fateful history. The parallel suggests that only by this same act of liberation can we attain a renewed openness to God such as that of primitive Christian witnesses.

This parallelism of theology to philosophy has already been pressed too far. Furthermore, Heidegger's view that the moment in which philosophy began is that in which thinking was most pure and in relation to which all subsequent philosophy is a devolution is highly questionable, and Protestants must be cautious of affirming its theological parallel for its polemical value against Catholicism. Still the discussion does suggest that the rejection of

Ott's thesis, that *the* poem of all the Biblical witnesses is the same, leads in the direction of much greater parallelism to Heidegger's own thought. From this point of view Ott has erred in having failed to carry through consistently the implications of Heidegger's "thinking about thinking" for theology as a kind of thinking.

III

Thus far this essay has attempted to defend the relevance of Heidegger for theology by claiming that theology can understand itself fruitfully as primal thinking. Ott's understanding of the implications of Heidegger's thought for exegetical theology has been accepted while his interpretation of systematic theology has been rejected as unwarranted and un-Heideggerian. Since the three American critics have pointed out a variety of problems in the use of the later Heidegger by theologians, we must determine whether their objections to Ott's thesis also apply to the more modest one defended in this essay.

Come's most emphatic objections to Ott's proposal that theology find new directions through dialogue with Heidegger center around the relation this seems to imply between being and God. Come supposes that the influence of the later Heidegger must lead to an understanding of man's relation to God analogous to Heidegger's view of man's relation to being. This he sees as wholly unacceptable to Christian faith.[5] Ott's personal position at this point is obscure and at present he disavows commitment to any particular solution to the problem. Hence we may conclude that insofar as the general project of gaining assistance from the later Heidegger depends upon formulating a doctrine of God or of God's relation to man in Heideggerian categories, the project as a whole is in difficulty.

Come's view is that Heidegger's thinking about thinking cannot be separated from Heidegger's thinking about being. This

[5] Cf. above, Come, *"Advocatus Dei—Advocatus Hominis et Mundi,"* pp. 124–125.

leads him to the conclusion that theology cannot understand itself fruitfully as primal thinking in Heidegger's terms.[6] In the earlier part of this essay, on the contrary, the Heideggerian analysis of primal thinking has been abstracted from major aspects of Heidegger's view of being and in this abstracted form, it has been claimed to be relevant for theology's self-understanding. It must be granted that this abstraction is a drastic one and that Come's insistence on the unity of Heidegger's thinking about thinking and his thinking about being is well taken. However, such abstraction appears to be in the spirit both of Ott's proposal and of Come's understanding of the theologian's proper use of a philosopher's ideas.

The thesis maintained in this essay is that real parallels are to be found between the work of the interpreter of poetry, the theologian, and the philosopher. Come addresses himself only to the relation of the latter two. There he acknowledges that there may be some parallelism, but he denies that it has more than incidental significance for the theologian.

The question of Heidegger's relevance for theology can only be answered clearly by examining the analogy of proportionality between theology and philosophy that is proposed. The analogy suggested by Heidegger at the 1960 meeting of "old Marburgers" was that philosophical thinking is to being as theological thinking is to the self-revealing God, and Ott has expressed approval of this suggestion. At the same time, the analogy actually underlying Ott's essay in this volume is both more complex and more adequate, although it is clearer in respect to poetry than to philosophy. First, the self-disclosure of being is to *the* poem of a poet as the self-disclosure of God is to *the* gospel. Secondly, *the* poem of a poet is to all his poems as *the* gospel is to all the writings that witness to it. Thirdly, the poems of a poet are to their primal hearing and interpretation as the Scriptures are to their primal hearing and exegetical theology. Fourthly, the interpretation of the poems of a poet is to the interpretation of *the* poem of the poet as exegetical theology is to systematic theology.

[6] *Ibid.*, pp. 125 ff.

If a similar parallel to philosophy is wanted, it will work best if we appeal to the favored position accorded by Heidegger to primitive Greek philosophy. Although these analogies are not suggested by Ott, we may try the following. First, the self-disclosure of being is to the primitive Greek apprehension of being as the self-disclosure of God is to *the* gospel. Secondly, the primitive Greek vision of being is to primitive Greek philosophical writings as *the* gospel is to all the writings that witness to it. Third, the primitive Greek philosophical writings are to their primal hearing and interpretation as the Scriptures are to their primal hearing and exegetical theology. Fourth, the interpretation of primitive Greek philosophical writings is to the interpretation of the primitive Greek vision of being as exegetical theology is to systematic theology.

One remarkable feature of Ott's proposal is that it leads to support of a theological position much like that of Barth and Come. However, the proposal developed in the early part of this essay moves sharply away from the common ground of Barth, Come, and Ott through its employment of a more complex analogy of proportionality which is actually a more appropriate parallel with Heidegger. This analogy of proportionality may be formulated as follows. First, the self-disclosure of being is to *the* poem as the self-disclosure of God is to the vision of saving reality of a particular witness. Secondly, *the* poem of a poet is to all his poems as the vision of a particular witness is to all his writings. Thirdly, the poems of a poet are to their primal hearing and interpretation as the writings of a witness are to their primal hearing and exegesis. Fourthly, the interpretation of the poems of a poet is to the interpretation of *the* poem of the poet as the interpretation of the writings of a witness is to the interpretation of his vision of saving reality. Fifthly, the interpretation of *the* poem of each of the poets of a given school or national tradition in their unity and diversity is to the interpretation of *the* poem of each member of that school as the interpretation of the visions of saving reality of the Biblical witness in their unity and diversity is to the interpretation of the vision of each witness severally.

Analogies three, four, and five in the outline above afford a way of thinking of the functions of exegetical theology, but they only point to, without answering, the question to which Ott addresses his essay, "What is Systematic Theology?" An answer to this question was hinted at above in a parallel drawn to the fresh work of the contemporary philosopher and the relation of that work to his study of the history of philosophy and its origins. This parallel is indicated better by Heidegger's suggestion of a simple analogy of proportionality than by the more elaborate one underlying Ott's essay. But the question as to the method of systematic theology can emphatically not be answered by such a parallelism, and its further discussion falls outside the scope of this essay.

Michalson sees the chief threat of the later Heidegger for theology in the precedence he gives to the question of being.[7] Against this he defends a radically historical understanding of faith and theology. Against Tillich and as a warning to some who might try to build upon the later Heidegger, his argument has force. Whether it is relevant to Ott's understanding of the proper relation of theology to the later Heidegger, Ott will be free to say in his final statement. But in the use by theology of the Heideggerian model proposed in this essay, the question of being need not be central to the theological enterprise. Neither being nor human existence is the horizon of hermeneutical interrogation but rather the self-revealing God.

Michalson's objection, however, is not only to the primacy in theology of the question of being but also to Ott's insistence on the unity of the Bible. Michalson notes that Ott gives to the Bible as canon priority over the Bible as history.[8] He shows that this leads to an unhistorical reading of the Old Testament in terms of New Testament presuppositions.

It has been argued at length above that this feature of Ott's thought does not derive from his adoption of a Heideggerian model but rather stands in some tension with that model. The

---

[7] Cf. above, Michalson, "Theology as Ontology and as History," pp. 138, 153.

[8] *Ibid.*, p. 149.

freeing of Ott's formulation from this un-Heideggerian element should operate to restore the Bible as history to its proper priority over the Bible as canon. The diversity of the modes of relationship to the one God to which Michalson points was also insisted upon in slightly different terms above. The major thrust of the proposed method is to guarantee that the text shall be set free to be what it really is.

A third criticism by Michalson of Heidegger and Ott is directed against their rejection of the creative role of the subject in thinking.[9] A subjectivism that has played a prime role in existentialism is repudiated. Man must, of course, discipline himself to the utmost to attain the requisite openness to being for primal thinking to occur, but the occurrence of this thinking requires freedom from the distorting influence of pragmatic purpose and preconception. In the moment of primal thinking the initiative is with that which gives itself to be thought.

This aspect of Heidegger's thought *is* carried over in the analogies of proportionality suggested in this essay. However, what is required for this proportionality is something less specific than full acceptance of Heidegger's understanding of the relation of being and thought. All that is strictly required is that we suppose that in the relation of the first witnesses to God's self-revealing the initiative was with God and that their witness came to be in some degree of openness to this divine initiative. Further, we must suppose that it is possible for us to approach a text with the intention of entering into the experience of the writer and that to some degree this intention can be realized.

Ott supposes that systematic theology also can come to be in this non-objectifying kind of thinking *with* the Biblical writers. Against this Michalson calls for an articulation of the faith that avoids the esotericism of poetry through the medium of history.[10] The argument of the present essay is compatible with that of Michalson but also compatible with an understanding of systematic theology (in distinction from exegetical theology) more like

9 *Ibid.*, pp. 139, 151–152.
10 *Ibid.*, p. 154.

that of Ogden. The position maintained is that whereas Ott points us to a relevant understanding of exegetical theology through a Heideggerian analogy, the still more difficult question of the function and method of systematic theology remains to be faced.

Ogden takes a more positive view of Ott's proposal than does either Come or Michalson. He expresses approval of the intimate relation of theology with philosophy that it entails, and he agrees that the later Heidegger points toward freeing theology from the restrictively anthropological focus characteristic of some of Bultmann's works.[11]

Nevertheless, Ogden does not believe that the later Heidegger makes possible the formulation of theology in a non-objectifying way. This means, in the terminology of Heidegger and Ott, that he denies the possibility of a theology that is not metaphysical. Ogden summarizes his argument very succinctly as follows. "Insofar as all objective thinking and speaking are metaphysical and theology is necessarily objective, there can hardly be any such thing as a nonmetaphysical theology."[12] Since the first premise is little more than an accepted definition, the issue hinges entirely on the second premise.

Ogden's argument for the premise that theology is necessarily objectifying is that theology differs from faith, that this difference lies in its function of clarifying and communicating faith, and that clarification and communication require objectification.[13] Faith, as analogous to Heidegger's primal thinking, does not objectify, but theology, as an account of faith, cannot be paralleled with primal, non-objectifying thinking. Ogden sees that Ott's reply must consist in distinguishing levels of primal thinking, but he denies that Ott has shown how he can thereby claim a non-objectifying character for theology.

Ogden has here clearly focused the crucial issue with respect to Ott's whole project. This project can only be carried out suc-

[11] Cf. above, Ogden, "The Understanding of Theology in Ott and Bultmann," pp. 157–158.
[12] *Ibid.*, p. 167.
[13] *Ibid.*, pp. 166–167.

cessfully if much more attention is paid to the levels of non-objectifying thinking. In the suggestions made in the earlier part of this essay an attempt was made to distinguish such levels.[14] The initial apprehension by a poet of *the* poem is one such level, its expression in his several poems is another, the reader standing with the poet and apprehending the reality that grasped him is a third. All of these kinds of thinking have certain characteristics in common and in distinction from the natural sciences, and this unity may be described as their non-objectifying character. If so, an answer to Ogden's criticism is possible, and a non-objectifying and therefore nonmetaphysical theology can be formulated on the basis of a Heideggerian analogy.

It must be stressed again that *systematic* theology can be proposed by Ott on this analogy only by introducing an assumption about *the* gospel being one in spite of the variety of witnesses. This assumption is both un-Heideggerian and unhistorical. Hence the present defense against Ogden of non-objectifying theology is a defense only to a non-objectifying exegetical theology. Whether a systematic theology that takes seriously the profound diversity in the Biblical witness can retain this non-objectifying character is an open question.

Ogden also maintains that the distance between Ott and Bultmann on the issue of objectifying language is not as great as it might appear.[15] This is not a serious criticism of Ott's basic thesis but it does raise the question of the positive value of employing an analogy from the later Heidegger. If it were true that Bultmann, using the earlier Heidegger, arrived at essentially the same exegetical method as that now advocated by Ott, the introduction of the later Heidegger into the picture would be largely superfluous.

However, a real difference does seem to obtain between the method of Bultmann and the proposal of Ott. Bultmann's approach to the New Testament includes large elements of looking *at* as well as *with* the writings, and the removal of these elements

---

[14] Cf. above, pp. 180 ff.
[15] Ogden, *op. cit.*, pp. 162–163.

from his theological method and results would have far-reaching consequences.

Bultmann insists that the serious student of the New Testament must approach the study of the writings with questions arising out of his own existential situation. He then asks the Biblical writings for answers to these questions. The questions dominant in Bultmann's own work are questions about man and about the possibility of authentic existence. In the process of seeking answers to these questions in the New Testament records, Bultmann often looks *with* as well as *at* the writings. Indeed few exegetes have ever been more helpful in enabling others to find their way into the world of the primitive Christian experience. Nevertheless, one must insist that the focus upon the self-understanding of the Biblical writers has inhibited our sharing fully in their vision, a vision dominated by the self-revealing of God in Christ rather than by their own new existence.

The two methods approximate each other insofar as the questions with which the Bultmannian approaches the text have themselves arisen from the vision expressed in the text. Also, the Bultmannian acknowledges that the questions themselves are subject to continuous modification in the light of the text. This means that a student might be able to work through the Bultmannian approach until he came finally to identify himself with the question and hence also with the vision of the Biblical writer. Hence, the Bultmannian approach may offer no necessary block to achieving the end posed by treating exegetical theology as primal thinking. Nevertheless, the affirmation of this end has major importance. Its acceptance as a goal has the invaluable effect of turning attention away from its present focus on anthropology toward that which focused the attention of the primitive Christian witness—God himself and his saving work.

IV

The conclusion of this essay is that the Heideggerian model does point to a valuable clarification of one phase of exegesis.

This phase may well be the one most deserving of the name "exegetical theology." If this kind of exegesis can be freed from its association with an unhistorical doctrine of the unity of the Bible, it may provide a valuable corrective to both Barthian and existentialist forms of exegetical theology.

These conclusions are important, but they are far more modest than some of Ott's more enthusiastic claims suggest. In the first place, it is clear that essentially the same direction could be taken by exegetical theology without appeal to Heidegger. In the second place, the results of operating with this exegetical method may be little more than a minor correction of existing methods or a modification of their emphases. In the third place, and most important, the diversity of visions of saving reality from which the Biblical witnesses arise can only pose again the normative question as to the structure of authentic faith in the twentieth century. On this most important question it is not yet clear that the Heideggerian analogies throw light.

7. Response to the American Discussion

HEINRICH OTT

University of Basel

I

I agree with James M. Robinson that the debate within German theology concerning the theological relevance of the later Heidegger's thought is still fully open and fluid.[1] The contributions by American theologians brought together in this volume undoubtedly constitute a valuable contribution that advances the discussion. The points of view, questions, and emphases are to a large extent new, and they lead beyond the previous state of the discussion in German theology.

The latter is determined largely by the dualism of law and gospel, which is understood in Protestant theology of the Lutheran type as the basic structure of theological thinking as a whole. Indeed the theologians associated with Rudolf Bultmann are today elevating it to a formal principle of ontological and hermeneutical relevance. It is along this line that my attempt to show the thinking of the later Heidegger to be significant for theology has been countered in Germany. This is clearest in Gerhard Ebeling's series of theses entitled "Faith's Responsibility in the Encounter with the Thought of Martin Heidegger."[2] Here the "law-gospel" pattern is immediately applied. Heidegger's philosophy is "interpretation of the law"—and this simply because it is

[1] Cf. above, p. 76.
[2] Cf. above, pp. 75 f.

not gospel. "Law" here becomes the ontological horizon in which everything that is not gospel has its place. From this point of view my project must evidently be rejected since I at least begin by trying to see Heidegger's thinking about thought and language in full neutrality with regard to faith, and to be on the lookout for correspondences fruitful for theology.

This reaction is understandable and could scarcely have turned out otherwise. Where the alternative "law or gospel" is in this way brought into play from the very beginning, there cannot be, even temporarily, a neutral position for philosophy. Hence Bultmann is also arguing quite consistently when he objects that there can be no continuity of theological and philosophical inquiry such as I seek, and that instead the theologian has a completely different theme from that of the philosopher, namely the one question: How can man as a sinner stand before God? According to Bultmann, a relation of theology to philosophy is possible only to the extent that theology is dependent on the understanding of historicness worked out by philosophy. On this point I would like to comment: For Bultmann this stands in analogy to the assumption that the gospel, in order to be gospel, must be dialectically related to the law.

I myself am in a position to enter upon another path, since I— as a Reformed theologian and a pupil of Karl Barth—do not think on the premise of the law-gospel pattern. I am able to take philosophy seriously as a theologian, without being forced by immediate application of the law-gospel alternative to regard it as an "interpretation of the law," and, on the other hand, without binding myself to any philosophical "results." Thus one can test from case to case the extent to which philosophy has perhaps discovered something that the theologian too can acknowledge as suitable and helpful and hence can appropriate.

Thus we have two different axiomatic points of departure for theology that stand over against each other. According to the axiom that a given theological thinker employs, philosophy will appear for him in a different light. A more detailed testing of the hermeneutical range of the law-gospel pattern will in due time shed more light on the situation in which this discussion finds itself. But one can already say that the opposing position of my critics from the Bultmannian direction appears most vulnerable in Ernst Fuchs' review of *Denken und Sein*.[3] Here "word" and "thought" are set over against each other as parallel to "gospel" and "law," so that one gains the impression that for Fuchs word is actually equal to gospel and thought is actually equal to law. Hence, in the name of the "word" for which he as theologian is responsible, he stands in opposition to Heideggerian "thought." But he in no way takes into consideration what Heidegger has already thought with regard to the structural connection of word and thinking. Yet the nature of thinking is after all a problem for the theologian too, since the theologian also *thinks*. But Heidegger has brought basic clarification as to the connection, the continuity, the "interaction" (if I may put it this way) between thought and language. To be sure he may not yet have attained thereby the essence of *theological* thinking and speaking. But nevertheless it seems to me that theology would be better advised to think *further* along with Heidegger rather than, as does Fuchs, to bring immediately into play the law-gospel antithesis. This antithesis does not even belong here, and it renders impossible *further* thinking oriented to the phenomena of word and thought.

I have been reproached in the same context, and from a different side as well, for being too uncritical with regard to Heidegger. I cannot acknowledge this as a genuine criticism. For if Heidegger has not said certain things, or has not said them yet, or has not stressed them adequately, or if perhaps as a non-theologian has not been able to say some things, this is far from implying that what he in fact has said must for this reason be false or in need of criticism. Surely we may at first simply listen to Heidegger's analyses in their whole incompleteness—of which, incidentally, he himself is fully aware. And among other things it belongs to real listening that one does not immediately assume a stance of opposition.

[3] Cf. above, pp. 69 f.

To be sure, Bultmann is right in saying that in Heidegger—especially in the later Heidegger—the personal and ethical dimension, concepts such as guilt, responsibility, etc., are hardly to be found. In the early Heidegger it seems on first glance to be different. Yet I think I have proved that with regard to its main intention *Being and Time* was already conceived entirely in the direction of the great theme of the later Heidegger.[4]

Is a dimension lacking here in Heidegger? Heidegger would not deny this. For my part, I would not for a moment hesitate to designate reflection upon this dimension which is still lacking in Heidegger as indispensable for theology. Heidegger has achieved his insights into the nature of language thus far not from the personal, interpersonal sphere, but rather in the area of man's relation to the world—to things—in the area of the philosophical question as to being. But what he has worked out here can, to say the least, be illuminating for what we as theologians have to do beyond what he has done. His insights will make our own task not harder, but easier. It will be our task to inquire into the nature of language not only in the interpersonal sphere, but especially in the divine-human sphere opened by the revelation. Whereas Heidegger for the purposes of his limited objective confines himself to texts of such poets as Hölderlin or Trakl, we will have to hold to Biblical texts and take our point of departure in them. But for me there is no doubt that the task of making this inquiry really does lie before us theologians, and that one cannot do justice to it by hastily applying pat formulae. And no one is better able to remind us of this duty of ours than Heidegger.

For the rest, Robinson seems to me correct when he emphasizes that my apparently uncritical presentation in fact also poses a critical question to Heidegger: Is he in the position to enter into the discussion with theology begun in *this* way and himself to think *further* in this discussion?[5] A critical debate does not neces-

---

[4] It seems to me that Carl Michalson in his essay has not taken this factor fully into account.

[5] Cf. above, p. 34.

sarily have to take the form of the debaters' contradicting each other and of assuming, in whole or in part, an opposing "position."

The fact that I myself am not in the least willing to stop with Heidegger can be made clear in my discussion with Cobb.

II

Among my American discussion partners I would like first to confront John B. Cobb, Jr. This is partly because he himself enters into discussion with the three other contributors, and because I would like to concede at the beginning that I find myself in agreement with his argument over against Michalson, Come, and Ogden. But this is also because Cobb's own criticism of my attempt seems to be especially new and important with regard to the previous debate about Heidegger's significance for theology. I believe that Cobb's train of thought leads us to a very basic problem of all theological hermeneutic.

Cobb confronts me with the fact that in an important point I do not remain in conformity to Heidegger. I would concede to him that he is right—if it were our duty as theologians to remain wholly within the framework of Heidegger's previous thought. But precisely at this point I as a theologian must diverge from Heidegger, that is, I must go beyond him in making certain differentiations. For Heidegger is not a theologian and his hermeneutic is not theological hermeneutic.

The model in terms of which Cobb argues is, in my opinion, quite correctly chosen. It is the "one poem" of each profound poet[6] into which it is the real task of genuine understanding to penetrate, in order that from there the individual poems of the poet may really first become understandable. I have indeed spoken of the one (unspoken) "poem" of all Biblical witnesses,

---

[6] Incidentally Heidegger also speaks occasionally of the "one thought" of each profound thinker. See his pamphlet *Aus der Erfahrung des Denkens* (Pfullingen: Günther Neske, 1954), pp. 7, 19.

the gospel, out of which they all "compose." And I am indeed of
the opinion that this one poem is common to them all, since they
all have to do with the one, identical God, who reveals himself.
Cobb confronts me with the following: "The identity of the
[Christ] event and the shared experience of the event . . . does
not guarantee *a priori* an identity of visions."[7] He goes on to say:
"The identity of initial datum does not determine an identity of
prehension."[8] And he proposes to me, as a way more appropriate
to Heidegger, the following conception: Each Biblical witness has
his own, specific "unspoken poem," out of which he delivers his
witness to God, who is of course identical for all. Only in this way
would justice be done to the variety of the Biblical witnesses—and
indeed this first is a really appropriate application of the fruitful
point of departure residing in Heidegger's hermeneutic. If, on
the other hand, one were to reckon with a "poem" common to
all witnesses as I do, then the whole witness of Holy Scripture
would be flattened out in a completely unhistorical way and
would be harmonized *a priori* by constructing a standard Biblical
or at least New Testament theology. This is in substance Cobb's
argument.

I agree fully with Cobb when he says: "To argue that the
Christ event constitutes an exception requires special argument
not fully developed in Ott."[9] Here is exactly where the problem
lies! This is exactly where we must think further! I agree also
with Cobb's proposal to me as to how to defend my own procedure by reference to Karl Barth: "The Christ event is the
self-presenting of God to man. The witness is one for whom
personally this event constitutes such a self-presenting by God.
Since the initiative here is with God . . . , it must be always
self-identical."[10]

Yet Cobb has here left out of consideration a factor fundamen-

---

[7] Cf. above, Cobb, "Is the Later Heidegger Relevant for Theology?" p.
184.
[8] *Ibid.*, p. 185.
[9] *Ibid.*, p. 184.
[10] *Ibid.*, p. 184.

tal for all theological hermeneutic, namely the *communio sanctorum*. In my view it is not at all the case that the outcome is the production of a uniformly harmonized standard theology of the New Testament, not to speak of the whole Bible. The differences and antitheses between the Biblical authors continue to exist and must be taken very seriously. Yet the historian who thinks outside the church sees only these differences and occasional affinities. To be sure he may also concede—what he as a historian can hardly avoid—that ultimately these very different witnesses at least *envisage* (intend) the same identical subject matter, namely the same, identical God. But seen this way Cobb would still be right: The identity of what is envisaged does not in the least guarantee the identity of the views!

But the theological exegete thinks from beginning to end within the area of the church, within the horizon of the *communio sanctorum*. He finds himself together with all Biblical witnesses within the bond and the fellowship of the people of God. This situation is for him unavoidable and becomes his hermeneutical principle. Hence the situation presents itself to him quite differently. He not only sees the variety (and of course an identity of what is envisaged), but, standing as he does in the same community, he is also in a position to relate the Biblical witnesses to each other with all their variety and partial contradictoriness and to perceive from the interaction of the divergences a word valid for him in his own here and now. It is not a matter of a standard theology that would already have the Biblical witnesses in harmony with each other, but rather of a word that manifests itself in a theological answer valid for his day, an answer that he *himself* gives and *must* give. For the word of the witnesses demands an answer from him, standing as he does in the same *communio*. He gives this answer as his own and hence of necessity as his coherent answer to the calls of the Biblical witnesses in their full variety. He hears them all, Paul and James, John and Luke, and so on, and he takes them all seriously as God's witnesses, and hence to this extent he attributes authority to them. But he does not *take over* Paul or James, etc., but rather, after listening to them all and learning from them what he is able to learn, he formulates responsibly his own answer.

The historian who stands outside the church is not able to do this. For him the Biblical witnesses are merely historical phenomena. They demand of him no answer, and, since he is not in the same communion, he would not even be capable of such an answer—unless perchance in reading the texts he were suddenly to hear the demand, and thus, perhaps still doubting and questioning, were nonetheless to be drawn already into the area of the *communio!*

On the other hand, one cannot in the least say that the theological exegete, when he relates the witnesses to each other in their differences and then forms his own answer, is thereby operating in an unhistorical way. Such a criticism would be straining the concept "history," and hence would be a misunderstanding of historic reality, as if history consisted merely in the views of men and not rather in the interaction between the views and what is envisaged.[11] The theological exegete does not in the least ignore the historical differences—even when he proceeds to relate the witnesses to each other. For him the Biblical witnesses do not automatically have a formal authority simply because they are in the canon—except for the formal authority that consists in his proposing to listen seriously in the expectation that a witness to God and his revelation will be given him. But this simple expectation need not have an unhistorical procedure as its consequence. The witness of the individual witness must of course first prove itself as a witness, and this happens or manifests itself as the exegete's answer takes place.

To return to Heidegger, I would reply to Cobb that in the case of theological hermeneutic *both* statements are true: Each individual Biblical witness has his own, specific "unspoken poem" out of which he speaks. And also all Biblical witnesses together have the same "unspoken poem" out of which they bear witness. It is one and the same subject matter, which is not only *intended*

[11] This danger seems to me to be present for Michalson, who stresses the concept of history a great deal.

by them all but which *inspires* them all and sets in motion their thinking and speaking, namely God in his revelation.[12]

In this special situation there is no contradiction in the fact that I would like on the one hand to retain Heidegger's hermeneutical model of the "unspoken poem," but on the other hand to affirm *both* possibilities. For God's witness is on the one hand the individual, but on the other hand the *communio sanctorum*, the people of God as a whole. The church in this broadest sense is no collection or sum of believing individuals. Rather the church is *a single subject*, in which the individuals participate. Faith and the church belong so closely together that the church is a structural element of faith. That is to say, we cannot in our thinking describe what faith is without immediately striking upon the concept of the church and including it as a constitutive element in our description. We should not let our concept of faith be determined so much by modern, individualistic humanism!

This structural tie between the individual's faith and the church's faith is the reason why I cannot see any genuine alternative in Cobb's question whether each Biblical witness has his own unspoken poem or whether they all have a common poem, but can only affirm both. But I heartily agree with Cobb that this difficult question relative to faith and hermeneutic is far from being adequately clarified.

III

In the spirited presentation by Carl Michalson the concept "history" plays the decisive role. "History is an horizon so inescapable that being is itself a derivative of history."[13]

Michalson sees in the later Heidegger (whose material continuity with the earlier Heidegger he apparently does not concede) an ontological enterprise at work that does not take this

---

[12] This would then be the place to reflect further upon the problem of the inspiration of Scripture—which to be sure cannot be a verbal inspiration and also not a personal inspiration.

[13] Cf. above, Michalson, "Theology as Ontology and as History," p. 147.

inescapability of history with sufficient seriousness. Rather history is the sole medium in which reality appears[14] and consequently may not be bypassed in this way. He reproaches me for setting up, with reference to the later Heidegger, an ontological hermeneutic for theology, and hence for surrendering again one of the most essential attainments of Protestant theology, namely consistent historic thinking.

It seems to me that "history" is thus elevated into the dogma above all dogmas. It becomes so much the medium of all occurrence that one can no longer ask, and does not even need to ask, what history itself is.[15] But Heidegger in his thinking is driven by precisely this question as to what the nature of history is. His question as to being is not an ontological transcending of history. Actually it is precisely: What is history really? How does the occurrence of history ever come about? This does not in the least mean history should be traced back to an unhistoric or suprahistoric first principle. Rather it is precisely the historicness of history that is to be correctly understood. In my opinion Michalson associates Heidegger's fundamentally historic concept of being too closely with Paul Tillich's unhistoric "Being itself." He fails to see the transcendental character of Heidegger's question as to being.[16] What is history? How does it happen? The train of thought which should begin here does not intend to reduce history to a non-historic principle, but rather to describe history in its structures as history.

[14] *Ibid.,* p. 137.

[15] Incidentally this is an interesting parallel to the beginning of *Being and Time,* where Heidegger exposes the dogma of Western metaphysics, to the effect that "being" is the most universal and most obvious concept, which is neither subject to nor in need of further inquiry and clarification.

[16] Objections have been frequently expressed in the German debate, for example by E. Jüngel (Cf. above, p. 69), to my use of the term "transcendental" to characterize the way Heidegger poses his question. These objections have not succeeded in convincing me. I use "transcendental" in a purely formalized way and am not seeking as did Kant principles immanent to reason. Heidegger himself, who usually repudiates fully a reduction of his thinking to an idealistic transcendental philosophy, has expressed his agreement with me on this point.

Hence it is precisely in the name of really radical historic thinking that I believe I have to oppose Michalson. In rejecting the direction of the later Heidegger's thought, and affirming the absolute universality of history, he is actually leaving undiscussed the question as to the nature of history itself. Nor can the obvious fact that the questioner's position is itself historic, a fact to which Michalson quite correctly points, justify in any way the neglect of this question. It is precisely the outstanding characteristic of Heidegger's thinking that it reflects upon the nature of "history," in full consciousness of its own historicness and without the illusory desire to overcome this historicness.

But how can "history" be designated the theme of Heidegger's thinking? Is not his theme rather being? Is Michalson not correct in setting "ontology" and "historic thinking" over against each other? Here one must keep in mind the context in which "being" is relevant for Heidegger. It is the history of Western thought. Its great theme and at the same time its great fate is "being." Hence, to understand the nature of this history, Heidegger has to inquire as to the meaning of "being." But Heidegger's reflection ultimately goes beyond this theme. In his dialogue with a Japanese professor about the possibility of the West and the Far East understanding each other, the topic is no longer being but rather language and hermeneutic.[17] Similarly in the address, "Der Weg zur Sprache,"[18] and in other recent statements Heidegger no longer speaks of being but rather of "e-vent" (*"Er-eignis"*).[19] The theme of language as history's room, the theme of thinking as historic hermeneutic, is broader than the theme of being. The latter is limited to the inquiry as to the nature of the history of Western thought. Hence on occasion Heidegger could even say that the concept "being" should not even occur in theology.

To this extent the title of my book, "Thinking and Being"[20] might be misleading for some. "Being" does not play for Hei-

[17] "Aus einem Gespräch von der Sprache," *Unterwegs zur Sprache,* (Pfullingen: Günther Neske, 1959), pp. 83–155.
[18] *Ibid.,* pp. 239–268.
[19] Cf. above, pp. 57 f.
[20] *Denken und Sein* (Zürich: EVZ-Verlag, 1959).

degger himself the dominant role that has been attributed to it, and this is all the more true of the confrontation of Heideggerian thinking with theological thinking. To this extent my remarks on Heidegger's concept of being and on the *analogia entis* are intended to have an experimental and hypothetical character more than that of theses. *If* one wishes to inquire about the being of *God* within the framework of Western thinking about being (and Christian theology has indeed done just that for centuries), then how would the matter have to appear in view of Heidegger's understanding of being? It is obvious that Heidegger himself does not pose this hypothetical question, since he apparently does not consider Western thinking about being as a suitable horizon for talking about God. But Heidegger is not a theologian. In distinction from the theologian he does not stand in his thinking under the necessity of having to give account of his faith in his time. He can afford to be silent here. Hence it is difficult to discuss with him. For my part, I consider it too early to maintain a thesis on this question.

In the approach taken in my book, *Denken und Sein,* I followed Heidegger's own path. He occasionally designates the actual, primal, and continuing theme of his thinking as "the hermeneutical" theme.[21] He himself approaches this theme along the guiding line of his hermeneutic of the history of Western thinking, that is to say, along the guiding line of the question as to being. But the theme itself leads further. As his dialogue with the Japanese professor shows, it can lead beyond Western civilization. Doubtless it can also lead beyond philosophy into the domain of theology, as various written and especially oral statements of Heidegger indicate. But here everything still remains open. Incidentally, this larger dimension of the theme going beyond the question of being has become evident only in the most recent period. Even the "later Heidegger" seemed at first to be dominated by the question as to being.

I emphasize all this over against Michalson, who in my opinion uses the concept "ontological" in all too traditional and sche-

---

[21] *Unterwegs zur Sprache,* pp. 95 ff.

matic a way to designate Heidegger's undertaking.[22] But my remarks about the broader scope of Heidegger's theme are also intended to relate to the view developed by Arnold B. Come. In my opinion he, too, has attributed to the concept of being a position all too central in our discussion. For the rest I am in complete agreement with him when he wishes to take up the discussion with Heidegger as with an *advocatus hominis et mundi*. I see the situation with regard to the discussion between theology and philosophy just as he does. I am also in agreement with his requirement that we must see the limits of a theological discussion with a philosopher such as Heidegger.

If I have tried in discussion with Michalson to designate the broader and more primal theme of Heidegger's thinking with the term "history," I do not mean at all that Heidegger has completely clarified for us theologians what history is, or what language is.[23] But surely Heidegger has taught us really to pose the questions.

On one further point I must speak to Michalson's presentation. He sets "historic" and "ontological" thinking over against each other correlatively with "word" and "mysticism." Michalson rightly points to Heidegger's affinity to Meister Eckhart. I myself do think that the problem of mysticism must be taken seriously in theology, and precisely for the sake of correctly understanding what *word* means, and that an overdone "theology of the word" that is only apparently the "consistently Reformation" theology of the word will not lead us further. He who really wishes to understand the mystery of the word—namely, that it does not merely communicate information but rather is itself an event— will have to take silence into consideration. Of course for the time being all this can be no more than an indication of where I stand.

[22] For a long time Heidegger himself has completely avoided the term "ontological."

[23] For language is the room of human history. The two themes "language" and "history" are congruent. Heidegger himself prefers to speak of language and only rarely of history. This is doubtless a more precise designation of the one problem which is really involved.

IV

Schubert M. Ogden in his investigation aims exactly at what was of primary importance to me in my confrontation of Heidegger's philosophy with the situation in theological thinking: Heidegger's understanding of primal thinking as non-objectifying thinking. I welcome Ogden's observation that on the question of the relation between faith, preaching, and theology, I am not very far from my teacher Bultmann. This is true. Bultmann is, of course, aware of the inseparable relatedness of theology and preaching, and I for my part have never maintained the absolute identity and indistinguishability of the two.

Quite correctly both Ogden and Cobb (in his criticism of Ogden) insist that if Heidegger's understanding of essential thinking is to be introduced here, one would have to be able to speak of different stages or levels of primal thinking, such as preaching and theology; but they insist that I have not adequately clarified this problem. I see the situation just as they do. My talk about levels of understanding was merely an indication of a problem. Nonetheless it seems to me premature for Ogden to say: "That he nowhere solves the problem strongly suggests that Bultmann is correct in insisting it is insolvable."[24]

I am of the opinion that both Bultmann and Ogden are able to see and take hold of the problem only on the premise that there is in any case such a thing as objectifying thinking and speaking, and that one already knows exactly the nature of this thinking and speaking. For both, this is the fixed point of departure on the basis of which it should be immediately apparent that theological talking, like all "talking about . . . ," is of an objectifying nature. For the time being I can only assert that in terms of Heidegger it is precisely this premise that is no longer obvious to me. Rather for me the big question has become: What really happens when a *word* or a *thought* occurs? (Both belong very close together, as I have emphasized over against

[24] Cf. above, Ogden, "The Understanding of Theology in Ott and Bultmann," p. 165.

Ernst Fuchs.) Actually we do not even know what "objectifying thinking and speaking" is. These premises belong to the traditional conceptual constructions and dogmas that Heidegger describes in *Being and Time* in explaining the nature of the phenomenological method. Here he says that thinking oriented to the phenomena themselves must decidedly break through these constructions. So we must seek to orient ourselves anew to the phenomena of word and thought. To be sure that requires considerable mental exertion. Heidegger has already taught us to see that in their real nature both word and thought are not information but rather event. It will now be our theological task to clarify the event-character of the word in terms of the Biblical word and the event-character of the theological thinking involved in it in terms of the great thoughts of the theological tradition. I do not doubt that in this matter we are still at the beginning and that the steps that lead us further will be taken only slowly.

I would like my last word to be a word of genuine thanks to all my American discussion partners, whose thoughts were very valuable and fruitful even when I was not able to agree with them.